GOVERNMENT AND THE GOVERNED

GOVERNMENT
AND THE GOVERNED

A HISTORY OF POLITICAL
IDEAS AND POLITICAL PRACTICE

By
R. H. S. CROSSMAN
LATE FELLOW OF NEW COLLEGE, OXFORD

With a Foreword by
THE RT. HON.
H. A. L. FISHER
O.M., F.R.S., F.B.A.

LONDON
CHRISTOPHERS
22 BERNERS STREET, W.1
CAPE TOWN : MELBOURNE : SYDNEY : WELLINGTON : TORONTO

First Published - - *May*, 1939
Reprinted - - - *August*, 1939
,,   - - - - -*September*, 1942
,,   - - - - - -*March*, 1945

CONTENTS

vi CONTENTS

FOREWORD

THIS spirited and challenging survey of the course of political thought from the Renaissance to the present age is the work of a young apostle of democratic principles, who after winning philosophical laurels in an Oxford College is now embarked on the open sea of politics. A book on political philosophy suffers no harm from such enlivening and contrasted experiences. When the College Don becomes Town Councillor or parliamentary candidate the exchange is not all loss. The fact that Mr. Crossman is not purely academic gives to his work a sense of animation and actuality often wanting to the nicely balanced treatise of the philosophical recluse. A lively concern for the happenings of to-day and to-morrow lends meaning to the thoughts and occurrences of the past. Mr. Crossman travels easily over a wide tract of time. If some of his judgements may seem to need qualification, he has a good eye for the general features of the landscape and a gift for describing contemporary movements of opinion and of disengaging those which are of special moment.

Political theories do not descend from the sky, but are conditioned by many earthy things such as the circumstances of the age, the place, the moment and the historical antecedents, personal constitution and natural proclivities of the thinker. Fashions in thought continually change. In political philosophy nobody says the last word. If Marx is now the prophet of the disinherited, his empire already begins to crumble. Other prophets will succeed him, other political religions will capture mankind. Political philosophy is always the reaction of thinkers, a reaction which is sometimes deliberate, but sometimes, as in the case of the Nazis, passionate and headlong, to the stress and strain of contemporary events. Theory does not dictate facts. Facts dictate theory. That Mr. Crossman has so firm a grasp of this fundamental truth gives value to his treatise as an introduction to political philosophy. He sets his philosophers in the stream of time and shows how their views were moulded by the pressure of its moving waters. Yet though the world is in ceaseless flux, and every day brings new surprises, human nature remains much the same, and so too do the truths which may most profitably be spoken about it. If there are changing fashions in thought, there is also a body of dateless wisdom. The modern world will find more healing mixtures in Aristotle than in Ricardo or Spencer, Sorel or Rosenberg.

In a time, such as ours, of revolutionary agitation, philosophies are rapidly shaped or borrowed to express the purposes of dominant men. When Lenin was reading in the British Museum he told a friend that he was in search of a philosophy to support his plans. As all the world knows his need was satisfied by Karl

Marx. It was otherwise with Mussolini. No suit of philosophical old clothes exactly fitted that portly shape. The philosophy of Fascism was a body of doctrine invented ex post facto to explain, to justify and to consecrate the polity which had risen from the violent scuffles of the North Italian streets. Not very different was the course of affairs in revolutionary Germany. Mr. Crossman rightly points out that, despite some philosophical precursors, the Nazi movement owes most of its peculiar character to the Leader who was brought up amid those fiery racial hatreds which tore at the vitals of the old Austrian Empire so strongly as to plunge all Europe into war.

The reader of this volume will naturally ask at the end of it how all this is going to develop. Do we stand on the eve of an iron age ? Are we looking into the grave of the civilization which we know ? Will the new accelerated tempo of politics, stimulated by aeroplanes and sustained by Dictatorships and mechanized propaganda, extinguish the prudent and deliberate processes of parliamentary Government ? Will a tyrannous xenophobe totalitarian militarism reduce us all to a dead level of dull animal brutality ? Are the Christian virtues obsolete ? Is cruelty to be an object of worship ? Are we to be faced with the prospect of a new Armageddon more terrible than the last war,—the democracies of the world pitted against their three totalitarian adversaries ?—and if nothing is left of us after that, shall we, as Mr. Wells has dreamed, at last consent to sacrifice the costly luxury of the nation state ?

It is rash to prophesy. The downfall of Britain is proclaimed in every age. It has not come. Lenin and Trotsky were confident of a world-wide revolution. It has not come. Less assuredly, but still hopefully, the friends of the League of Nations predicted an era of democratic peace and disarmament. It has not come. In the general uncertainty three observations may perhaps be safely made. First, that such mythologies as are here described provide no solid foundation for a state; second, that hysteria and megalomania are never permanent; and third, that beneath the winter frost of international suspicion and hostility, which for the moment covers the greater part of the globe, innumerable seeds of charity and goodwill await the opportunity of a favouring gleam of common sense in high places to burst into flower.

H. A. L. FISHER

AUTHOR'S NOTE

Acknowledgments are due to the King's Printers for permission to quote from the Authorised Version on page 39, and to Professor Tawney and Mr. Murray for the extract on page 30.

CHAPTER I

INTRODUCTORY

POLITICAL theory is a dangerous sort of thinking : it is neither a science which tries to understand, predict and control the workings of nature, nor a pure philosophy which tries to define the character of thinking and of reality itself. Nor again is it simply historical. The political theorist cannot, however hard he tries, confine himself to a catalogue of the various forms of state which have existed, or the various ideas about the state which men have held. He must not only state facts, but interpret them, and the way he does so depends, partly at least, on his own feelings and philosophy of life.

To understand this, let us take a simple analogy. At the bottom of my garden runs a stream, and one day I decide to dam it and divert its waters into a new channel. If I am wise, I shall apply certain scientific principles in doing the job. The stream is something which, if I understand its nature, I can utilize for the fulfilment of my plans. What my plans are, whether they are morally good or bad, does not affect my power over it or my understanding of its nature. But now imagine a fish swimming in that stream. Let us suppose that it too is miraculously endowed with human powers, that it can reason and love and hope and fear. The stream is the element in which it lives and all its aspirations are limited by the nature of its watery existence. It cannot get out of the stream and control it from outside, nor can it really think in terms of a way of life like mine on land. It may by tremendous efforts of abstraction try to do so, and those efforts will no doubt be useful. But nothing will divest its thinking altogether of an aqueous flavour. Its concepts of right and wrong, its hopes of paradise and its fears of hell, will always be "fishy" and spring from its experiences in the stream at the bottom of my garden. Though it can be objective and scientific in planning life below the surface, it can never reach a really objective view of water or mud as I can, because it can never look at them from outside.

We human beings sometimes look with contempt on the poor dumb fishes, and conceive of ourselves as creatures uncircumscribed in our powers of thought. But actually we can never think ourselves even into the world of fishes, though we understand all about them. We can only think how a human being would behave there, which is a very different thing. And in the second place we too are in a stream in which we live and breathe and have our being.

That stream is the process of history upon this planet. Here we swim for a time, plan and scheme, love and hate and beget children who will swim after us. Though we can understand and control much that is in it, we can never get outside it and plan the stream itself, as I can plan the course of the stream at the bottom of the garden. Studying the quality of the water, we may learn to predict floods and cataclysms which will sweep away our homes and destroy our civilization : studying each other, we may preach that this social system is preferable to that and seek to enforce the one we approve. But because the stream of history is beyond our control, and essential to our nature, we must always remember the relativity of all our planning.

Political theory is the attempt to think out the best way of organizing life for human beings living in the historical process. It can never reach final conclusions, because the environment in which we live is constantly being changed, partly by uncontrolled natural processes, partly by human effort. Proud as we are, we should remember we cannot control all nature : if a comet collided with the earth, it might so change our circumstances that we should need entirely different types of political organization. We can only plan, direct and control so long as our environment does not change too rapidly or too violently. Even the laws of gravity are not unalterable ; they have only remained unaltered for a long time in a considerable area of the universe.

The limiting conditions then of political theory are first the physical environment in which we live, the whole material universe which is in constant if general change ; and secondly, the human environment which is also changing. Man, with his unique gifts of language and memory, has been able in the course of a few thousand years to build up a great social tradition, which enables every child to start adult life with the collected wisdom of generations. This social tradition is as much a fact as the physical world : it is *the* human fact, the supreme accomplishment of mankind. The New Hebrides native, the Chinese peasant, and the American millionaire breathe in the same physical air, but a different social atmosphere. They have not made it or constructed it or thought it out : it has made them what they are, and their spiritual life is as impossible without it as physical life is without physical air. It has given to them, each in a different way, the scale of values, the religion, the interests which they possess; and, though they may change it slightly or criticize it, they can no more think themselves out of it than they can think themselves out of breathing.

Clearly then political theory cannot be an absolute science. It cannot think out and lay down once and for all how men should live, and how states should be organized. It can only, after studying the existing physical conditions and the existing social environment, suggest the ways and means for ordering existence. With changes in either or both of these limiting conditions, political theory will go out of date and become an interesting historical phenomenon.

For this reason it is of little profit to study political theory in the abstract. You cannot remove a little slice of life called politics or a slab of organization called the state from the intricate structure of human society and hope to understand it. It is no use making a list of the theories of the state held by Plato, St. Augustine, Machiavelli, Rousseau, and Marx, comparing one with another and asking, " which was right ? " Nor will you learn much by studying the methods of famous statesmen and asking which was the best. We have got to see politics as one aspect of the life of an epoch, and political theory as one aspect of the thought of an epoch. Right and wrong, good and bad gain meaning for us first from reflection on our own problems: we cannot reflect them back into the past until we have discovered in what ways the problems of our epoch are analogous to those of past ages.

If anyone enquires, "what then is the use of studying the political ideas of past generations ? " there are two answers to be made. In the first place, if our present phase of the historical process is unique and different from all others, it has also grown out of the past and is unintelligible without it. To study the history of political ideas is to study our own ideas and see how we came to hold them. Mostly they are not ours in the sense that we thought them out for ourselves. Like all other ideas, we received them in a jumble as we grew up : we got them out of poetry we learnt, out of hymns and newspapers and out of our parents' conversation. They do not fit together into an orderly pattern, but are little better than a heap of fragmentary prejudices, which school and university education try unsuccessfully to fit together, but which real life usually knocks into its final shape. From this point of view the life of the individual is not unlike the life of society. For here too political ideas are not nice little packets of logic. In modern England and modern America, the ideas which really stir people are not clear-cut theories, but an astonishing amalgam of religion, economics, social ethics and personal likes and dislikes. A nation does not think ; it feels and it feels as inconsequently as it feels passionately. To understand these feelings both in yourself and in society as a whole you must turn to history and study the forces at work which produced this confusion of feelings in yourself and in your people. If you can once understand that, you can clear up your own mind and decide not only what ought to be done, but how best to persuade other people that it ought to be done.

In the second place, from time to time in our history men have arisen who have taken the jumble of ideas and tried to reduce them to order. Sometimes they have done it as statesmen, like Napoleon or Lenin, by legislation which shapes the lives of their countrymen, and sometimes like Hobbes and Marx, they have been content to think out the way in which order could be accomplished. More rarely men like Paine and Woodrow Wilson and Masaryk have tried to do both. It is the ideas of men such as these which political theory studies. It concentrates not on the chaotic welter of public opinion, or the actions of statesmen, but on the speculations of great thinkers who tried to understand the problems of society and to think out the best way of ordering human relations. Such men are never typical or representative : the typical thinker about politics is shallow, prejudiced and confused. They are always abnormal, usually unpopular, and often ineffective in their own times, because they see too far for practical politics— Plato was no more a typical Greek than Hegel was a typical 19th-century German—and for this reason, if their theories are to become really influential in moulding public opinion they must be simplified and organized almost beyond recognition. Marx was a great political theorist, but Marxism had to become shallow, prejudiced and confused before it could be made into an influential political creed. We must distinguish therefore the study of great political theorists from the study of influential political ideas, even if the second often bear the name of the first. We read the works of the great thinkers in order to train ourselves to think clearly, not merely to understand the epoch in which they lived. We study the confused ideas which have moved men in politics in order to understand our own confusion and learn how to put it right. We can do the two together, provided only that we learn to distinguish them clearly one from another.

CHAPTER II

THE BEGINNINGS OF THE MODERN STATE

I. NATION AND STATE

WE live in a world of deadly political conflicts in which Democracy, Fascism and Communism are creeds passionately defended and passionately attacked. In the name of each of them statesmen are prepared to risk war and the death of millions. These conflicts are not only internal, but external too. It is not only Americans or Englishmen who dispute among themselves which is the best form of government; nation stands ranged against nation in the war of ideologies.

No doubt it is true that we are all vitally affected by the form of government under which we live—or die. For in the modern world the state influences our most private lives. The size of our family, the education we get at school, the money we earn, the books and newspapers we read will all be very largely determined by the form of government set over us. And for this reason the intelligent citizen must make up his mind which he prefers and how much he will risk for the cause he has decided to champion. But if he is wise he will note one remarkable fact. However deep the differences between the various forms of government, the resemblances are still more remarkable. Fascist Germany, Communist Russia and Democratic

America are infinitely more closely related to one another than they are to any political organization which existed in any of those three countries two hundred years ago. It is because the resemblances are so great that the differences arouse such passionate feeling.

This fact is quite natural. It is only possible to compare things and to contrast them when they belong to the same family, or at least have certain elements in common. In so far as dogs and cats are both animals we can see their *generic* resemblance and their *specific* differences, but it is not much good to argue whether you prefer dogs or cats. When, however, you start comparing different sorts of dogs, comparison becomes both fruitful and acrimonious. For here you have a closely related group which yet still permits of an infinite variety of types. So there is a great deal more argument among dog fanciers than there is between dog fanciers and cat fanciers. The same thing is true of forms of government. It would be difficult to arrange an intelligent debate between a Polynesian savage and an American of the Middle West, simply because their ways of life are so remote from one another ; and again, an English workman has infinitely more in common with a German or Russian workman of to-day than he has with any Englishman who lived in 1200 A.D. For all the differences, the modern state in England and America and Russia is of one type and can be studied as such.

Let us consider some of these resemblances. In the first place compare the life of the worker in a motor-car factory in America, Russia and England. No doubt we shall find important differences between them, but these differences are all within the frame-

work of one common fact, industrialization. How insignificant they look when we compare life in a Ford
factory with that of the coachbuilder only four hundred
years ago. Directly we do that we see that the rational-
ized factory system of mass-production is a universal
feature of modern life and that most of our political
arguments are directly or indirectly concerned with
the best way of organizing this system which is
common to every modern state. Or again, consider
means of communication (railroads, aeroplanes, wireless,
telephones, etc.), and we shall draw the same conclusion. The *technique of production* is the same everywhere. Or consider health services and war services :
again we find that the technique of maintaining and
destroying human life is common to all modern states,
and is totally unlike anything which existed five hundred
years ago. Or lastly, consider the modes of recreation
and leisure, cinema, radio, gambling, dancing, detective
stories, and so on. We are faced by the same fact :
underlying all differences between our modern states
is a common civilization which separates them all from
the mediæval social system, the life of the Chinese
peasant or of the Polynesian native. Only on the land,
in places where our modern industrial order has not
won complete predominance, do the old ways of life
survive.

But these basic resemblances can also be found in
the political systems themselves. All our Western forms
of government are species of the *nation state*. Before
the sixteenth century this type of centralized authority
was unknown ; since then it has developed and spread
over the world until it is the normal political system of
Western civilization.

Most of us believe that we know what we mean by the words "nation" and "state"; and yet very few people could give any satisfactory definition of either of them. What is a nation? "A people belonging to a single biological stock", says the Nazi as he confiscates Jewish property and exiles thousands of German citizens. "A people bound together by ties of history, language and culture", says the Englishman, looking uneasily at Southern Ireland. "A free assemblage of individuals, irrespective of race and language, who are willing to live under a single government", says the American citizen, and hopes that no one will mention the negro problem, or the immigration laws.

All these definitions are unsatisfactory, because they all attempt to define by logic what has grown by an historical process. No actual nation will fit any of the logical definitions because no actual nation can be what the system builders would like it to be. Race, language, culture and free choice have all played their part in the formation of nations, but so have geography, economics, strategy, statesmanship and war. Countless factors have contributed to this process, so many and so various that the only safe definition of a nation is "a people living under a single central government strong enough to maintain its independence of other powers". Under this definition it is clear that Abyssinia is not a nation, and the existence of Czecho-Slovakia, as it now remains, is still in the balance, while that of Austria is ended for the present.

Unsatisfactory as this account of "the nation" may be, it has one advantage. It indicates the connection between the modern nation and the modern state. Nationality [1] is something which depends on a central government. War can and does change your nationality whatever your race or language or free choice may be : and so can the decision of the government set over you. On the other hand a government which flouts too far the free choice of its citizens or violates too flagrantly their racial and cultural feelings *may* be unable to maintain its authority. " Nation " and " state " are two aspects of the Western social order and each is unintelligible without the other. A state must possess or bring into being some basis of nationality, a nation must submit itself to some form of centralized control, if either of them is to endure.

For this reason, before we can start to analyse the different types of modern government we must first study the nation state itself. This is the bottle into which the new wines of capitalism, nationalism, democracy and so on have been poured. Their strange mixture is straining it to bursting point, and yet it persists as the container of them all. Historically, it was the first of the modern phenomena to appear ; logically it is the basis on which most political theory and practice has been based.

What we take for granted is always more difficult to understand than anything we question or doubt. Nationality and state authority are elemental factors in our way of life, and we rarely pause to analyse the conditions which they imply. But directly we do begin to reflect we see that they are by no means so self-evident or necessary as we supposed them to be. Why

---

[1] Though *nationalism* does not. But we have lately learnt by bitter experience that a sense of national unity is not a sufficient basis for a nation state.

should mankind be divided up into nations, each with its own laws and customs ? Why should each national government have its own army, navy and air force ? Why should boundaries be drawn between peoples of kindred stock ? Or why again should they become obstacles to communication and trade ? We have seen already that no satisfactory definition of a nation is possible, except the statement that it is a people under a common government. But why should the government be common to these millions of individuals and exclude those ? Is it merely a matter of power politics or is there some principle of division ?

No simple answer can be given to this question, which is indeed *the* question of modern political theory. The nation state was brought into being less by human planning than by blind forces outside our control : it was not based upon clearly-thought-out principles, but caused by certain economic and social changes which occurred in Europe between the thirteenth and the sixteenth centuries. To understand its nature, we must understand these changes first of all.

II. THE MEDIÆVAL ORDER

Mediæval society differed from our own in two ways. In the first place we live in a world in which the failure of the rubber crop of Malaya affects the worker in Birmingham or in Detroit, while a deal on the New York Stock Exchange may ruin the cocoa producers of West Africa, who have hardly heard of London and certainly know nothing of stocks and shares. Science has enabled us to travel where we please and to trade where we have the will and the power to do so. This ease of communication more perhaps than any other single factor has produced the economic interdependence of our world society.

Mediæval man, on the other hand, was tied to the country he lived in. His roads were far worse than they had been under the Roman Empire, and his trade was mostly confined to the local market town. His was a self-sufficient agricultural economy in which the village itself catered for most of its wants, and the towns depended on the country districts around them for their foodstuffs. The feudal system was the natural expression of this localized agricultural economy. A powerful central government needs speedy communications : where these are lacking, government is bound to be decentralized and fall into the hands of the local gentry ; and the king becomes at best a final court of appeal, at worst one feudal lord among others. For this reason in the Middle Ages there was gradually built up a magnificent hierarchy of social classes, in which each grade owed immediate allegiance to its immediate superior, and only indirect and secondary allegiance to the higher grades. This social pyramid of allegiance was at the same time a pyramid of property rights and of obligations. In theory the king owned everything : in fact he handed most of the land over to the barons and lords in return for certain services. They in turn passed most of it on to those beneath them again in return for services rendered, until at last you reached the serf with a multitude of obligations and very few rights. In such a society law will remain a matter of custom and tradition. Centralization can only be of benefit to the lowest classes ; to the local gentry it can only appear as a dangerous threat by the king to their proper privileges and power.

The stability of such a society depends on the power of the feudal lords to maintain order throughout the country while checking the encroachments of the Crown. The King, on the other hand, can only increase his power either by an appeal to the serfs against their over-lords, which is very unlikely, or by relying on the support of another group which is composed neither of serfs nor gentry. If ever such a group comes into existence the feudal system is bound to crack.

Here then is one aspect of the mediæval world, its slow-moving economic system, and its decentralized and graduated distribution of political power. But if in the fields of economics and politics the mediæval outlook was deeply parochial, there was one institution more universal and more international than anything we possess. The Catholic Church was the spiritual mistress of the civilized world. Centralized in the Vatican at Rome, with a magnificent civil service and an obedient emissary in every village, it could boast a complete control over the art, education, literature, philosophy and science of Western Christendom. For centuries it gave to Western Europe a common culture accepted by every king and baron. Civilization was Catholic, and Catholicism was civilization. Tied to the soil, limited in his trade and traditional in his law, mediæval man was a citizen of a religious country which embraced the whole of the Western world. For this reason, his thought, like his painting and music, was essentially ecclesiastical. In it, there was nothing beyond theology, as there was no land beyond the claims of the Catholic Church. Theology was its all-embracing wisdom, as the Pope was its spiritual lord. Theology could delegate to science or architecture or logic certain special fields of study, as the Pope could grant to princes the charge of the temporal protection of their subjects. There could be disputes about the division of office, and quarrels between kings and popes, but the fundamental principle remained unquestioned : in all matters spiritual the Church was supreme. Moreover, the universality of the Christian faith was paralleled on the temporal side by the belief in the universal nature of Law. Law was not something enacted by the will of a sovereign or a popular assembly, but the all-pervasive atmosphere of social life. It was natural to man, just as it was natural for him to breathe and eat and drink : it was not dependent on human reason for existence, but an eternal truth to be discovered by patient study. We think of a law as the result of a decision by a parliament or a dictator : the Middle Ages felt it to be the framework within which prince and baron and serf alike must decide everything. It was one of God's gifts to man, as unchanging and independent of human whim as the dogmas of Christianity.

This belief in the reality of natural law enabled the Middle Ages to develop a spirit of constitutionalism and even a type of representative institution. Since Law was not the perquisite of princes or a product of sovereignty, there was a real sense in which all men were felt to be equal in their ability to grasp it. Since it belonged to the people as a whole, the people must take some part in the election of their kings, and in some cases the king entered into a contract with his people to observe it. Traces of this theory of kingship are still to be found in the English coronation service, just as the popular theory of Law still survives in trial by jury.

The political institution which corresponded to this notion of Law was the Holy Roman Empire. Universal Church, Universal Law, Universal Emperor, this was the Trinity of Western Europe, the framework of the feudal system. Emperor and Pope divided the authority which had once been united under the Roman Emperors, the first as the temporal, the second as the spiritual over-lord. But the position of the Emperor was far more uncertain than that of the Pope. Not only must he wage war against the encroachments of the papacy, but also against the independence of territorial kings and princes. In fact, the power of the Emperor (generally centred in Germany) varied enormously from time to time, and was hardly felt in countries as remote as England. A poet like Dante could write of a Roman emperor restored to the glory and influence of earlier days ; but such a synthesis was mere day-dreaming in a world of primitive communications and divided loyalties. Whereas the Church exerted universal control, the emperors only longed for it, and came to grief whenever they tried to win it. From 1300 onwards the growth of French, Spanish and English national unity under national monarchs put an end to all such dreams, and the real struggle began between territorial kingdoms and the imperial Church.

The mediæval ideas of Church and Empire, of representation and authority, of property and freedom, are remote from us and difficult to grasp. We, in England, have kept much of them in our institutions and laws and particularly in our social life : we still *feel* in some ways as mediæval man *thought*, but those feelings do not fit in with our modern world or the modern political theories which we claim to act on. This unconscious traditionalism makes it difficult for Americans to understand English politics. America is a new country and its institutions and social philosophy are entirely those of the modern nation state. They do not flow out of an unbroken process of development from Alfred to George VI ; on the contrary, they are results of a deliberate act of choice by which numbers of Englishmen broke with the Western world and built a new society across the water. For this reason, in America, politics is politics and business is business : things are what they seem because they are coherent ; whereas in England the subtle influence of an antique philosophy is still strong enough to make any simple statement about English political life almost certainly untrue or at least misleading.

Only one aspect of mediæval life was entirely destroyed by the Reformation in England—the Papal and Imperial supremacy. On every other point the new state compromised with the old order and accepted it as the basis on which to build. But the pressure of circumstances forced even an Englishman to decisive action with regard to Rome. It was not a question of doctrine or reform of abuses or even of marriage-convenience, but simply whether England was to become a nation, and English traders were to gain that freedom of enterprise for which they longed. To attain this, the old universal culture of Christendom and the institution which gave that culture its frame-work of dogma and organization was destroyed. The Tudor attitude to Rome is the clearest proof of the fundamental importance of the Papacy to the mediæval order.

This supremacy of the Church is also seen in mediæval political theory. Strictly speaking this did not exist as a separate branch of philosophy but was merely one aspect of theology. Although, by the distinction which was made between the temporal and the spiritual sphere, it was admitted that kings and princes could act as they deemed fit in matters which did not affect the salvation of their subjects, yet this division of power was made by the Church itself, and kings and emperors needed the papal blessing to legitimise their rule. This meant that, although there was in practice a real conflict of power between for instance Emperor and Pope, in theory all power was derived from God through His Church; and the theoretical harmony between the spiritual and the temporal could only be maintained so long as the kings could find no permanent basis of power in their own countries strong enough to challenge interference by the Church. Directly this happened they were bound to ask how the spiritual charge of men's souls could really be separated from the temporal charge of their bodies, and how within one territory there could be two supreme rulers. Merely to ask this question was to discover that the Church's power was by no means purely spiritual. A world-wide organization, which was also in most countries the richest landowner, must obviously possess a certain temporal influence; just as a king who has any strength at all will affect the spiritual welfare of his subjects.

In short, the mediæval compromise between a world-wide Church and territorial princes depended for its stability upon the static and parochial character of the feudal system, and upon the inability of any king or emperor to break the local power of the feudal lords. Both in theory and in practice such a system was bound to break down, directly the balance of power altered decisively in favour of the kings. For when this happened, any attempt by the Church to exert her old authority would be felt to be a political manœuvre by a rival temporal power.

The Middle Ages did not collapse in a year or a decade or even a century. The transition to the epoch of the nation state was slow, and in some countries like Germany and Spain it is still going on to-day. To begin with, the conflict was fought in mediæval terminology and the changes occurred within the old order. Not till the process was nearly completed did the Renaissance and the Reformation accelerate the tempo and make the break complete. Then suddenly men began to feel the spirit of a new age and to frame concepts which gave recognition to the changes which had been going on for generations. Political revolutions are always the end of a process : they come when social and economic changes have been so great that the old ways of thought and the old balance of power have become unworkable. So too new philosophies arise, not at the beginning of a development, but at the end, when man's innate conservatism has brought him to a point where idea and reality have scarcely any points of contact left.

This point was reached in Western Europe in the 16th century. As the strength of the kings increased, so the theories of papal and imperial supremacy developed too. The close of the Middle Ages brought a decline in the actual power of Pope and Holy Roman Empire combined with an increase of their universal claims. Men looked for unity and central authority because they felt the need for it. Pope and emperor asserted each his world domain because they were in danger of losing it. At last in Italy a man appeared who was suddenly to speak in a new language and to discover a set of new concepts and definitions with which to describe facts long since waiting for recognition.

III. THE ABSOLUTE MONARCH : MACHIAVELLI

Niccolo Machiavelli was born at Florence on May 3rd, 1469, and died on June 22nd, 1527. A practical politician and an experienced diplomat, he only began to write when the return of the Medici destroyed the free republic which he had served for nearly twenty years, For this reason he cannot be reckoned among the academic theorists of politics. He wrote of practical politics as he saw them, of the art of winning power and keeping it, of the errors which lead to a prince's downfall. For him the means were so fascinating that he never seemed to worry about the end. That was left for the Prince to decide for himself : his adviser, as Machiavelli conceived himself to be, was only concerned to enable him to achieve whatever he willed.

It was in this spirit that *The Prince*, his most famous book, was written. Unconcerned with morality, or religion or scientific method, *The Prince* is a handbook, not of statesmanship, but of statecraft, which expresses in a few pages the essence of the Renaissance in which the nation state was born. The mediæval world order had been shattered, the alliance of spiritual and temporal power had broken down, and in the anarchy of Northern Italy it was evident that it could never be rebuilt in its ancient form. For here the free cities which had resisted the imperial designs of the German Emperor were struggling to survive in a world which had outgrown them. The expansion of trade, better communications and the rise of the merchant adventurer were all by the 16th century demanding a larger scale, a more centralized political system than feudalism permitted. What had seemed for centuries the protection of fair wages, of social justice and of spiritual salvation now appeared as a clog and a hindrance to human initiative. Everywhere, therefore, kings began to gather to themselves more and more power and, with the backing of the new traders and financiers, to exert supreme authority over the feudal barons. The reign of absolute monarchy had begun in France and Spain, and was soon to come in England with the Tudors.

Looking backwards it is easy to see such a transition as a stage in the progress of human society. We forget the anarchy, the cruelty, the upsetting of established institutions, the destruction of that law and order upon which the common man depends. Because our ideas of right and wrong are founded upon the new ideas and institutions of the period, we forget that the new, when it came, must have seemed wicked and inhuman. To read *The Prince* is to remember the darker side of the change. Machiavelli was not a bad man, or a cold-blooded schemer. On the contrary, he was a passionate supporter of republican institutions, who saw more clearly than most that no state could prosper where morals had collapsed as they had collapsed in Italy. He understood the value of freedom and impartial law and sound religion, but he also felt that the Church could no longer provide them as she had done in the past. Recognizing the need for a moral order, he saw the rottenness of the existing moral order : desiring freedom, he saw that the freedom of the free city was too small for the modern world. In an epoch of shattered institutions he realized that constitutionalism and kindliness and traditional morality were no longer the basis for a stable society. And for this reason he preached the *doctrine of power*.

In so doing he discovered one of the basic principles of modern political theory. Whatever our intentions, be they humane or inhuman, Christian or pagan, a government which is to survive must have power at its disposal and must understand the technique of employing that power. "The first job of a government is to govern." "Machiavellian" is now a term of abuse : we in England and America have become so used to the relative stability of modern society that we can afford to make our first demand that a government shall be just or constitutional. For this reason we are shocked when a revolutionary government in Russia or Spain puts order first and justice second, and we protest against its inhumanity. But humanity in some situations may give victory to the other side. In a revolutionary crisis or in a war, a ruler or a general can only afford to be humane and forbearing if it pays. That is the reason why most of us hate wars and revolutions ; but it is useless, because we hate them, to refuse to realize that, when they occur, power becomes the only weapon which anyone can employ. Moreover, it is still more important to see that humanity and justice are only possible in societies where some central authority

can exact obedience. If the power of the established
authority is flouted by a rival force there is an end of
law and order.

Because conditions in Italy were so desperate,
Machiavelli saw this ugly fact quite clearly, and his
new conception of the state could be more precise than
that of his English contemporaries. The lines which
are blurred in English history by the continuity of our
development were sharp and clear for him because
Italy called for sharp and clear decisions. The philosophy which lives behind the advice of *The Prince* can
be summed up in two points :—

1. *In every state there is a supreme power, the Sovereign.*

Machiavelli saw that the Papacy was the chief cause
of Italy's weakness. As he put it in one of his writings :

We Italians then owe to the Church of Rome and to
her priests our having become irreligious and bad ; but
we owe her a still greater debt, and that one that will be
the cause of our ruin, namely, that the Church has kept
and still keeps our country divided. And certainly a country
can never be united and happy, except when it obeys wholly
one government, whether a republic or a monarchy, as is
the case in France and in Spain ; and the sole cause why
Italy is not in the same condition, and is not governed by
either one republic or one sovereign, is the Church. . . .
The Church, then, not having been powerful enough to be
able to master all Italy, nor having permitted any other
power to do so, has been the cause why Italy has never been
able to unite under one head, but has always remained
under a number of princes and lords, which occasioned her
so many dissensions and so much weakness that she became
a prey not only to the powerful barbarians, but of whoever
chose to assail her.[1]

[1] Quoted in Sabine's *History of Political Theory* from
Machiavelli's " Discourse on the First Ten Books of Titus
Livius," translated by Detmold.

Machiavelli was not against the temporal power of
the Pope: if he could have become monarch of
Italy, all would have been well. But in that case he
would have been a sovereign king like other kings.
Whether it were Pope or prince who achieved the supreme
authority was a matter of indifference to him as long as
someone achieved it. With this argument Machiavelli
welcomed the nation state which refuses to recognize any
limitation of its authority by an outside power, be it a
rival prince or an international Church. For it the
Church is either a voluntary organization alongside
others (which, if it has the right of protection, has also
the duty of obedience) or else a part of the state itself.

This claim that no spiritual power should challenge
the state destroyed once and for all the old world
order. For though the Catholic Church and the emperor
still survived, they survived not as the supreme arbiters
over kings and parliaments, and over the thoughts
of civilized mankind, but as institutions which must
adapt themselves to the new national states. From
now on the world would be divided into territories or
states (to use the word first popularized by Machiavelli)
whose laws would be promulgated by one single central
government.

2. *The control of power is the justification of sovereignty.* But if the old dispensation was shattered, what
was to replace it? Mediæval man had been a limited
parochial creature, but at least he had evolved a system
of laws and customs universally respected by kings and
priests and by rich and poor. Because Law and Religion
stood above every power, he could trust his neighbour
and appeal to them if he was wronged. Now with the
breakdown of the Church's supremacy, security had

disappeared. The Renaissance Italian had to rely on his wits and his weapons : if they failed there was no higher court of appeal. Machiavelli is the incarnation of this new spirit of independence. Man, he assumes, is dominated by one motive, ambition. He is a free creature, a law unto himself, for whom the rest of mankind are obstacles to or instruments of his will ; not self-preservation but self-assertion is his creed and trade and science and military strategy are the tools with which he accomplishes his aggrandizement.

The Machiavellian man was anti-religious and anti-social. Bound by no laws which did not benefit himself, he was morally free to think and do anything : the only limits on his freedom were his own capacity and the ambitions of his neighbours : the only world he recognized was the world of human endeavour. No wonder he regarded the Middle Ages as an epoch of superstition and spiritual confinement, and found back in the cities of Ancient Greece the model for his behaviour. There, he felt, men had lived by reason in free communities. The clear-cut lines of their architecture were rational assertions of human will ; their philosophies had been human philosophies, not theological abstractions. He turned instinctively to them, and in his architecture, his painting and his writing derided the grotesque other-worldliness, the humble spirituality, the meek self-abnegation of Gothic Cathedrals and the theology of monks. This world was not a vale of tears, where devils and demons beset him and where he must humbly seek the salvation of his soul, but a new classical world open for the free rational man to conquer and to mould to his will.

This ruthless spirit of self-assertion was not of

course the spirit of the common man. Only a tiny minority was inspired by it, traders and adventurers, kings and bishops. It was the spirit of a new ruling class, which harried and devastated the common folk of Italy more mercilessly than ever ; and in Machiavelli we find a sharp distinction between the amoral ruler and the masses. The masses need morality and religion : the ruler must provide them, but he need not himself feel bound by their rules. He is the supreme legislator above all laws, and law is the instrument of his sovereignty. Of course there is an inconsistency in such a philosophy. If the ruler is free and rational and above all law, why should not his subject be the same ? Machiavelli has no answer to this question. Declaring the prince free from all restraints of law and morality, preaching the new gospel of humanism, he could only argue that force was the sole justification of power. But that is to say that power has no justification at all.

Although he was inconsistent, or rather because he was inconsistent, Machiavelli was right in his diagnosis of the character of Renaissance society. It was the creature of a new oligarchy ; it was based on force, and the ideal it preached of the free rational man was only open to the ruler. In the mediæval world all were subject to God ; in the new secular world a few men had become gods to rule omnipotently over their fellow-men and to use them as instruments of their will. These new rulers were restrained neither from heaven above nor by their subjects beneath them. They were free precisely because they held the vast majority of their fellow men in thraldom. Religion and morality, instead of binding ruler and subject into an organized society, had become the instruments for the subjection of the masses.

Machiavelli's Prince therefore has two distinct problems of government : (1) How to imbue the masses with sound morality and religion, to educate them and inspire them to become useful members of the state. (2) How to deal with the minority of free men, princes of foreign states and rivals within his own. But both these problems are solved, in so far as they are solved, in terms of power politics, and neither solution squares fully with his passionate belief in republicanism and freedom. In the period in which he lived it was impossible to reconcile them.

It would be wrong to suppose that Machiavelli was typical of his age. For many centuries mankind would still think not in terms of secular politics but of theology, and regard as blasphemy Machiavelli's philosophy of life. He was realistic, not in the sense that he showed how mankind was really thinking, but because he perceived the realities underlying their thoughts and actions. But this perspicacity was also blindness. A realism which disregards our actual thoughts, disregards a very vital element in the real situation. Power may be a dominant factor in politics and make religion its tool, but if men believe that religion not power is their motive, they are not pure power politicians. Machiavelli was deeply influenced by his Italian environment, and of Italy his diagnosis was largely correct. But Italy was precisely the country which had failed to establish a nation state. Of France and Spain and England, where the nation state was successfully created, Machiavelli's picture is fantastically untrue. Can it be that it was

because their outlook was not so logically Machiavellian that they succeeded where Machiavelli failed ?

IV. THE ECONOMIC REVOLUTION AND THE
REFORMATION

In Machiavelli's writings we find the first recognition of the political revolution which was to bring
into being the Nation State. We must now turn our
attention to the social and economic changes which
accompanied it. These changes were four in number :
the discovery of new sources of wealth overseas, the
development of international finance, a revolution in
the methods of farming and in the law of property,
and the Reformation.

We have seen that mediæval Europe was a closed
economic system. Its only contact with the distant
lands was through the Levant to the East, and these
trade routes had long been controlled by the Venetians,
who passed on their merchandise to the free cities of
Germany. At the end of the 14th and the beginning
of the 15th centuries, this monopoly of trade began to
break down. Portuguese and Spanish merchants found
new lands to conquer. India, Africa and America
began to pour in an ever-increasing flow of silver and
spices, and the centre of balance began to shift from
Venice to the west. When the Turks sacked Con-
stantinople in 1453 and closed the routes to the East,
they only completed the process.

The result of this shift was a gradual increase in
the importance both of England and of the Netherlands. What had previously been a remote island

became in the sixteenth century a central point between the old world and the new : but it was in Holland and Belgium that the full force of the change was felt, for here Antwerp became the metropolis of world trade, and the German cities now looked to her and not to Venice as the source of their merchandise. The Portuguese chose it as their trading centre, and later Charles V of Spain made it the commercial capital of the Spanish Empire.

Here then is the first of the great changes. Western European nations had started upon the course of Empire, discovering new continents, stripping them of their treasures and bringing them in exchange the Catholic creed. And as a result the Western seaboard became the economic centre of the world. But this sudden influx of wealth (and especially of silver) produced deeper convulsions. The new merchant enterprises needed capital and contrariwise there was money to be made by investment. The sudden expansion of trade could not adapt itself to the old parochial economics of feudalism, and a new international banking system was developed to satisfy its needs. With the rise of the bankers and merchants, there came into being in every country a new class, the bourgeoisie, neither kings nor aristocrats nor peasants, nor yet the craftsmen and local traders of mediæval days, but an independent body on whom every other class from king to serf was soon to depend. The bourgeoisie was essentially the monied class. They controlled the means of exchange : it was their capital which financed the campaigns of kings, their ships which trafficked with east and west, and their business houses which arranged the exchange of goods between the countries of Europe. Here is an account of some of the activities of their financiers :

The financier received his payment partly in cash, partly in concessions, which still further elaborated the network of financial connections that were making Europe an economic unity. The range of interests in which the German banking houses were involved is astonishing. The Welsers had invested in the Portuguese voyage of 1505 to the East Indies, financed an expedition, half commercial, half military, to Venezuela in 1527, were engaged in the spice trade between Lisbon, Antwerp and South Germany, were partners in silver and copper mines in the Tirol and Hungary, and had establishments, not only at Lisbon and Antwerp, but in the principal cities of Germany, Italy and Switzerland. The Fuggers, thanks to judicious loans to Maximilian, had acquired enormous concessions of mineral property, farmed a large part of the receipts drawn by the Spanish Crown from its estates, held silver and quicksilver mines in Spain, controlled banking and commercial businesses in Italy, and, above all, at Antwerp. They advanced the money which made Albrecht of Brandenberg archbishop of Mainz ; repaid themselves by sending their agent to accompany Tetzel on his campaign to raise money by indulgences and taking half the proceeds ; provided the funds with which Charles V bought the imperial crown, after an election conducted with the publicity of an auction and the morals of a gambling hell ; browbeat him, when the debt was not paid, in the tone of a pawnbroker rating a necessitous client ; and found the money with which Charles raised troops to fight the Protestants in 1552.[1]

The rise of capitalism has sometimes been closely connected with the Reformation which occurred about the same time, but it is an oversimplification to speak of the one as the cause of the other. Naturally the growing importance of a new class throughout Europe

[1] *Religion and the Rise of Capitalism*, by R. H. Tawney (Murray).

was bound to affect the religious problem. But capitalism is not a specifically Protestant phenomenon. Spain and Portugal, the first imperial countries, remain Catholic to this day, and there were Protestant countries such as Scotland which had little connection with the new economic movements.[1] Irrespective of religion, the economic revolution spread through Europe and, wherever it went, it undermined the existing order by its demand that the pursuit of wealth should be considered a respectable career for a Christian. Just as international finance upset the economic equilibrium of Europe, so the philosophy of property upset the moral equilibrium of the world.

Mediæval man had conceived of property as subordinate to the rule of law. His guilds had laid down *a fair price* for the articles they made, and had maintained that usury was wicked. In condemning usury they had condemned all transactions where one man came off worse than another; the fruits of the earth and the product of man's industry were good things which could be bartered and exchanged for money, but not for profit.

Of course there was profiteering in the Middle Ages, and there was usury too. But the Christian tradition denounced them, and both the kings and the Church were guided by this tradition. Living under a stable, parochial economy, men could welcome such limits on private enterprise as protection against exploitation, because the world had no need either of free capital or of capitalists. But the vast expansion

---

[1] The Scottish Reformation is really more comparable with the mediæval revolts against the extortion of Rome than with its contemporary movements on the Continent.

of international trade and the advances of science and technology demanded precisely these things ; and soon emperors and kings and popes began to depend on the bourgeoisie, on usury and on capital, although they were still denouncing them officially. The corruption of the Church, which Luther exposed and against which the whole movement of the Reformation was directed, was an inevitable result of this contradiction between the morality and the economics of the age.

Once again let us avoid the danger of moralizing after the event. The fact that in the later Middle Ages men were tacitly permitting the sins which they denounced was not due so much to their individual dishonesty as to their circumstances. Whenever a moral or legal code is maintained in force, after the economic system to which it was adapted has been revolutionized, a contradiction between theory and practice is bound to arise. In such a situation, it is impossible to be both intellectually honest and morally good. The fifteenth and sixteenth centuries were precisely such a period, and however high man's intentions might be, it was bound to be an age of moral collapse.

Thus while the new national sovereigns rejected the imperial pretensions of Rome and asserted their supreme authority within their territories, moral reformers began an attack upon the spiritual power of the Church. Denouncing its worldliness, its riches, and the corruption of its manners, they began to feel that individual men and women could live really Christian lives only if they freed themselves from its domination. And the invention of printing gave them a rule of life which was to replace the dogmas of Catholic tradition. The printed Bible was open now to all who could read :

through it truth could be revealed direct to the layman without the mediation of the priest. Education, which had been a monopoly of the Church, was now open to all who could afford to read books, and the new middle classes in Germany, France, the Netherlands and England became the backbone of the Reformation. The Bible, not the Catholic Church, as the source of truth, the nation, not the Pope or Emperor, as the source of power—these were the two driving motives of the movement which Martin Luther's action precipitated in the year 1517.

But the Reformation in its early stages did little to solve the social problem. Disgusted by what he held to be the corruption of the Catholic Church, Luther failed to see the reasons for that corruption. In revolt against all institutions, and preaching a message of personal salvation by God's grace, he was too incoherent a thinker to work out a social code adapted to the new capitalist age. Instead he preached a reversion to a simple peasant morality which was as mediæval as the Catholicism he denounced. He inveighed against usury like any monk, but since he also urged the destruction of those religious institutions which had once checked it, the real result of his crusade was to free the Church from papal control and surrender it to the control of secular princes, who could twist his pliable gospel into any form which suited them. Lutheran protestantism, which began as a revolt against institutions and forms, ended as a department of state : passive obedience to the civil authorities was its absolute command, and peasant revolts which sought a social gospel in the teaching of Christ were ruthlessly crushed by the new reformed Churches. Fundamentally the

D

absolutism of Catholic Spain and of Protestant Germany had much in common.

It was therefore the indirect effects of the Reformation which were of permanent significance. The Church had been the richest institution in the world : when its riches were confiscated and distributed among the *nouveaux riches*, a vast accumulation of capital was suddenly freed for investment, and huge estates previously managed by the monasteries became the personal property of hard-headed business men. The mediæval theory that the right of ownership implied corresponding duties disappeared with the hierarchy of feudal classes, and the new masters of society began to regard land as a chattel to be bought and sold like any other merchandise : it was simply a form of wealth be to accumulated like any other property. By disregarding or by twisting the law they began to build up large estates and to push the villein into the waste lands which had not yet been cultivated.

With this new idea of exclusive private ownership came new ideas of applied science and up-to-date business methods. The economic revolution was accompanied by revolutionary changes in industry. Private property, science and banking went hand in hand, and ruthlessly destroyed the mediæval ideal of the social organism, to replace it with a new society of individual property owners, applying human reason to the increase of the earth's riches—and of their own.

Somehow European man had to accommodate his religion and law and social morality to these new conditions. As we have seen, his first reaction was to denounce them, and look backwards to a mythical golden age of feudal happiness, with the result that he was quite unable to restrict or control the evils to which they gave rise. The Lutheran Reformation and the Counter-Reformation, in which the Catholic Church put her house in order, were not really constructive movements and ended merely in the recognition of the inevitability of the new order, without legislating for it. It was only from the middle class itself that a new social morality could spring, forged by their actual experience of the problems of the modern world— neither kings nor churchmen could do the job—and the beginnings of this new philosophy of life are to be found in the Calvinist Movement.

John Calvin was born in France in 1509, and died in Geneva in 1564. Scholarly, calm and precise, he was a very different personality from the fierce, romantic and incoherent Luther; and he is important to us not for any great originality in his thinking, but because he started a movement which was to mould the minds of the new business class in France, Switzerland, Holland and Great Britain and ultimately America. Without surrendering, like Luther, to the power of the new secular princes, he founded a Church in which merchants and bankers could feel themselves at home. The model for this reformed Church was the city of Geneva, in which Calvin ruled for close on twenty years as the appointed minister of God's word. Here it was that the new business classes were to work out their own morality of austere and ruthless severity. Without popes or emperors to give them orders, the citizens of Geneva subjected themselves voluntarily to the dictates of their own elders, the interpreters of God's command.

The Calvinist reformers by no means fully understood the changes which had taken place, nor did they wholeheartedly reject the mediæval way of life. In the crucial matter of usury Calvin himself was conservative, though he made the vital distinction between usury and a fair return on capital. He still believed that religion must rule man's whole life and that the Church was the supreme authority. But he replaced the great world church of Rome by the elected ministers of Geneva and substituted the Bible for the Catholic tradition as the final source of truth.

These changes were, however, sufficient to enable a beginning to be made with the construction of a modern moral and political theory. The sober merchants of Antwerp and Lyons and Geneva, liberated from Rome, and freed from the restrictions of feudal economics gradually evolved that philosophy of industry, thrift and good works which was to be the basis of business confidence and private enterprise in England and America. The gloomy doctrine of Predestination told them that it was fore-ordained by God's decree who was to be saved. But to ensure that he was among the elect, each man was forced to discipline himself to a rigid ethic. With this sense of personal responsibility to inspire them the Calvinists showed an energy as great as that of the modern communist, who also believes in the omnipotence of a force greater than himself. Nothing enables a man to be strong and resolute and dynamic so much as the belief that he is but clay in the hands of his Maker.

Of democracy, however, and individualism, there is no trace in Calvin's writings. He was authoritarian and theocratic through and through, freeing men from subjugation to Rome in order to let them be slaves of God in subordination to his chosen rulers. That this

type of " fundamentalism " suited the temperament of
the new middle classes and gave them a morality which
made their business prosper is an accident of history.
Calvin's influence is due not to his perspicacity, but to
the fact that he disregarded politics and economics
and sought quite simply to teach the good life to the
respectable business man. In so doing he helped to
create a stable basis of social morality on which later
a stable political structure could be built by men profoundly different in their ways of thought from the
early Protestant reformers.

V. POLITICAL THEORY OF ABSOLUTISM

We can see already that the emergence of the nation
state was a complicated and lengthy process. By the
end of the 16th century the Reformation and Counter-
Reformation had divided Europe into a number of
territorial states, some Catholic, some Protestant, and
all with large religious minorities ruthlessly suppressed
by the reigning power. On the other hand the economic
revolution had developed with very varying speeds in
different countries. Roughly speaking, the Protestant
countries were those in which the bourgeoisie had gained
permanent influence and were already threatening the
absolute supremacy of the kings, while the Catholic
monarchs, by checking the development of capitalism,
were sowing the seeds of their imperial decay. Spain
and Portugal and Italy were now to be replaced by the
Netherlands and England as the leaders of European
commerce and trade, while Germany, lacerated by
religious wars and unable to achieve any national unity,

was to sink into the background. Alone of the Catholic states France began to develop the characteristics of the modern state, but even here the suppression of Protestantism was to cost her dear.

The first political theories of the nation state reflect the transient character of the compromise between centralized despotism and the new financial capitalism of the bourgeoisie. In the introduction I distinguished between theories which influenced historical change, and theories which showed an understanding of it. Machiavelli's account of the state belonged to the latter class. Though it was incomplete and one-sided it did at least point to one unescapable fact, that modern government is ultimately based on centralized force, and that without a backing of force no justice or morality can prevail. But few of Machiavelli's contemporaries understood the implications of this theory; and the ideas which were influential in the building of nation states were usually attempts to avoid this awkward fact by adapting mediæval philosophy to the new conditions.

The most influential of these new theories was that of the *Divine Right of Kings*, and the duty of *Passive Obedience*. This theory was simple, popular and fundamentally irrational. It was helped by few philosophers of any distinction, and yet from the end of the 16th century right down to 1914 it was of widespread importance. Not only James I of England, but the last Emperor of Germany and the Czar of Russia, claimed to rule by Divine Right and demanded of their subjects obedience to that divinity.

To begin with, the theory depended chiefly on biblical quotations. " Render unto Cæsar the things that are

Cæsar's," said Jesus Christ, and Paul had amplified this in his Epistle to the Romans :

Let every soul be subject unto the higher powers. For there is no power but of God : the powers that be are ordained of God.

Whosoever therefore resisteth the power, resisteth the ordinance of God : and they that resist shall receive to themselves damnation.

For rulers are not a terror to good works, but to the evil. Wilt thou then not be afraid of the power ? Do that which is good, and thou shalt have praise of the same.

For he is the minister of God to thee for good. But if thou do that which is evil, be afraid ; for he beareth not the sword in vain : for he is the minister of God, a revenger to execute wrath upon him that doeth evil.

Wherefore ye must needs be subject, not only for wrath, but also for conscience sake.

For this cause pay ye tribute also ; for they are God's ministers, attending continually upon this very thing.

Render therefore to all their dues : tribute to whom tribute is due ; custom to whom custom ; fear to whom fear ; honour to whom honour.[1]

Here were direct and precise instructions to the faithful. Although the Roman Empire was a pagan empire, Paul had ordered Christians to accept its authority as derived from God, and had, it was argued, thus admitted that the state, whatever the personal morality of its monarch, was divinely ordained. " Kings ", wrote James I of England, " are breathing images of God ". This new and startling theory was necessitated by the break-up of the mediæval world-order, and it was to be held by kings of both the Protestant and Catholic faith. Just because the new state depended ultimately

[1] Romans xiii. 1 – 7.

on force concentrated in one central government, that central government was bound to claim absolute obedience from its subjects, so long as large sections of them refused to recognize its authority. It could not permit the religious conscience to question its commands without precipitating civil war : nor could it permit men to accept the doctrines of Machiavelli. For although it was true that the state rested on force, to accept this doctrine was to admit that any rival power had the right to overthrow the existing government. Thus the Divine Right of Kings became the justification of the *status quo* in an epoch racked by a succession of religious wars. Catholic governments used it against Protestant minorities, and Protestant governments against Catholic ; Catholic minorities in Protestant countries would denounce it, though with rather different arguments from those used by Protestants under Catholic rule. It was a convenient doctrine provided that your side happened to be in power.

But if you were not in power, new political theories had to be found to justify resistance. The Huguenot in France and the Catholic in England were equally interested in denying Divine Right and finding reasons why no state should persecute its subjects for their religious convictions. For this purpose they went back to the old mediæval notion of a contract between king and people and tried to show that, though the king's power was derived from God, it was also dependent on an agreement to maintain true religion. Once this was admitted, the Catholic or Protestant minority could argue that, if the king preached false religion, it was their duty to destroy him. This theory was as absolutist as that of Divine Right. It claimed not toleration for religious sects, but the absolute right of the upholder of " true religion " to rebel.

We must notice two important features of these new political theories to which the conflicts of the nation state gave rise. In the first place all of them are still theological : unlike Machiavelli's, they do not recognize the secular character of politics but still claim the absolute right of organized religion to control governments. While this claim was made, there was no room for freedom or democracy or constitutionalism, and there was bound to be a permanent state of civil and international war. For these theories were as totalitarian as modern Fascism or Communism. They asserted the right and the duty of those who know the truth to enforce that truth on everyone else. Not till Europe had been exhausted by the wars of religion, and it was clear that heresy could never be extirpated by violent oppression, did the idea of toleration begin to creep in ; and this idea could only come if the state became a secular power (as Machiavelli had conceived it) which left religion to the conscience of the individual.

In the second place, the Reformation had produced a situation where the established governments differed in the religion they tried to enforce, while everyone still maintained that a universal religion must be enforced. This meant that political theory became entirely opportunist. What theory you held depended on whether you agreed with the government or were against it. In fact, political theory was not an attempt to analyse what society is and how it should be organized for the common good, but an instrument of propaganda for and against the established order. Because both sides were seeking the impossible—absolute uniformity of religious belief—they were unable to perceive those basic facts about the nation state to which Machiavelli had pointed long before.

It is unnecessary to analyze in detail any of these arguments either for passive obedience or for the right of resistance. Though many of their advocates were able pamphleteers, they did not do much more than serve a special cause. The great advances in human thought were now being made in science and pure philosophy, and the great social changes were the work of statesmen, not of theorists, of scientists not of political philosophers. But by the beginning of the 17th century the time was ripe for the first self-conscious analysis of the modern state. Western Europe had settled down to its new territorial states, each with its bureaucracy, its armed forces and its absolute monarch. The new financial system was now a recognized and respectable institution, and the exclusive rights of private property were universally admitted. The basis of the modern state had been securely built.

CHAPTER III

THE ENGLISH REVOLUTION

I. THE BACKGROUND

WE have seen already that the development of political ideas in England has always been somewhat different from that on the continent of Europe. During Roman times the remoteness of the British Isles from the " world's centre " in Italy meant that the British people were conquered late and deserted early by the legions, while the Scots were scarcely touched by Roman influence. Civilization was then swept away in the disaster of the Saxon invasions only to be brought back once more in 597 by Augustine and the Catholic Church, but still Britain remained a distant province of Christendom, living now by its simple Saxon customs and suffering continually under the wars of rival kings. Then came the second period of invasion. From 800 to 900 the Norsemen harried the land in spite of Alfred's desperate resistance, and this invasion was renewed at the end of the 10th century, with the result that Canute became King of England, Norway and Denmark in 1018. But this unification did not last, and it was a Saxon king, Harold, whom William the Norman conquered. In 1066 England became for the third time a province of the Latin world.

The Norman conquest resulted in the imposition of the feudal system from above. England, unlike 'most countries, was " feudalized " by a small ruling class, and this meant that it was far more centralized. The king really owned the land and let it out to his vassals, taking good care to scatter their estates and retaining sufficient to maintain his over-lordship against all rivals. For this reason the beginnings of a nation state are to be found in England as early as 1100, and already the king's central power is welcomed as a defence of the common people against the local lords. This alliance of a Norman king with his subject Saxons did much to unify the nation. It brought with it two other features of the nation state : in the first place the old Saxon usages were elaborated into the structure of a Common Law whose administration was retained by the monarchy, and in the second place a King's Council was formed of temporal and spiritual dignitaries which was the beginning of representative government. Only in his battle against Rome was the King of England unsuccessful, and the murder of Thomas à Becket resulted in the establishment by the Church of her rights to decide all criminal charges against clerics in her own courts. Meanwhile, the king's sheriffs presided over county courts, and the efficiency of his commissioners is proved by the meticulous accuracy of Domesday Book.

This centralizing tendency received a check in 1215 when John, who had unwisely attacked the privileges of the Church, the barons and the town merchants, was compelled to grant *Magna Carta*. Though it was not constitutional in the sense that it laid down the rights of the British citizen—that was impossible in a land of serfs—it did include a constitutional principle, since it admitted that the kingly power was limited by traditional rights and forbade arbitrary taxation. Magna Carta established the principle that taxation should be a matter for consultation between the king and the feudal lords, and this in its turn implied the beginnings of Parliament. In future, though the central executive spent the taxes, it would be the tax-payers who levied them upon themselves.

The development of this division of functions between the Executive and the Legislature is paralleled by a decline in the feudal system. As trade and industry increased in England, its Norman kings became more and more English kings, for whom France was not the centre of their domains but a province of England. Moreover, the growth of the towns, many with Royal Charters freeing them from feudal exactions, meant that the importance of the great barons decreased proportionately. A middle class of landowners, merchants and craftsmen was arising who were content to leave law and administration to the central power, and slowly the lesser barons too became, not feudal lords, but landowners under the state's authority. We can see this development also in the growth of the wool trade. England by 1300 was the greatest exporter of wool, and the produce of Lincolnshire and the West was shipped across to the mills of Flanders. The old self-sufficient economy was beginning to slip away.

This growth of a class of small landowners and merchants, distinct from the great barons and the bishops, is reflected in the division of Parliament into Lords and Commons; and the growing wealth of the latter gave them increasing influence with the kings who were always in need of money for their wars. The feudal system, though it remained the political structure of the country, was being slowly undermined by economic factors. Only in Scotland and in Wales, which were still conquered territories, was the old feudalism still undisputed master.

It is unnecessary to trace in detail the turbid history of England from 1300 to 1485 when the first of the Tudor kings gained the throne by force of arms and set about the systematic destruction of the old nobility. It is a period of violent transition, in which the loss of the French provinces after a hundred years of fruitless war forced the kings at last to grasp that the destiny of their country was not to be found in the conquest of Europe but in the development of their island's own resources. For now the power and the wealth of the middle classes was steadily increasing and the manufacture of cloth was replacing the export of wool and making England a mercantile country in the full sense of the word. This change was shown by her participation in the voyages of discovery, and in 1497 John Cabot sailed from Bristol to discover Newfoundland. From now on the accumulation of silver and the security of export markets became important motives of British policy, and England was ready for those political changes which we have described in the first chapter.

But Tudor absolutism and the ensuing Reformation did not cause such radical convulsions as in other countries. The king had always wielded more power and the Pope less than elsewhere : the agricultural revolution from feudal to private property had been under way for generations, and the squires and merchants had long challenged the power of the feudal lords and assumed for themselves some of the functions

of local government and national legislation. When
Henry VIII, by declaring himself both the temporal
and spiritual head of England, finally broke with
Rome, his people were behind him. Nor did his absolutism go to such lengths as that of Spain and Portugal.
Parliament, which had survived the Wars of the Roses,
survived the Tudors too ; while the new nobility of
wealth created by them succeeded the older feudal
lords. There was violence in plenty, but it was all
within a framework of national unity.

Nevertheless Tudor absolutism meant a decrease
in the influence of free institutions. Just as the Church
became a department of state, and the parson in the vill
age almost a state official, so the Privy Council and the
Justices of the Peace became executors of the royal will.
Thus the political form under which the nation was
" freed " from feudalism and papal supremacy was in
fact far more despotic than anything which preceded it.
But this political subjection was accompanied by a
spiritual liberation. The energies of the nation were un-
chained. In literature, science and business there was a
sudden burst of individual enterprise, which came
to a head in the Elizabethan era.

The framework within which this new life grew was
Mercantilism or the transfer to the state of that supervision of economic life previously held by the Church.
The Tudor era is not a period of free trade but of state-
controlled trade, in which a new bureaucracy directs
the activities of private enterprise. The state inter-
venes to grant monopolies, fix wages and prices, manage
the currency, determine tariffs and, by a new poor
law, to tackle the problem of unemployment. Here,
too, the centralizing tendency is at work to destroy

feudalism and sweep away the barriers against internal and international trade. The methods used are despotic, the understanding of economic law is small, but in the course of half a century Tudor energy has transformed the economic system and established the principle that the accumulation of wealth, in particular bullion, is a major national interest. Where previously money-making had been restricted by religion and law, now Church and state co-operated to facilitate the process, and law became the protector and assistant of private property and private enterprise both at home and abroad. The riches of the Church were ruthlessly confiscated and sold by the crown to business men who could get a quick return on the capital suddenly made available. Not yet, however, have we reached the period where the commercial classes are so secure that they can agitate against state interference and demand " free trade " : in the 16th century they needed state control and were content that a state, sympathetic to their interests, should replace the Church as the supreme controller of their activities.

This combination of political dictatorship and individual enterprise should be carefully observed. To-day analogies are being drawn between Tudor England and Nazi Germany in order to justify the form of government in the latter, and it is often argued that Germany has been liberated by Hitler, as England was liberated by the Tudors. It is of course true that free institutions can be accompanied by spiritual apathy and even enslavement, and that political absolutism is frequently an accompaniment of any violent revolutionary change. But it does not follow that the imposition of a dictatorship is always a liberation

of the spirit. Indeed it is never so unless the dictatorship does in fact enable a new class to expand its activities or a new form of life to be developed. Tudor
absolutism only justified itself finally in the Civil Wars
when the free spirit of the middle classes threw off
an absolutism mild in comparison with that of Henry
or Elizabeth. Whether the Nazis look forward to this
completion of their revolution I do not know.

In matters of religion, too, there was a curtailment
of liberty. Under Elizabeth's settlement the Church
retained the episcopate and much of the ceremony of
the Roman Mass while discarding its subordination
to the Pope. The spread of Protestantism, whether in
its Calvinist or Lutheran form, was checked by state
action, and non-conformists became an heretical body
persecuted and imprisoned like Roman Catholics. This
development was to be of immense importance for
British political thought. For whereas economic changes
were accelerated by Tudor policy, the moral reformation was checked by the new national Church. This
created a deep division in the ranks of the middle
classes. Those who were set on worldly success were
happy to accept the dictates of the Church of England ;
but the few who had religious scruples were cast out.
As a result the fight for religious freedom became a
question of personal conviction. For whereas a Catholic
would be accused of disloyalty to the British Crown right
into the 18th century, non-conformity brought with it
no questions of national or international significance.
Thus the creation of a National Church, which was
neither Roman nor Protestant but English, enabled the
fight for religious toleration to be freed from the dip-
lomatic considerations which influenced it so deeply

E

in France and Germany, and to become the genuine struggle of loyal British subjects to gain freedom to worship God in their own way. It is to this fact that British liberalism and American democracy owe their peculiar character. They are based not only on economic interests but on moral convictions and the demands of the religious conscience.

In spite, and partly because of the curtailment of political and religious freedom, England under the Tudors was moulded into a modern nation; and the failure of the Catholic restoration, engineered by Philip of Spain, completed the process. Previously the middle classes had had economic and moral motives for their attack on Rome; now patriotism demanded they should defend their country against internal and external foes. The defeat of the Armada in 1588 meant that the new régime of national independence had come to stay, and that from now on patriotism would always be on the side of the new commercial and land-owning class against any king who tried to thwart its will or impose an alien Catholic faith. The balance of power was already swinging away from the central government to the bourgeoisie. Previously the latter had looked to the former for protection, now the former must realize that without the latter it could accomplish nothing. England was passing out of the era of Machiavelli's Prince, who must by his personal sovereignty reign supreme, into that new state of free institutions of which, as we have seen, Machiavelli himself had dreamed. The Prince had fulfilled his function.

It was, however, to take many years of civil war and dictatorship before this fact was realized. Indeed the first stage of British development, after the Armada, was an attempt to confirm and enlarge the authority of the Crown. This attempt was begun by James I who, as we have seen in the first chapter, was the first British exponent of the theory of the Divine Right of Kings. The Tudor epoch was essentially a period of action and of expansion. Men were so busy making the new state that they had no time to speculate about it. Neither Henry nor Elizabeth explicitly claimed Divine Right for their sovereignty or explicitly demanded passive obedience. They ruled as secular autocrats on the model of Machiavelli, and they were prudent enough to placate their supporters and often to submit to their wishes. But James I came to the English throne from Scotland, where he had had bitter experience of the tyranny of a Calvinist Church. Scotch Calvinism had sprung up as a popular national movement on the continental model combining a religious reformation with an attack on the French troops which the Queen Regent, Mary of Guise, had introduced. Led by John Knox, the Calvinists in a few months had converted the yeomen, the craftsmen, the middle classes and some of the feudal lords. The struggle between the reformers and the Catholic Crown had culminated in the execution of Mary Queen of Scots, and the General Assembly of the Scottish Church had become the dominant power in a land where representative institutions had had no chance to grow. In this narrow sectarian atmosphere James had grown up, to succeed in 1603 to the English throne, and thus to unite the two kingdoms. He came to London with a bitter hatred of religious self-assertion, a high opinion of the obligations of kingship, a great deal of book learning and very little sense. Least of all could he understand the wealth, power and independence of the new men of substance, though the subservience of the Anglican Church was much to his taste. At a moment when Parliament was bound to claim a greater influence on policy, the King of England asserted his Divine Right and, to implement his claim, was bound to rely precisely on those reactionary elements which the Tudors had sought to suppress. The Anglican Church, the great landowners and their retainers rallied to the support of the new doctrine, while those classes which had served the Tudor despots loyally became now the upholders of constitutional liberty and the right of resistance. Moreover, by forcing the middle classes to the left, the Stuarts drove them into an alliance with all those nonconformist and puritan sects which had been fighting for religious freedom. The result was that by the time Charles I began to assert his kingly authority, he found himself in opposition, not only to many business interests, but to the burning zeal of the religious reformers.

The essentially conservative character of the Roundhead opposition to the Stuarts cannot be overemphasized. It is to be found once more in the Glorious Revolution of 1688, which threw out the last of the Stuarts and established once and for all both the rights of Parliament against the king and the refusal of England to permit political Catholicism. The revolutionary features we find in Cromwell's army are not causes but results of the civil wars. Both the gospel of the Levellers and the execution of the king are explicable only in terms of the anarchy caused by the war itself. But the extremism, which war always breeds and which forced even Cromwell into extreme action, was in advance of its time. England was not ripe for

equalitarian democracy though Cromwell's soldiers
could dream nobly of it.

This phenomenon is not uncommon in epochs of
violence. Revolutions can never go faster or further
than the social structure permits. The deep balance
of forces will assert themselves in the end despite the
sermons and ideologies and bloodshed. You can put
the clock back (for a time) but you cannot put it forward
except in theory. We can illustrate this from two
modern countries. Russia has attempted to skip
whole generations in the development of modern
industry and political organization. But the absence
of a strong bourgeoisie to supply the civil servants
of her new industrial state has endangered her attempts
to reach socialism without going through the stage
of bourgeois democracy. You can produce tractors
of a sort by a Five Year Plan, but you cannot produce
an administrative class so easily. The Spanish Civil
War gives us also an illuminating analogy. The Spanish
bourgeoisie was probably weaker and the Church
stronger than their equivalents in the time of Henry
VIII. Yet because the issue had been postponed so
long, what was accomplished in England by centralized
despotism was attempted in Spain by Liberal Democracy. Russia has tried to push through industrialization without a middle class by ruthless dictatorship.
Spain attempted to crush feudalism by constitutional
means. As a result civil war broke out and was transformed into an international war on Spanish soil.
Whereas in England the bourgeoisie opposed despotism
only after the despotism had broken its most formidable opponent, the Church, in Spain it found itself
matched against the Church, the army and their foreign

supporters. No wonder that it failed to overcome them.

In England, at least, the real revolution occurred, not in the Cromwellian but in the Tudor epoch, and the Civil Wars and Glorious Revolution confirmed the strength of the new order, exploded Utopian theories of popular democracy and finally defeated the forces of reaction. What *was* changed was the temper of both sides : a period which started with theological controversy based on passionate religious conviction ended in toleration, scepticism and the rule of reason. It is as though war and anarchy had purged the struggle of all its ideological paraphernalia and left the combatants face to face with the sober material issues. By a process of sheer exhaustion both sides came to see that no principle and no religion was worth a civil war. In short, *the idea of toleration* was the chief result of a war between two parties both intolerant in their claims.

II.   CONTRASTING PERSONALITIES

The changes in English society between the accession of James I in 1603 and the flight of James II in 1688 are illustrated by the writings of the two greatest students of political theory which this country has produced. Thomas Hobbes and John Locke were contemporaries[1]; only thirty-nine years separates the date of publication of their most famous works, and yet

[1] Hobbes 1588-1679, published the *Leviathan* in 1651.   Locke 1632-1704, published *Civil Government* in 1690.

the difference between them is a difference of epochs, almost of civilizations. The *Leviathan* is the last great product of the Renaissance, *Civil Government* the first forerunner of the Age of Enlightenment. A comparison and contrast of these authors will enable us to see something of the nature of the English Revolution.

Both Hobbes and Locke came of middle-class families. Hobbes' father was an Elizabethan parson, ignorant and hot-tempered, who had to fly for his life after a scuffle, and his son Thomas was brought up by a prosperous west country glover. Locke was the son of a small country lawyer who found the collection of ship-money for Charles I so distasteful that he joyfully joined the Parliamentarian army in 1642. Both boys in spite of their humble birth were sent to Oxford, Hobbes becoming a member of Magdalen Hall in 1603, and Locke of Christ Church in 1652. If fifty years changed many things in England, they did not change Oxford, and Hobbes and Locke both reacted violently against the logic which the professors there still taught in the scholastic tradition. They got out of Oxford what later generations were to get, a hearty contempt for dons and a number of useful friends.

But here we must notice our first point of difference. The young Hobbes turned naturally from the quibbles of logic to the classics. It was in the study, among others, of Thucydides that he found both his emancipation and his real education, and it was not till long afterwards in 1629, when he was over forty, that geometry first excited his interest and turned him from literature to science and the new philosophy of Descartes (1596-1650). Locke on the other hand studied

Descartes as an undergraduate, soon became an intimate of the famous scientist Boyle, and began to practise medicine in Oxford after taking his degree. This difference in the intellectual development of the two men is of profound importance. Hobbes, still in the Renaissance tradition, started as a humanist, worshipping the Greek and Roman authors because they disclosed to him a secular civilization in which theology and priests played no part at all and things were measured by the standard of human reason. Thus he was a true descendent of Machiavelli, chiefly interested in destroying mediæval superstition ; and the science which he later studied was not natural science in our sense, but geometry and philosophical speculation on the Greek model. Against mediæval scholasticism he was determined to erect a system of abstract principles, proved by pure reason alone ; and although he preached a materialist philosophy of natural science, he remained not a scientist but a metaphysician who saw in the mathematical method of reasoning from first principles the instrument for achieving human mastery over nature and over his fellow-men. Locke, on the other hand, was thrown from earliest days into the company of natural scientists working by the method of experiment, prediction and control. The work of Boyle in his laboratory began to undermine his faith in logic. Starting from the Cartesian method, which for Hobbes was the summit of man's achievement, he then attempted to evolve a system which would reconcile philosophy with the methods of experimental science.

The contrast between the pure reason of the Renaissance and the empiricism of the 18th century is to be found also in the styles of the two writers. Locke writes an easy, flowing English, colloquial, occasionally pithy, always clear. The simplicity of his style and its verbal precision indeed often disguise the confusion of his thought. In Hobbes, prose has not yet separated itself from poetry, and the *Leviathan* contains much of the majestic rhythm of the Authorized Version of the Bible. Even when it attacks religion and preaches scientific materialism, it uses the phrases of its opponents; and even where it pleads for a new scientific language, the plea has the eloquence of biblical prophecy.

There be so many words in use at this day in the English Tongue, that though of magnifique sound, yet (like the windy blisters of a troubled water) have no sense at all.[1]

In short Hobbes belonged to the age when men were destroying the supremacy of theology by philosophical argument, and still trying to construct a modern scientific language : Locke to the age of Newton himself.[2]

But we must return to Oxford. After taking his degree, Hobbes became tutor to the Cavendish family and remained attached to it, apart from short intervals, to the end of his life, living in their country houses, making the Grand Tour with his pupils, and meeting and conversing with the leading men of his time. He became a satellite of the aristocracy and never had any experience of business, government or administration. This explains to a great extent his pessimism and contempt for his fellow-men. With a hearty dislike for breeding without brains, he could not help

[1] From " Answer to Davenant " quoted in Michael Roberts' The *Modern Mind*, Chap. III.

[2] The *Principia* was published in 1687 and Locke's *Human Understanding* in 1690.

pouring scorn on the theological arguments by which
the Royalists defended their cause : and yet he was
unable to appreciate the strength or quality of their
opponents. The man who could declare " The value
or worth of a man is, as of all other things, his price. . . .
Honour consisteth only in the opinion of Power "
was not likely to be loved by Cavaliers, even if he could
confound the arguments of the other side.

Hobbes thus became a defender of the Royal Prerogative, whose arguments were acceptable to none
of its protagonists. He gave Machiavellian support
to a king who believed that Machiavelli was a blas-
phemer, and in the name of science and pure reason
denounced the forces of progress. As a result his
influence on the practical politics of his own day was
negligible ; how negligible is proved by the fact that
he was executed by neither side, although he first
returned to England during the Protectorate, and
then stayed there when Charles II was restored, being
rightly confident that Charles, who was a former pupil,
would protect him. In a very true sense Hobbes was
the first *academic* philosopher, so profound in his
thought so remote from practical politics, that no man
of action could take him seriously. Regarded as an
amusing eccentric, he attained the freedom of thought
which was once the perquisite of the mediæval
jester.

Again here, we find a contrast with Locke, who
was not only a practical scientist but a man of affairs
as well. As secretary to the Earl of Shaftesbury he
became an important official in the Lord Chancellor's
office in 1672, and had to leave England when his
master was incriminated in the Monmouth plot. The

Glorious Revolution of 1688 enabled him to return
and spend his last years in semi-retirement as Com-
missioner of Appeals. Throughout his life he participated actively in the day-to-day tasks of administration and finance, and studied the problem of
handling his fellow-men, not in the classic writings
of Thucydides but in the committee room. Unlike
Hobbes' writings, Locke's are the occasional essays
of a busy man of affairs. Whether he is writing of
toleration, or education, or the implications of the
new science for Christian theology, or politics or even
economics, he has an eye on the immediate practical
issues involved. He does not try to build a monumental edifice of human reason, but throws together
his reflections on the burning issues of the day. But
though he is unsystematic by academic standards,
he is intensely scientific in his method and outlook ;
he tests his hypotheses by an objective study of current
fact, has a half-hearted suspicion of argument from
first principles, and has no wish to say the final word on
any subject because he feels that for science finality
is impossible. Thus, though there is far less system
in his political theory than in that of Hobbes, he shows
far more understanding of politics : and contrariwise,
because the *Treatise of Civil Government* is more immediately applicable, it is now far more " dated " than
the *Leviathan*. Hobbes was so remote from immediate
reality that he perceived certain factors deep below
the surface, while Locke was primarily engaged in the
solution of current problems. The *Leviathan* sums
up the profoundest wisdom of the Renaissance, *Civil
Government* introduces us to the level-headed, unen-
thusiastic common sense of the 18th century.

III. THE *LEVIATHAN*

It is sometimes argued that the pessimism which permeates Hobbes' theory of government was caused by his experience of civil war. Such a suggestion is both a belittlement of the *Leviathan* and a historical impossibility. Hobbes was not the man to weave his theories under the pressure of circumstance : although his life was one of compromise and prevarication, his mind was incisive and unyielding, and the chief ideas which he developed in the *Leviathan* are to be found in an earlier work written before the war began. Already in 1640 he had outlined a theory of the nation state which summed up the whole Renaissance spirit, and gave a philosophical basis to the movement whose origin we saw in *The Prince*.

The motive of this movement was, as we have seen, its " realism ". Machiavelli had tried to see man stripped of all theological trappings as a human being with purely mundane interests. The difference between him and Dante is the difference between Michael Angelo and the sculptor of the western façade of Chartres. The one sees through the flesh to the anatomy of muscle and bone, the other expresses in human form the supernatural essence of the spirit. Strictly one is no more realistic than the other, but each sees a different reality and calls it man. Each has a different philosophy of life, and in the *Leviathan* the anatomical outlook of the Renaissance is developed into a fully-fledged political system.

Listen to the opening sentences of his introduction :

Nature (the Art whereby God hath made and governes
the World) is by the *Art* of man, as in many other things, so
in this also imitated, that it can make an Artificiall Animal.
For seeing life is but a motion of Limbs, the begining whereof
is in some principall part within ; why may we not say,
that all *Automata* (Engines that move themselves by springs
and wheeles as doth a watch) have an artificiall life ? For
what is the *Heart*, but a *Spring* ; and the *Nerves*, but so
many *Strings* ; and the *Joynts*, but so many *Wheeles*, giving
motion to the whole Body, such as was intended by the
Artificer ? *Art* goes further, imitating that Rationall and
most excellent worke of Nature, *Man*. For by Art is created
that great LEVIATHAN called a COMMON-WEALTH, or STATE,
(in latine CIVITAS) which is but an Artificiall Man.

Here in briefest outline you have Hobbes' philosophy.
Man is something which reason can understand like a
clock or a chemical compound. He works like a machine
and there is nothing supernatural about him. And
human society is equally rational : it, too, is a piece of
machinery, more elaborate, more imposing but at
bottom a product of human activity, and nothing else.
To run the machine correctly, all you need to do is to
understand its structure, and the structure of its component parts. There are laws which regulate both, and
they are to be found not by studying scripture or the
dogmas of the Church, but by studying the nature of
the state and of human beings. The art of government
must be based on the science of psychology.

Swiftly and precisely Hobbes then describes the
nature of man. His is composed of two parts, reason
and passions, and both of these are natural phenomena
which science can describe. Reason is a machinery
which associates the ideas which we receive through

our senses. It is not an active creative power, but a sorting office of the letters sent in by our ears and eyes and noses; and the sorting takes place automatically by laws as simple as the laws of gravity which Newton was soon to discover. The real force, however, which moves human beings is passion, and this again can be divided into a number of simple driving impulses, whether desires or aversions, some primal and some derived from experience.

It is unnecessary to analyse Hobbes' psychology further. In broad outline it is the famous Theory of Association which was to remain the chief Science of the Mind until the end of the 19th century. We only need to note that, though it is scientific in the sense that it looks for natural causes and excludes all supernatural explanations, it is not based on experiment or verification. Indeed, it is an hypothesis as little proven as the theology which it replaces. Against the dogma of revelation and Divine Law, it poses the dogma of the human machine and of human reason as the instrument of passion. [Reason, says Hobbes, is not a faculty granted by God so that man should know Him, but the tool which our desires employ to accomplish their purposes.] Instead of a cosmos ruled by God, he conceives an anarchy driven by desire.

And human society is man writ large. As man is the battlefield of competing passions, so society is the battle of competing men. [The state of nature, says Hobbes, is a state of war.] For [the driving motives of man in society are two, ambition of power and fear of defeat.] Desiring the satisfaction of his passions, he seeks the wealth and power over others which are necessary to their satisfaction. Fearing the attacks of his neighbours, he seeks security for the property which he has won. It is the uncertain seesaw of these two motives which makes human society so unpolitical compared to that of ants. Since they have no ambition and no reason by which they can compare themselves one with another, ants do not have that envy and ambition which make it so difficult for men to live at peace in a community.

This picture of his fellow-men is drawn from life, but it is not the work of a man of affairs. As description of the sober merchant or farmer or Parliamentarian it is fantastic and frankly unrealistic. But Hobbes was concerned, not with outward appearances, but with " psychological laws ". Mere fact he pushes aside like the flesh which impedes the anatomist's knife, until he reaches the hard bone of psychological structure for which he searches. At last he finds, despite all evidence, the motives which he decided to find before the operation ; and with mathematical logic demonstrates the anatomy of the human soul.

Hobbes' argument can be stated quite simply. Assume man a creature driven by envy, ambition, and fear and you have a state of war. But man has also reasoning powers which tell him that such a state is undesirable since it provides no security of enjoyment. Reason, moreover, can think out in the abstract a number of rules of behaviour which, if they were universally respected, would be of benefit to all. These rules are the old *Laws of Nature*, and also correspond roughly to the Christian ethic, " Do as you would be done by " Hobbes sees that, if all men respected them, all men would be happier ; but he also sees that a creature with the psychology which he has ascribed to man will not respect them himself unless it pays to do so, and will not trust others to respect them, unless it pays them also.

Here then are the factors with which a statesman must contend, and the *Leviathan* is the construction which Hobbes demonstrates to be necessary in order to reconcile anti-social man to social life. In the manner of a true geometer he proves it in a series of logical steps :

1. All men would like to live under the Laws of Nature if only each could be sure that others would observe them.

2. This is only possible if there is a coercive power, supreme above all, enforcing the Laws of Nature in a positive detailed code of law. Such a code of law is only binding because and in so far as it satisfies the universal desire for security.

3. A state therefore comes into being *through a social contract* between all the inhabitants of any one territory by which each resigns his rights of self-defence to the state on condition that all the rest do the same.

4. To be effective, such a social contract must demand the surrender of every right, and grant omnipotence to the state. If an individual or a group retains any bargaining power or right of appeal to a higher authority, then the others can no longer feel sure of securing equal treatment.

5. It is immaterial whether the sovereign is one man or a group of men, provided they or he have supreme coercive power. The sovereign must be above the law, and make it ; he must command the armed forces, have power over all property and control all public opinion. Without these powers he will not be supreme, and if he is not supreme then the social contract is no longer binding and a state of war once more exists.

6. Finally, if all this is proven, the Church must be the servant of the state, and the Papacy is the chief enemy of peace.

Such is the formidable construction of the *Leviathan*.
Starting from the hypothesis of a " free " man untram-
melled by conscience, the slave of passion, [it concludes
with a secure man under the dictates of a totalitarian
state,] free to think what he likes but not to speak it,
to do what he likes provided the sovereign permits it,
to hold what property he likes provided the exigencies
of statecraft do not demand its surrender.   Losing all
his rights, the individual has the supreme satisfaction
of knowing that all others have lost them too ; and it
is this knowledge which turns him into an obedient,
law-abiding citizen.

This argument shows at least what a profound insight Hobbes had gained into the working of the cen- [*or gov.*
tralized monarchy. Under the new despotism, the king
had become supreme over Church and state : he had
seized property where it pleased him, he had enforced
the public acceptance of religious dogmas established
by him alone, he had made a positive law along the
lines which seemed good to him.   And although
theoretically he was an arbitrary tyrant, his tyranny
had meant emancipation from the chaos of decrepit
mediævalism. In a real sense the Tudors, in spite of
their despotism, were more democratic than any ruler
who preceded them, since they relied on their personal
prestige and power as no ruler before them had done.
Taking all responsibility upon itself, the new régime
demanded and got a national assent to its autocracy.
The Church and a few thousands of individuals with
religious consciences or treasonable designs or unfortunately useful property suffered the stings of despotism,
but the nation as a whole felt the benefits of it.
Thus the paradox of an absolute sovereignty founded

upon a social contract had its reason in history even if its logic was a little slippery. Hobbes had grasped the inmost nature of the new state just at the moment when it was beginning to change into an entirely new form.

Much time and trouble has been spent in exposing the false reasoning in the argument of the *Leviathan*. If we leave the matter there, we fail to grasp its importance. For its logical contradictions arise from the inner stresses of the nation state, and Hobbes is often most to the point where he is most contradictory. Roughly speaking, the motives which he ascribed to all men were the motives of the creators of the new society : Tudor despotism had to deal with men of this temper, and was of this temper itself. For this reason his psychology, though it is a bad general theory, describes quite correctly the politics of the period. The statesman, instead of relying on " men of goodwill ", had to assume that force and fraud were necessities of government. Hobbes saw that the Divine Right of Kings was no longer accepted by many of the people who really counted : they demanded that the state should do a job for them and be based on their will. He saw that, since the old order was broken, all were now equal, ordered not by eternal class divisions but according to the power and property which each possessed, and anyone might win. In short, he recognized that bourgeois society was replacing feudal society.

This new individualistic society needed above all strong centralized government, and the more he stressed the competition of all against all, the more urgent this need appeared. Where no one is recognized as innately superior, a superior power must be constructed and imposed for the common good : where every hallowed custom and institution is challenged, new customs must be laid down and institutions formed. The economic and social changes which we analyzed in the first chapter must be recognized as facts, and state, religion and morality must be constructed anew with power sufficient to control them.

Hence arises the paradox of *absolute government based on a social contract*, which is the centre of Hobbes' system. Though it was a contradiction, it was also a necessity of thought which will recur in every revolutionary situation in modern history. The contradiction proves not that Hobbes was wrong but that the social order was in a phase of violent transition in which no state could legitimate its power and no philosopher who understood the problem could remain consistent. Not till the ideals of bourgeois society had been accepted as self-evident by theorists and absorbed as habits by ordinary men, was a consistent theory of government to be once more possible.

But even when this happened two aspects of the *Leviathan* would remain deeply significant. In the first place it would remain true that in emergencies no government could survive which did not retain power to crush opposition. Even the most democratic government, based wholly on the will of the people and hedged round with constitutional safeguards, must be able to suppress attacks on the Constitution. Within a modern state we have no rights which can be absolutely safeguarded by constitutional means, and, if we protect them by civil war, then we have violated the constitution and destroyed democracy. In this sense every modern

state is either a Leviathan which can crush us, or a
weapon which can be used by one group to destroy
the rights of others.

In the second place, even those who disagree with
Hobbes' account of the relation between the state
and the subject must admit the acuteness of his
analysis of international relations. Here he correctly
finds a " state of war " in which there is no security
because there is no sovereign over all, and he concludes
that foreign policy must be dictated by the needs of
self-preservation so long as this condition lasts.

> So in States, and Common-wealths not dependent on
> one another, every Common-wealth, (not every man) has
> an absolute Libertie, to doe what it shall judge (that is
> to say, what that Man, or Assemblie that representeth it,
> shall judge) most conducing to their benefit. But withall,
> they live in the condition of a perpetuall war, and upon
> the confines of battel, with their frontiers armed, and
> canons planted against their neighbours round about.[1]

The *Leviathan*, however, is not merely of interest
to students of modern international relations; it has
much to teach us about Nazism and Fascism, and
Communism too. For it discloses the basic reason
both for their origins and for their continuance. [Since
ordinary men and women want peace and security
much more than they care for political principles,
a system of liberty which cannot guarantee security
may be replaced by a totalitarian state and gain the
consent of the masses.] Political freedom is a luxury
which can only be enjoyed in very favourable circumstances : once it permits a deadlock and seems to be

---

[1] *Leviathan*, ii. 21.

lapsing into anarchy, any democracy may democratically vote itself out of existence. and, for a time at least, the people may prefer to be freed from their freedom. Hobbes gives us not the dictator's justification for his despotism, but the reasons which impel his subjects to accept it. The ⌊Leviathan⌋ is the first democratic attack upon democracy.⌉ As such it is of lasting interest, especially in regard to the nature both of liberty and of ourselves.

IV. CIVIL GOVERNMENT

Locke's *Treatise on Civil Government* has been often regarded as the final refutation of Hobbes' argument, and the ⌈perfect justification of representative democracy.⌉ But in certain ways it is not so democratic a book as the *Leviathan* and certainly does not refute it. What it does display is a brilliant insight into the practical problems of government in a country where the despotism of kings had been decisively challenged by a fairly homogeneous ruling class. For Hobbes' mistake was not in his logic but in his ignorance of the character and needs of the new men of substance. Having exploded the Divine Right of Kings and the claims of the church to challenge the state, he had concluded that the despotism which had prevailed in Europe for over a hundred years was the only possible form of government. Treating all men as equal, he had not noticed that every government, however totalitarian it may look, depends on the support of some at least of its subjects. The truth is that the form of government in any country largely

Conservatives — need a Leviathan to benefit their interests & don't really need local gov.

depends on the needs of those classes which are influential enough to challenge its power. If they do not need a Leviathan such as Hobbes described, they will not tolerate it for long.

This is what happened in England between 1603, when James I came to the throne, and 1688, when James II was forced to fly the land, to be succeeded by a Dutchman more amenable to orders. When Hobbes was writing his justification of absolutism, absolutism was already an anachronism in his own country. The civil wars were proving that since the Revolution effected by the Tudors had become part of the settled life of the country, centralized monarchy was no longer needed for the preservation of peace. On the contrary, for peace and prosperity toleration of differences within the limits of national unity was the demand of those sober Englishmen who had defended their religious and their political liberties against royal encroachment.

This demand John Locke recognized, though he understood even less than Hobbes the reasons for it. The refutation of the theory of Divine Right, which occupies the first half of his treatise, is a dreary piece of argumentation, lacking much of Hobbes' insight into the nature of political power, while his justification of representative institutions leaves most of the basic problems of government untouched. Locke was a brilliant politician but he was not a profound political philosopher.

Let us see how he sets about his demonstration that law and order can be preserved without accepting slavery to *Leviathan*. His first argument against Hobbes is that *Leviathan* only substitutes for the

war of all against all, the war of the despot against
his subjects.[1] No reasonable man, to gain security
against his neighbour, will put himself wholly in the
power of the state. " This freedom from absolute
arbitrary power is so necessary to and closely joined
with a man's preservation that he cannot part with it
but by what forfeits his preservation and life together ".[2]
Locke sums up this argument in a famous passage :

Who would not think it an admirable peace betwixt
the mighty and the mean, when the lamb, without resistance, yielded his throat to be torn by the imperious wolf ?
Polyphemus's den gives a perfect pattern of such a peace.
Such a government wherein Ulysses and his companions
had nothing to do but quietly to suffer themselves to be
devoured. And no doubt Ulysses, who was a prudent
man, preached up passive obedience, and exhorted them
to a quiet submission by representing to them of what
concernment peace was to mankind, and by showing that
inconveniences might happen if they should offer to resist
Polyphemus, who had now the power over them.
The end of the government is the good of mankind ; and
which is best for mankind, that the people should be always
exposed to the boundless will of tyranny, or that the rulers
should be sometimes liable to be opposed when they grow
exorbitant in the use of their power, and employ it for the
destruction, and not the preservation, of the properties
of their people ? [3]

The limitation of sovereignty is thus the main
objective of rational man, and we must search for the
principles of that limitation. Locke finds them in
the *natural rights* inherent in us as men. Thus whereas
Hobbes looked for some power strong enough to restrain
wilful man, Locke is trying to find a safeguard for
rational man against the wilfulness of princes. He

[1] § *Treatise* 17.   [2] § 22.   [3] § 228 and 229,

refutes Hobbes only by asserting that man's needs are not what Hobbes said they were ; and he is right, not about men in general, but about the English gentlemen of his day.

In 1688 there had been a revolution. A king had been expelled, a new king had been selected and his sovereignty hedged round with parliamentary safeguards. But this revolution had resulted in none of the dire consequences Hobbes foretold. When the machinery of state broke down, man had not immediately reverted to a state of war : on the contrary, the country had been united in one common purpose—to defend its constitutional rights against royal trespass. By asserting the right of revolution it had saved itself from civil war. In fact, the gentlemen of England had freed themselves from the Leviathan and felt better for it ; they had proved that England was now a nation which needed no centralized despotism to hold it together, and refused to tolerate a king whose religion it disliked.

It is from this idea of a nation united by a common interest that Locke starts. He expresses it in the generalization : "In the state of nature, men have natural rights to life, liberty and property : civil society only comes into being for the preservation of those rights and can justifiably be dissolved whenever the government violates them". This theory means in simple language that, quite apart from fear of the policeman, men respect each others' civil rights out of ordinary common sense. The policeman is only there to punish a criminal minority and to relieve the sensible majority of the duty of self-defence ; the judge in order to enable the law-abiding citizens to have an impartial decision on matters in disagreement ; the army to protect a peaceful social order from external aggression.   On all fundamental matters, we are in agreement about what we want and the state is only a convenient machinery for facilitating the protection of our peaceful activities.

What is the nature of this peaceful social order which Locke assumes to be desired by all ?   The answer is given in Chapter V of *Civil Government*, where he deals with the Right of Property.   In this chapter he puts forward a theory that private ownership is derived not from the state but from the individual's own rights.   Once a man has " mixed his labour " with a field or a mill or a shop it is his absolutely and he can bequeath it to anyone he likes.   Whether Locke was right in asserting that property originates in this way is unimportant. What matters is the principle that property is the exclusive possession of the proprietor and carries no obligations with it, and the corollary that one function of the state is the preservation of this exclusive property system.

A comparison with Chapter II will indicate how completely different this theory is from any mediæval philosophy :   it is indeed the first clear account both of bourgeois morality and the bourgeois state, in which the amassing of private wealth is held to be one of the chief activities of sensible men.   Locke is the prophet of private enterprise, and of freedom of contract, and he showed his real boldness of spirit in extending this principle even to marriage.[1]   He conceived of England as a nation of free property owners intent on the amassing and free enjoyment of wealth.

[1] § 81.

For such a people the Leviathan has become a use-less and a dangerous burden. They do not cry for a despot to win them their rights from the Church or the feudal lord : their rights are established, unchallenged by men of position, and they fear only encroachment by a king with too much power. Thus Locke abolishes sovereignty and replaces it with a division of powers between the legislature and the executive (i.e. the new constitutional monarch). By splitting the Leviathan into two and making each a check on the other, he ensures that each fulfils its proper function and neither is strong enough to encroach on the people's natural rights.

Civil Government is based on the assumption that the citizens of a state will be men of property who assent to government freely because they recognize its utility for so long as it continues to be useful. But what of the minority (if it exists) who disagree with its institution, or the minority in the legislature who vote against a law ? Locke replies that they too must recognize that, since unanimity is imposs-ible, the majority must prevail. No sensible man will upset constitutional government by resorting to revolution against the considered opinion of a majority of his fellow citizens. The principle of majority rule, so vital to future developments of the democratic idea, is here introduced as a relatively unimportant detail of political procedure. Locke believes not in the will of the majority, but in the will of all, which he is con-vinced is well-nigh unanimous in defence of natural rights.

It is on this fundamental agreement of all men of good will and substance that respect for law and govern-ment by discussion must be founded. The nation can afford toleration (except of Catholicism) because the nation has one common interest : it can permit freedom of thought and speech as long as they do not violate this common interest ; and lastly, since the risk of disturbing this harmonious society comes not from the people below but from the powers above, it can permit more freedom to the private individual than it can to any branch of the government itself.

The ideas which Locke built up into the system of civil government were to be the inspiration not only of English but of American Liberalism ; and, through borrowing them without asking too carefully about their applicability, continental Liberals were to pay a heavy price. Indeed it is difficult to find a political theory which has been more readily welcomed and more grossly misapplied. The fault for this is partly Locke's : the system which fitted England so admirably was not suited to countries with quite different histories. But because Locke generalized its principles into a universal form and offered it as a rational panacea for all political problems, this was not easily understood. Moreover, it was not noticed that to two fundamental problems he gave no answer at all. For in the first place what is to happen when, under the constitutional system he outlines, a section of the community begins to realize that it has no natural rights to defend ? Locke had legislated for men of property, but what of the labourer without possessions who was rapidly replacing the peasant proprietor ? It is not sufficient to declare all men equal when the vast majority are disfranchised, uneducated and without wealth. A belief in natural rights might stimulate such as these not to accept civil government but to overthrow it. To this problem

Locke's answer is unsatisfactory and inconsistent. Sometimes [1] he says that the people are the judge of the adequacy of government. When he does this, he makes the majority will the final arbiter in the state and identifies the rights of the majority with the natural rights of all. Sometimes he holds that, once civil government has been established, the people have no right to modify the constitution [2] or even to restore it to its original perfection. On this view civil government is a static form of society which is bound to degenerate into oligarchy. But it is this second view which is the real basis of Locke's thought. Just as the mixing of labour is only the original justification of property and is soon lost sight of, so democracy is only the origin, not the *raison d'être*, of his system. The people must be content to feel that they are virtually represented by the men of property who are their legislators, and it is for the preservation of the social order, not for its improvement, that Locke is really anxious.

The second problem follows naturally from the first. Locke defined the aim of civil government as the defence of natural rights, but he made no mention of natural *duties*, or social obligations. It is as though he envisaged the nation as a network of private estates, each carefully fenced from the next, in which the only duty of a citizen was to keep off his neighbour's ground, the only job of the legislature to perfect the law of " privacy ". If Hobbes' natural man was savagely anti-social, Locke's was high-mindedly so. He had not even the vaguest idea of government as a force for positive good—education, social services, etc.—or of

[1] § 240.   [2] § 158.

men as co-operative creatures; and the virtuous egot-
ism of his representative oligarchy has a chilly air of
rationalism and exclusiveness which will repel the
reformer and the democrat of later days when they
dream of the social state.

But these are defects inherent both in his system
and in the liberalism of his age and its successor. When
Burke denounced [1] those democrats who justified the
French Revolution by references to the Glorious Revolution, he was on firm ground, and his interpretation of
its motive was the correct one. Locke was the prophet
not of popular government but of government by consent, not of democratic rights but of humane oligarchy,
not of liberty but of " privacy ". Directly his theory
was adapted to the demands of a landless people it
became not a defence of constitutionalism but a justification of popular dictatorship. Robespierre might
claim to have acted on Lockean principles, but he
would have received small mercy from Locke himself
or from the Whigs he spoke for.

And yet as we shall see, much of his philosophy
survives to this day as the guiding principles of British
political life. The exclusive rights of property may be
challenged but they are still a potent force. Government
as the perquisite of a small political élite is a fact, if
not a theory, of our modern life, even though the in-
gredients of the élite have changed. The Englishman
is still, as in 1688, an unpolitical creature, who consents
to government by others as long as his vital interests
are undisturbed; he is still suspicious of centralized
authority, still believes in the principle " set a thief to
catch a thief ", still instinctively forgets that political

[1] *Appeal from New Whigs to the Old.*

rights bring political obligations too, whether in the sphere of national defence or of property management. In brief, he is still, as Locke suggested, a person who regards politics not as the centre of his life, but as a bothersome duty which had best be entrusted to a few and changed as little as possible.

It is easy to smile at Locke's picture of a society of free citizens, each happily cultivating his own back garden and leaving his neighbours to cultivate theirs. But we shall underrate *Civil Government* if we regard it merely as an expression of English character and a complacent defence of the Glorious Revolution. For although it was written as a tract for the times, it remains a classic example of bourgeois political theory, and its ideal of social life is shared by most democrats and socialists to this day. Eighteenth-century England did not aim at a high ethical standard, but its temper was rational and tolerant, and these qualities Locke rightly believed to be essential to any civilized society. He saw that it is the aim of civilization not to harness our noblest emotions in the service of a splendid and all-powerful state, but to enable us as individuals each to develop in his own way. Thus when he stressed the unimportance of politics compared with private life, he was expounding the ideal not only of English Whigs in the seventeenth century, but of Western civilization as a whole. The economic changes, which culminated in the industrial revolution, would make its realization increasingly difficult and accentuate the conflict between the right of property and the rights of life and liberty which Locke had failed to notice in his own day; but through all these changes the ordinary men and women of America and England and Western Europe would still dream of a kindly, tolerant society which should secure to each equality before the law and freedom to live his life as he thought best. Like the later Liberals, Locke was unduly optimistic ; he believed that representative institutions were only needed to guarantee existing rights and failed to observe that, for the mass of the people, the economic conditions of freedom must be created by the state before they can be guaranteed.

For there is a deep distinction between representative institutions and democracy, between the *Rechstaat* and government of the people. A well-ordered democracy will adopt the principle of equality before the law and institutions of the Lockean state but, in making the common people participators in government, it will change them profoundly. The bourgeois ideal, for which Locke spoke, assumed the existence of an enlightened upper class, ruling in the interests of all and representing the common people. Aristotle, who had experience of states where the voice of the people prevailed, was shrewd enough to see that representative institutions and an independent judiciary are in the interests of men of substance, and labelled them " oligarchic ". They can only be made the servants of democracy when the people are educated and organized to defend their interests, and when, through taxation and the provision of social services, they have realized some measure of economic security. Thus, though democracy can be achieved through representative institutions, it is not identical with them. Civil Government can be transformed into popular government, but in itself it is oligarchic in temper, and Locke in his day was the protagonist not of the people's rights, but of humane and enlightened government by a class which he assumed without question was the virtual representative of the nation as a whole. That the mass of the people might actively participate in self-government never occurred to him.

But though we should, from our twentieth-century standpoint, observe this failure and notice how it would enable the defenders of privilege in the future to pretend that they were the advocates of freedom, we should not blame Locke for the faults of his successors. In his own day, he was a sane progressive, whose writings tempered the arrogance of the social oligarchy and taught it the discipline of representative institutions. And, if later he was to inspire Burke's conservatism, he inspired Paine and Rousseau—and even Karl Marx as well.

CHAPTER IV

THE AMERICAN REVOLUTION

I.   THE AGE OF REASON

THE century between the Glorious Revolution which established the Whig oligarchy in England, and the revolutions which transformed France and the United States of America into modern nation states, was marked by the development of a Lockean philosophy in France and America. For a hundred years England was a country admired by all progressive thinkers, the home of prosperity, liberty and justice ; and two Englishmen, Locke and Newton, were regarded as prophets of the age. In the realm of physics Newton had demonstrated the power of the mind to discover simple universal laws applicable, despite apparent differences, to all material bodies ; and it was natural that men should believe that similar laws governed the movements of human society. In the 18th century it seemed as though mankind was on the edge of discoveries, which would display both the mechanism of the universe and the structure of human society as simple rational creations of a benevolent deity : while on the other hand it seemed equally clear that, if passion and prejudice could be suppressed and human reason released from bondage, then man could both master nature and attain his true, social happiness.

This belief in the infallibility of reason and the simplicity of its task is the keynote of the philosophy of the *Aufklärung*, which became the gospel both of the critics of despotism in Europe, and of the framers of the American constitution. Perhaps the Americans did not appreciate the perfections of the British Constitution quite as fully as the French philosophers Voltaire and Montesquieu, who visited England to behold and admire. But then the Americans suffered under it and the French did not. Be that as it may, Lockean principles came to America via France and inspired the revolutionaries both in their struggle for independence and in the elaboration of their constitution.

Thus we are faced with yet another paradox in the development of political ideas. Locke had formulated in *Civil Government* the justification of the Whig resistance to James II; and so in his own country the theory of natural rights, of representative government and of checks and balances became a conservative defence against radicalism. But force of circumstance and a monarch who knew no English soon evoked a system of cabinet responsibility to Parliament which deprived the king of most of his executive powers and made the government in effect the monopoly of a small ruling class. For the battle of the representatives of the people against the despot was substituted the party warfare of Whigs and Tories, based on a spoils system of quite open corruption. The natural rights of free and equal citizens were enjoyed by a class of not more than ten thousand, the " virtual representatives " of a people oppressed by a vindictive code of law. In the 18th century the toleration which Locke had lauded was not made available to the Non-conformist and the Catholic, who suffered under the privileged tyranny of the Anglican Church. The latter was forbidden to worship in public till 1779 ; the former could not be a candidate for Parliament till 1828, or enter the Universities of Oxford and Cambridge till 1871. Granted that the Whig oligarchy in its local government was often both responsible and humane, granted even (which is probable) that it served the country better than any alternative class, it is still a strange fact that it justified its ascendancy by speeches about natural rights and the social contract, and by a theory of checks and balances which bore little relation to the facts.

Stranger still, it was this British constitution and British theory of government which became the watchword of Liberal revolution in Europe and America. Even Rousseau and Paine were deeply influenced by it, and there are still self-styled democrats who believe that Locke spoke the last word about the character of good government. But this paradox has its explanation. In no country, outside England, had the bourgeois revolution been achieved. The French Revolution, from its first year to the expulsion of Napoleon, accomplished by civil strife what in England had been achieved largely by peaceful change ; while the makers of the American Constitution tried to ordain by law for the United States the predominance of those social classes which in England achieved supremacy by a continuous development through three hundred years. Neither they nor the forces which won the French Revolution really wished to go further than Locke had desired. That they were forced to do so and to inaugurate democracy was due to the pressure of new forces which they disliked as intensely as the British aristocracy of landowners and merchants disliked them. In brief, the American and French revolutions were both bourgeois revolutions which were so retarded that they occurred just when the bourgeois order was about to undergo a new social revolution as violent as that which had convulsed Tudor England ; and the ideas which inspired them became therefore the instruments of two conflicting tendencies, the one intent on creating bourgeois society on the Lockean model, the other pushing on to a new conception of national democracy.

Of the first tendency, Montesquieu is the outstanding example in France, Madison in America and Burke in England. Though differences of circumstances affected them profoundly, they all conceived of the civilized state as essentially oligarchic in character and feared " democracy " ; they all assumed that substantial property alone gave the right to political influence ; they all believed in free discussion and liberty of expression as essential to good government ; and lastly, they all held that politics was the art of securing the preservation of an essentially static social order. Each in his own way contributed new features to the study of politics, but they were nevertheless representatives of the old Lockean order, not of the new society of the 19th century. Against them we can set Paine and Jefferson and Rousseau as representatives of the new ideas.

At first sight it may seem surprising to class Edmund Burke with the Liberal critic of French autocracy. How, it may be asked, can we connect the apostle of British Conservatism with the French progressive ? But Burke was not—and no Conservative has ever been—a conservator of everything. In his early years [1] he launched

[1] See *Thoughts on our Present Discontents.*

violent attacks on George III for attempting to restore
the royal prerogative to its pristine glories. Against
such an attack on the constitution he stood firm. Again,
he defended the American colonies in their fight for
freedom, urging a far-sighted toleration which might
possibly have retained them within the Empire. In brief,
he stood not for the letter of any political theory, but
for the spirit of 1688. The balance of forces then
reached he held to be the perfect balance for the British
nation, and he was resolved to maintain it against
attacks from above and from below. Clothing it with
the robes of a semi-religious mysticism, he worshipped
it—but he also understood it profoundly and realized
at once, that, whatever their intentions, the French
revolutionaries would not be able to halt the revolution
there. They might use Locke's language and even
believe what they said, but Burke was acute enough
to observe things stirring in France which might endanger the British constitutional monarchy which he
loved. Such a constitution he believed could only
be the result of a long period of development ; it could
not be constructed artificially as the French liberals
desired. In brief, by his very denial of some of Locke's
principles, he remained to the end a staunch defender
of the civil government which Montesquieu admired
and which Madison was to see realized in the American
constitution. His condemnation of the French Revolution may have been futile and ill-judged, but it was
consistent with the rest of his political activity.

Burke realized that Locke's theory was as much in
need of reconstruction as the Whig party to which
he belonged. Both had arisen as a defence of constitutional rights against political Catholicism, and against

the enlargement of the power of the Executive. The defeat of the efforts of George III had shown once and for all that England had little to fear from the monarchy ; and, since the danger of a Stuart restoration was now remote, it became clear that the old distinction of Whigs and Tories had little reference to immediate issues. His new Conservatism was therefore an attempt to restate the principles of British Government in up-to-date terms. Locke's stress on the right of revolution had been caused by a danger which was overpast. Burke, seeing the new danger not on the right but on the left, realized that Locke could now be easily interpreted as advocating popular revolution against the existing system, that the social contract and natural rights were by now principles not of conservatism but of revolution against the settlement of 1688. For this reason he began a new analysis of the constitution which Europe so much admired, and developed his theory of its organic growth under the guidance of a benevolent providence.

In this work he was greatly helped by the sceptical analysis of David Hume, who had already in his *Political Essays* and *Treatise on Human Nature*, published in 1739, exploded both the theory of natural rights and that of the social contract and had based his theory of government on purely utilitarian considerations. Thus while *Civil Government* was still quoted in text-books as the true account of British liberties, and although a lawyer like Blackstone could still in 1765 repeat the old theory of checks and balances, the true defenders of 1688 had been forced to discard most of the principles of John Locke and to begin a new empirical analysis of the nature of the state. In so doing they found themselves moving steadily away from the Liberal thought of France and America; and this was only natural. For their job was to maintain the authority and dignity of Civil Government, whereas the French and Americans had still to establish it. Their revolution was already nearly one hundred years old, whereas the French and the Americans must still seek inspiration for the struggle.

II.   BACKGROUND OF THE AMERICAN REVOLUTION

We must now see how this ideal of Civil Government developed in the American colonies, what peculiar features it there put on and how it influenced the birth of the American nation. Among the many motives of British colonization of the Northern American coast, three only need here be stressed. In the first place several of the colonies were capitalist ventures, inaugurated and maintained either by companies or by individuals. Virginia and Massachusetts are instances of the first, Maryland and Georgia of the second. At first it seemed that America and India offered to the enterprising Englishman similar opportunities of combining personal profit with the cause of true religion. But it so happened that the agricultural wealth of the American coastlands could best be exploited by white imported labour, and the character of this labour was determined by our second factor, the religious conflicts of the period.

Ever since the establishment of the Anglican Church it had been clear that the reforming conscience was not satisfied by the English compromise. Calvinism drew its strength not only from Scotland but from England too, and its persecution by a supposedly reformed Church gave it its peculiar characteristic of Dissent or Nonconformity. Those who were not satisfied with Anglicanism were soon divided into countless sects and congregations, each striving to realize a perfect community of saints, one divided against another on matters both of organization and of dogma. The driving motives of the British Non-conformity—at least so long as it was in opposition—were its desire for religious toleration and its determination to purify the lives of its members of all traces of popish superstition.

Between the accession of James I and the Civil Wars the Dissenters found life hard in their mother country and they became the natural source for colonial emigration. Most of them small business men, craftsmen, shopkeepers or yeomen farmers, they sought in America a country where they could establish a rule of the Saints or at least worship as they pleased. Thus the colonies were populated by a strange assortment of classes ; gentlemen escaping from their creditors and speculators anxious to make their pile were mingled with Puritan and Catholic refugees, while below them were the vast mass of " indentured servants ", forced labour brought with them by the colonists as part of the price paid to the Trading Companies for their land. It is roughly true to say that the New England colonies were predominantly Puritan, while Virginia for instance was officially Anglican, and tried to maintain a Cavalier tradition. But both in the plantations of the South and in the merchant-enterprises of the North, the population was overwhelmingly derived from the lower stratum of the British bourgeoisie. Its culture, its religious factions and its social ideals were those of a country which had experienced the social revolution of the Tudor epoch, and of a class dissatisfied both with the Anglican compromise and with the reactionary economic policy of the Stuarts.

Thus the American colonies were indeed New England, but they were England with the top layer cut off. There was no aristocracy, no court, and few of those frequent feudal traditions which still survive in England. Here in fact was British bourgeois society perfected by the break with the past which emigration and the type of emigrant were bound to produce. It was no equalitarian paradise, no single-minded community, but the battle-ground of those forces which in England still opposed one another, but also were opposed by other traditional forces indigenous in the mother country. It is important, if we are to recognize the full force of the revolution, to appreciate the stability of the class-structure in the American colonies before the wars of independence. It was as rigid as in the mother country and more exclusively conditioned by the interests of land and trade. The hierarchy descended from the dominant merchant and land-holding families, through the small farmers and craftsmen to the mechanics and finally to the vast mass of indentured servants and slaves. This social system was confirmed in most states by an established Church, and by a government in the hands of the propertied classes. Unless he ventured out into the unknown, " the base mechanic " was not much freer in pre-revolutionary America than in England.

In the third place, the traditional element was represented by what in the course of time came to be looked upon as a foreign force, the British Crown and its representatives, the governors and their officials. As control by London companies or individuals was gradually replaced by that of the Crown and its ministry, the Board of Trade, American society became divided into Tories who stood for the British connection and mixed in government circles, and patriots who felt the connection an obstacle to their free development. The sense of independence of this patriotic movement was moreover stimulated by the factor which was to play such a decisive part in American history—the frontier. Even for the indentured labourer brought to the States against his will by a propertied emigrant, America was a land of hope, where courage and self-reliance could still hack out a path to freedom in the uncharted west. Here there was not, as in Europe, the sense of constraint engendered by a settled society with fixed boundaries. Locke had conceived of civil government as a community of men of substance formed by a social contract. In America such a view of the state had an immediate significance for the property-less as well as for the propertied. For, if a man could not find his natural rights in the settled order of New England or the South, he could strike west, and, by mixing his labour with the virgin soil, give an actual meaning to Locke's myth of the origin of property. Thus to the American citizen it was not only Locke's account of civil government, but also his description of the state of nature which rang true. He could himself take part in the life of nature, himself establish his natural rights and then in due time, accepting the social contract, submit to the jurisdiction of civil government.

This deep rift between the frontiersman's literal interpretation of Locke and the orthodox interpretation current among the settled communities on the eastern coast-line reflects the social conflict which was the background of the revolution. How far the Westerner was from a true understanding of Locke's intentions can be seen by a consideration of Locke's own suggestions for the constitution of Carolina. He proposed the distribution of land among a small group of proprietors headed by a Palatine, or prince ; one-fifth was to be held by them personally, another section laid out in manors held by an aristocracy and tilled by serfs, the rest to be small freeholds. Politically it was to be an oligarchy on the English model with a popular assembly. Such a constitution, however ridiculous it may seem to-day, must have been perfectly palatable to many American Tories, since it was not so very different from much that already existed both in the North and in the South. That it was unsuccessful was due not to its English origin, but to the spirit of the frontier which made itself felt even through the settled States.

We may sum up our conclusions as follows : The social structure of the American colonies did not differ fundamentally from that of the mother country save in the three particulars of the absence of an aristocracy, the existence of an expanding frontier, and the toleration of dissenting sects. The revolution therefore was not the revolt of a free equalitarian society from the tyranny of imperialism, nor yet on the other hand was it the work of a disgruntled minority of lawyers and politicians. It was a complicated movement in which we trace three different strands. In disentangling them we can learn something of the interplay between ideas and interests in revolutionary movements.

The immediate and proximate cause of the war was not so much the conflict of commercial interests between the mother country and its colonists, as the claim on the part of the latter to those rights for which the English Parliamentarians had fought. If they had refused to levy taxes for a royal autocrat, their American cousins could now use the same arguments and challenge the principle that colonial trade should be regulated to the advantage of the mother country. Such an attitude could prevail in India until well into the 20th century : it was bound to produce trouble far sooner in colonies whose population was chiefly of English stock and regarded itself as no whit inferior to its British rulers. In the second place there was the tradition of religious self-determination which arose out of the non-conformity of many of its inhabitants. This tradition, though no more essentially democratic than its British counterpart, gave a basis of principle to the political conflict, and, once the war had got under way, principles steadily increased in importance. The claim to civil rights widened into a War of Independence, and the war itself aroused a sense not of national unity but of anti-British solidarity which had not been apparent before it started. The war was not caused by a desire for independence, but the desire arose out of the war itself. In the third place the war precipitated a social conflict within America itself between the settled oligarchy of landowners and merchants and the apostles of the new doctrine of the Rights of Man and of demo-cracy preached by such men as Thomas Paine. Here again the same phenomenon is noticeable. What had been before the revolution a vague and inchoate feel-ing was crystallized by the struggle into a new and potent philosophy of life. The birth of the American nation and of American democracy was not the result of a rational plan on the part of the patriots but of a war commenced for quite different purposes. The colonists entered it as colonists with a grievance ; num-bers of the most influential opposed it and supported the British. They came out of it Americans dimly aware of a new national unity; and, since those who had borne the brunt of the fighting were not the men of property but the labourers and the small farmers, they came out of it with a strong leaning towards democracy.

National character and political ideas are usually forged in the fire of violence and bear the marks of their origin through generations of peaceful development, long after the feelings of revolutionary struggle have passed away. Of American civilization this is clearly true. The War of Independence became its tradition, the myth which no statesman could afford to disregard; the new United States gloried in the purely bourgeois character of its culture and institutions, and regarded itself as a free confederation established upon pure and revolutionary principles. It felt that it had willed the revolution, whereas in truth its new anti-British will had been created by the revolutionary act.

It was only after the war that the real problem of American national unity was solved, and that the democratic movement was strong enough in the northern states to sweep away those feudal characteristics which had been imported from England. In the first flush of victory royal perquisites were abolished or handed over to state legislatures. Tory properties were confiscated and divided into small-holdings, and the laws of primogeniture and entail were annulled. Furthermore, an attack on the established Churches of the various states was made, and in five the Anglican Church lost the privileges it had enjoyed. Within ten years the Americans had destroyed every vestige of the feudal system (or, as they felt it, the *British* system). The new force of nationalism, linked with the essential needs of a propertied community, had prevailed to establish a truly Lockean Civil Government, a free society of merchants and landowners secure in the enjoyment of their wealth and privacy.

III.   THE AMERICAN CONSTITUTION

But this stable bourgeois society was not to be erected on the basis of the ideas prevalent among many of the soldiers who had fought for independence. Thomas Paine, the English pamphleteer who had done so much to inspire the spirit of resistance, had begun to preach the ideas of popular democracy, and, as in the Cromwellian army, the feelings of the rank and file had surged far ahead of the prudence of their leaders. If we study the Constitution we shall find that it marks a reaction against the vehemence of revolution, a highly successful effort to call a halt on the progress towards popular rule, and to ensure that representative institutions should never threaten the natural right of property. As always a period of revolutionary action was to be followed by the re-establishment of settled government. When the visionaries have had their day, it is the time for the statesman to step in who will fix his eyes not on ideals but interests and consider security of more account than freedom.

We are singularly fortunate to possess an eye-witness account by a reliable person of the proceedings of the convention which drafted the American Constitution. A reading of the papers of James Madison gives us a rare insight into the minds of those capable business men who met at Philadelphia in 1787. Eight years of bitter experience had shown that freedom from British government was in itself no panacea. The radicals, loathing all traces of the Leviathan, had left the States under such loose Articles of Confederation that no central government was possible. Congress was powerless against the sovereign will of the autonomous states : with British rule had disappeared all the higher functions of government, and the radicals were too suspicious of government to dare to replace them. Significantly enough, none of them took part in the Philadelphia Assembly.

For the social revolution and the war against the British had been negative in their aims and ideals. The war had been not a positively nationalist movement but an insurrection against the denial of civil rights ; and the social revolution had been an attack on privilege, backed by few constructive ideas. In many of the state legislatures there were already signs of the agricultural democratic movement which would see its millennium not in a balanced system of civil government, but in a return to the state of nature where central control was virtually unnecessary. This frontier-mentality, which was later to find its prophet in Jefferson, was still raw and unformed. Its sturdy vigour had won the war, but eight years were sufficient to prove that it could not rule in the kingdom it had won because it did not really believe in government at all. A sound foreign policy, and a stable currency and credit policy, for instance, appeared in its eyes as a violation of natural rights, and those who demanded such things were denounced as American Tories still infected by the British virus. It had not thrown off

British economic imperialism only to accept service under a similar system, imposed by those very gentlemen who in many cases had been lukewarm in their Americanism at the beginning of the war. For eight years the small farmers harassed the merchant and creditor classes mercilessly in an agitation which culminated in 1786 in Shay's Rebellion. Once again as in Cromwellian England men of substance and hard business sense had to take control. But here the revolutionary spirit of the army was brought to heel, not by the short-lived protectorate of an opportunist general, but by a grand act of collective statesmanship.

Thus for the first time in history a body of men were faced with the task of constructing *de novo* the central organ of coercive authority, while preserving relative independence to the existing local authorities, the state legislatures. The Constitution could not be evolved under the beneficent guidance of a Burkean providence : it must be invented by the wit of man, and gain the approval of the separate states. Little can Locke have dreamed that less than a century after he had written, the myth of the origin of government which he sketched would be realized by men of his own blood.

In almost every particular the makers of the Constitution were true to Locke's spirit. Most of them were clear in their denunciation of democracy and must have echoed Madison's anxiety :—

There will be creditors and debtors, farmers, merchants and manufacturers. There will be particularly the distinction of rich and poor. . . . We cannot, however, be regarded even at this time as one homogeneous mass, in which everything that affects a part will affect in the same manner the whole. In framing a system which we wish to last for ages, we should not lose sight of the change which ages will produce. An increase of population will of necessity increase the proportion of those who will labour under all the hardships of life, and secretly sigh for a more equal distribution of its blessings. These may in time outnumber those who are placed above the feelings of indigence. According to the laws of suffrage, the power will slide into the hands of the former. No agrarian attempts have yet been made in this country, but symptoms of a lively spirit, as we have understood, have sufficiently appeared in certain quarters to give notice of the future danger. How is this danger to be guarded against on republican principles ? How is the danger in all cases of interested coalitions to oppress the minority to be guarded against ?

Many of them agreed with Hamilton's coarse dictum : " All communities divide themselves into the few and the many. The first are rich and well-born and the other the mass of the people who seldom judge or determine right." In short, the convention was faced with the problem of finding some substitute for that security of property which arose in England from popular subservience to the oligarchy. For the traditional obedience to authority of a submissive people they substituted a system of checks and balances so intricate that scarcely a drop of the popular wave could trickle through. What Montesquieu had wrongly praised as the precious secret of British Government became in fact the central feature of the American Constitution. Federalism, in its earliest form, was designed and worked as a bulwark against turbulent democracy in a land where equality was something more than a philosopher's phrase. The Supreme Court, the President, the Senate and Congress were set up as four federal powers checking one another. The first three were all checks upon the fourth democratic power, while the first, and to a certain extent the third, checked the executive powers of the President. Moreover, all four were to ensure by their federal activity that the state legislatures did not democratically destroy the natural rights of man. Though federal powers were limited, they were limited precisely to such things as foreign trade, foreign policy, currency control and command of the armed forces which were necessary to keep the turbulent democracy of the states within harmless limits.

The American Constitution marks a tremendous advance on the political thought of *Civil Government*. It not only follows Locke closely, but interprets and clarifies his doctrine. Locke in the traditional atmosphere of English politics saw no need for envisaging a conflict between the will of the majority and natural rights. The American Constitution faced this issue squarely. In the first place, in the written Constitution and its defender, the Supreme Court, it ensured there should be no new interpretation of " natural rights " pushed through by the people's representatives. The Constitution could be modified by the interpretation of expert lawyers, but an amendment of it was made as difficult as possible. In the second place the will of the people was split into a Federal and a State will and thereby weakened. In the third place foreign policy was removed wholly from the control of Congress. In the fourth place the Senate was set up as the most remote and refined product of the popular will.

In the mother country the system of King, Lords, and Commons as checking bodies was a fiction. The King was not the real executive, the Lords and Commons were but one single oligarchic interest and the people were virtually unrepresented. If the American system was not democratic, at least it included more democratic features than any government of its time. Its wisdom lay precisely in the fact that it did really make the maximum concessions to democracy compatible with private property. It legislated for a society which had rid itself of an Erastian Church and a savage penal code, a society predominantly consisting of landowners small and large who felt a degree of personal equality unknown in Europe. To such a society it offered the protection of a federal constitution and a complicated mechanism of government suitable to protect it against the frailty of human nature. Here for the first time the " natural law " of bourgeois society was realized in a positive system of law and a civil government specially constructed to maintain it. Man, it seemed, had freed himself from the chains of tradition and voluntarily subjected himself not to a Leviathan but to a rational balance of social power.

Seen in this light, the work of the Convention was the supreme manifestation of the spirit of the 18th century. Government had been taken out of the hands of warring kings and bishops and entrusted to the quiet deliberations of business men. England had shown that an oligarchy could rule with the consent of the masses and could formulate its policy by free discussion. Now America demonstrated that a Constitution could be constructed by the same businesslike process. Its makers were unaided by any of the paraphernalia of courts and titles or established religion in winning respect for its authority. Relying neither on the Divine Right of Kings nor on the force and fraud of the Leviathan, they had constructed a machinery of governmental law based solely upon the balance of human interests. Their success seemed to establish once and for all the secular nature of politics which Machiavelli had preached. It tore off the trappings of sovereignty, stripped it of its theological attributes and exposed the state as a simple business mechanism for satisfying business needs. To many suffering in Europe under arbitrary despotism it seemed that in America man had at last attained the full dignity of rational manhood. The virtue of a written constitution establishing once and for all the rights of man became the unquestioned faith of progressive thought in the whole Western world. England had given place to America as the home of reason and of tempered freedom.

CHAPTER V

THE FRENCH REVOLUTION

I. PERSPECTIVE OF THE REVOLUTION

IN the preceding chapters we have traced the development of political ideas in two countries where the bourgeoisie had already in the 17th century gained political influence. But the history of England and America is not typical of the whole Western World. In Germany, Russia, Austria, Italy, Spain and France, the principles of absolute monarchy retained their supremacy for generations ; and the first of these to experience a bourgeois revolution was France. For this reason, until the Russian Revolution of 1917, the French Revolution was felt to be *the* revolution which marked the division between modern and ancient history. So long as political democracy was thought to be the final stage in the development of the human race, this was natural enough ; it seemed so obvious that what France had accomplished in the revolutionary years must be accomplished, peacefully or by violence, in every other modern country not only in Europe but throughout the world. To-day, however, we are forced to view the events of 1789 in a different perspective. Germany, Russia, Italy and Japan have all either tried democracy and discarded it or omitted the experiment altogether ; and in these countries new forms of totalitarian state prevail.

Whatever their likelihood of life may be, few experts would prophesy that they will be replaced by representative democracies. The same can be said with even greater assurance of China and India. Though the French Revolution may be the introduction to 19th century history, its ideas are of declining importance in our own epoch. It was the herald of an age which is already passing away.

But a study of it has more than historical value, since it offers us a perspective for the consideration of our own age. Looking back at the controversies it aroused, we can see our own controversies in a new light and realize, for instance, the futility of many of our own arguments about the new Russia, or even the new Germany. By studying the battle-at-arms between Burke and Tom Paine, we can at least realize how little the contemporaries of a revolution understand of its lasting effects. Such a study will teach us as much about Russia to-day as the reading of a dozen pamphlets for and against the Five Year Plan. It will also reinforce the lesson of the Wars of Independence, that revolutionary political ideas are not the major causes of revolutions, but are generally products of the social ferment.

The French Revolution is particularly difficult to understand because it occurred in an epoch of economic transition. Already a generation before it began, England was becoming the workshop of the world and experiencing the sudden acceleration of the industrial revolution which was to transform the lives of millions of her people. To the financial structure of capitalism was being added its factory and machine basis, to the merchant and landowner the industrial capitalist as a potent political factor. The agrarian economy on which the representative institutions of England and America had been securely founded was already being undermined when Frenchmen tried to build up a similar political system. Some writers, particularly Marxists, have tried to interpret the French Revolution as the social and political reaction to this economic change, and view it as the lever by which capitalism asserted its right to rule ; others have seen in it a purely political movement for the establishment of modern democracy. But all such simple theories are ultimately untenable. French industry was by no means highly enough developed or self-conscious enough of its aims to take a lead in 1789 ; and as for political democracy, in the modern sense of the word, it was feared by many of the revolutionaries and was most certainly *not* established as a result of the revolution.

The truth is, that in the transitional period when it occurred the French Revolution could not establish any stable form of government. It could destroy absolute despotism, smash the privileges of the Church and the nobility, and give the land to the peasants, but, on the uncertain and shifting class-structure of France, it could not build political institutions of lasting value. Whereas the comparatively stable social systems of America and Britain withstood the shock of industrialization and maintained a continuity of political form through the transformation, this was impossible in France, once the *Ancien Régime* had been swept away. Not till long after the War of 1870 against Germany was the Frenchman to feel once more any considerable degree of political security, although, as we shall see, the structure of his social life was established in the Napoleonic era,

Thus the significance of the Revolution lies not in the political institutions which it set up, but in the ideas which it evoked throughout the whole world. For 128 years until the Russian Revolution those ideas were to be the basis of progressive thought, and their protagonists were to be on the offensive against privilege and despotism; for 135 years, till Fascism established itself, no counter-revolutionary movement could find a creed able to rouse the masses. The American revolution had aroused the hopes of millions; 1789 set them actively to work on the task of achieving the political Liberty, Equality and Fraternity of which they dreamed, and for which they were to scheme for over a hundred years.

II. ANCIEN REGIME AND OPPOSITION

What was the political and social system which the Revolution overthrew? This question must be answered, however briefly and inadequately, before we can understand the ideas of the Revolution. As we saw in the second chapter, the nation state found its first form in absolute monarchy, its first political theory in the Divine Right of Kings. The French monarchy reached the zenith of its glory in the reign of Louis XIV (1661-1715). Under him the nobles were no longer rebellious rivals but satellites of a luxurious court, the Church was an amenable instrument of policy, and the whole life of the nation was controlled in its every detail by a vast civil service. The aims and objects of the French national state can be summed up in two words, wealth and glory, its methods in one—bureaucracy. Louis and his famous minister Colbert desired to make France the wealthiest and most splendid state in the world, and they conceived that this was only possible by victories in war and the monopolization of empire and trade. The doctrines of economic nationalism and of planned trade, which sound so novel in the mouths of Fascists, are really echoes of the *Mercantilism* of 17th-century France, which maintained that wealth arose not from reciprocity of trade between countries, but by one country excluding all others and gathering to itself a mountain of gold. Just at the period when British merchants were beginning to murmur against such a view and to sigh for freedom of exchange. French business men were overwhelmed by the infinite efficiency of a state machine which ruthlessly regimented them for the ends of imperial glory.

The gold which flowed in from a world-wide empire, as meticulously organized as the home country, was used for two objects, wars and public works of unexampled magnificence. Since both of these were totally unproductive types of expenditure and contributed only to the happiness of the sovereign and of the bankers who financed him, it became clear that the interests of the French state were the antithesis of the interests of the French people. The finance capitalism, which in England and America was slowly being developed into an instrument for the facilitation of the production and distribution of goods, was exploited almost exclusively in 17th and 18th-century France for the aggrandizement of the monarch.

Moreover, the religious policy of Louis, the strict censorship of literature and the Press, and the expulsion of the Huguenots prevented the rise of the strong and independent bourgeois class which was the backbone of the Protestant countries. Even before his death, France was rapidly becoming an oppressed nation, crushed by a ruthless Leviathan, while the nobles and the clergy, remote from the mass of the people, enjoyed the pleasures of privilege and surrendered their responsibilities to the state bureaucracy. The analogy with pre-revolutionary Russia does not need to be underlined.

The period between the death of Louis in 1715 and the storming of the Bastille in 1789 is one of continuous decay. A people, driven and not led, showed no enthusiasm for glorious wars or for the wealth of Empire. Already, while Louis was alive, French imperial pretensions had created an alliance led by England which forced upon France the Treaty of Utrecht. Exhausted by these efforts, the French were bound to be defeated in the colonial wars which marked the 18th century, and during which England was gradually building up her naval strength and laying the foundations of her empire. It is easier to establish than to modify an autocracy, and by the end of the century a country groaning under a corrupt financial system was forced to realize that there was little hope either of the monarchy curing its ills or of constitutional reforms which would enable others to do the job.

Such in bare outline is the environment in which the ideas of the French Revolution grew. For simplicity's sake let us list the chief grievances :—

1. The existence of privileged classes immune from taxation, in particular the Church and the nobility.

2. The existence of a huge state machine useless either to the business man or to the peasant, who was not interested in war or glory.

3. The censorship of all forms of individual initiative whether in business, literature, science or religion.

If we compare these grievances with those of the American colonists, we notice chiefly two facts. In the first place the colonists were oppressed by a government outside their own territory, and in the second place that government had not prevented the growth of a strong and prosperous bourgeoisie, and had not supported a large privileged class upon the proceeds of taxation. Thus the French Revolution was bound to produce a civil war, in place of a war of independence ; and secondly, having destroyed the old order, it could not build the new one upon the basis of an experienced and capable bourgeoisie and a long-standing system of local government. When the absolute monarchy fell in France there was nothing at all to replace it except an inchoate body of ideas developed not by practical experience of government, but by years of theoretical opposition. These theories, which had grown up during the 18th century, deserve far more attention than we can give them here. They are typical of the views of an impotent political opposition, and for that reason they are specially attractive to that vast majority of mankind who have taken no part in government, but enjoy discussing it. Precisely because of their intellectual dogmatism they acted as an excellent corrodent of respect for state authority among the educated classes in every European state where absolute monarchy still prevailed.

Observe for instance the views of Voltaire (1694-1778). In spite of his immense influence, he had no positive theory of revolution or government. He was a critic pure and simple, with a passion for civil liberty, a quite uncritical appreciation of the British system, and a real

hatred of clerical censorship. But Voltaire was no democrat : he hated the stupidity of the mob and thought of
the poor as objects of sympathy not as his fellows and
equals. For this reason his influence was purely negative,
and his witticisms served only to undermine the existing
order, without preparing the minds of his countrymen
to think out a practical alternative.

Even when we turn to those writers who explicitly
dealt with political problems we find the same story.
Criticism of the despotism was based unanimously on
Locke's *Civil Government*, but, in the French environment, Locke's view took on a more radical and dogmatic
tone. With no tradition of self-government, with no
representative institutions or common law to guide
them, the French theorists were compelled to treat natural
rights as a body of doctrine, self-evident, rational,
and coherent, on which any statesman could construct
a constitution. Instead of relying on the interests of a
compact and self-confident bourgeoisie to direct their
theorizing, they legislated in the abstract for a purely
rational self-interested creature which they then identi-
fied with the individual Frenchman. Thus the dogmatism of the *ancien régime* was countered by a rationalism which was no whit less dogmatic. Of this tendency
the theories of the *Physiocrats* are an interesting example.
They based their criticisms of the economic policy of
the state on a supposed natural economic order, as
self-evident as the system of natural law. This natural
order is so providentially arranged that, if each man
seeks his own happiness, the good of all is achieved, and
it is as certain and immutable in its working as the
material universe whose law Newton had discovered.
The task of statesmanship therefore is, in Turgot's

words, " to recognize the primary and unique laws founded on nature itself by which all values in commerce
are balanced with each other and fixed at a definite
value." This natural order they conceived to be a
system based on private ownership of agricultural
property, and it was largely in the name of the landlord
that they argued for the destruction of privilege, for
freedom of contract, for the abolition of government
regulation, and for the application of science to the
problems of farming.

Turgot and his friends were of immense importance
in the history of social science. Their attempt to find
Newtonian laws operating in the economic order laid
the foundations of the modern science of economics,
and their conception of man as an economic creature,
chiefly concerned with the augmentation of his property,
was to be developed later into both Benthamism and
Marxism. In their hands natural law became not so
much a moral order arranged by God, according to which
man *ought* to regulate his life, as a scientific generalization about what must happen in the economic sphere
under given conditions. Though they were not fully
conscious of this change, they did a great deal to dissi-
pate the mediæval theories of society and to prepare the
way for a scientific analysis of society. Adam Smith
had only to transpose their theories from the sphere of
agriculture to that of commerce in order to provide
the gospel of the new industrial *entrepreneur* ; while
Marx, adopting their " materialism ", interpreted it in
the interests of the industrial worker.

In their political views the physiocrats stood for an
enlightened despotism and denounced democracy as
a threat to private property. With their unbounded

belief in reason they failed to grasp that Platonic philosopher kings stood no chance of reforming peacefully the *ancien régime*, and that a revolutionary movement was necessary if Mercantilism was to be swept away. They could persuade the bourgeoisie of the futility of the existing system, but they could not inspire the people to overthrow it.

Indeed, it is only when we look outside the ranks of the orthodox theorists that we find the seeds of the new movement which was to grow out of the Revolution. Its ideas are to be found unorganized, emotional but intensely alive in two writers, Rousseau and Tom Paine.

III. ROUSSEAU

Up till now we have followed the development of a movement which was fundamentally rational in character, and in which we could trace an orderly progress of ideas. The growth of representative institutions, scientific understanding and civil liberty was simultaneous and related, and it was paralleled by the rise of a new class to political influence. But with Rousseau our orderly development comes to a halt and a new element enters in. Mysticism and sentiment reappear in a new form, and *Romanticism* begins to influence the forces of progress.

Though Rousseau antedates the Romantic movement in literature, music, and politics by nearly a generation, his connection with it is unmistakable. Like Wordsworth, he seeks escape in nature from the egocentric rationalism of society, like Shelley and Godwin he dreams of a mystical equality of man, like the German romantics he feels in the nation (the Folk) a primitive sense of community and " togetherness " which no philosophy can describe and no philosopher can analyse out of existence.

Jean Jacques Rousseau (1712-78) was born at Geneva. His father was a watchmaker and he was educated at the village school. Apprenticed to an engraver, he had not the patience to settle down to a craftsman's life, and ran away into Savoy, where he found the first of the various ladies who were to take him under their maternal care. She sent him to a seminary for the training of Catholic priests, but such discipline did not suit him, and for ten years he lived on his patroness. In 1744 he came to Paris, was once more befriended by a married woman and for twelve years mixed with the Encyclopaedists, a circle of intellectuals centred round Diderot, who popularized the rationalism of Locke and his school. Against this rationalism Rousseau reacted as violently as he did to the tyranny of the absolute monarchy, and was soon in opposition not only to the existing system but also to its opponents. In his novels, his *Confessions* and his political writings, he expressed with a brilliant incoherence the bewilderment and dissatisfaction of the human soul which could not find contentment either in the Church or in rationalist philosophy. Curiously like D. H. Lawrence, though on a quite different plane, he was able to generalize his psychological problems into a Utopian attack upon the whole of society, and in a visionary state to find that sense of community which his own disposition debarred him from enjoying. In so doing he voiced the longings of a new class, for whom Civil

Government was a vain and hollow mockery of true freedom.

In his life and his writings alike Rousseau was always escaping from the trammels of logic and civilized society. He was the first modern thinker to detest civilization because of its rationality and to love primitive man because of his simple decency. In expressing these feelings, he originated no political or social movement, but he was the first spokesman of an emotional attitude which from now on we shall find recurring in every political movement of the left and of the right. Whether we look at German nationalism, anarchism, socialism or even French democracy we shall find traces not only of Rousseau's thought, but of the feelings which he first tried to put into words.

Perhaps his deepest feeling was his rejection of the 18th-century definition of man as a self-interested animal, whose morality springs from his awareness of rational rights. Against this view Rousseau appealed to nature in an entirely new sense. The natural for him was not the rational plan of the universe but the primitive and the emotional. Man's inmost nature was the simple moral sentiments and æsthetic tastes, and he saw these beautiful primitive qualities contorted and defiled by the imposition of civilization. Man was born free, like the child in Wordsworth's Ode, but—

> Shades of the prison house begin to close
>   Upon the growing boy. . . .
> The Youth who daily farther from the east
>   Must travel, still is Nature's priest,
>   And by the vision splendid
>   Is on his way attended;
> At length the Man perceives it die away
> And fade into the light of common day.

Thus the dream of the millennium is the dream of the restoration of a primitive natural community which is bound together by its moral sentiments, and whose law is the expression of those moral sentiments and of a new common will.

This appeal to sentiment as deeper than reason and as the mainspring of action was not only bound to find a widespread response but was also based on a sound (if unconscious) psychology. For the first time it recognized not a theoretical but a real " equality " in the human race, and it restored to the western world an outlet for the religious feelings of community and of worship. Rationalism had destroyed the mediæval mystique and had made of God a theological abstraction. Rousseau gave to his age a new object of worship —human nature—and a new unecclesiastical Church, the people acting as a community. From now on the religious emotions would be canalized into a secular religion—humanism: the state would take the place of the Church as the institution in which worship would take place, and politics would become the theology of the modern world.

Man an emotional being, the state his new religious community, humanity his secular god : this in brief is the vision which Rousseau poured out in his incoherent writings. The message is not rendered more intelligible by the fact that it is mixed with a welter of political theorizing in the true 18th-century tradition, and that Rousseau attempts to express his rejection of rationalism and bourgeois society in terms of a theory of the bourgeois state. The *Social Contract*, taken as it stands, is unreadable nonsense because it is a romantic vision transcribed into 18th-century terminology. But it is an excellent discipline to read it and to analyse out the incompatible elements of which it is composed. In so doing we shall come to understand the amazing confusions both in Rousseau's mind, and in our own.

Rousseau starts, true to tradition, with a social contract by which man passes out of a state of nature into obedience to the state. But his overlord is now no Hobbesian Leviathan, nor yet the Civil Government of Locke but " The General Will ". Already it is clear (1) that either Rousseau's natural man does not need a contract to become part of the mystical state, or (2) alternatively, if he wants a social contract, then it must be between men aware of the very system of rational rights which he so much abused. When we come to the General Will we are in still greater difficulties. This, says Rousseau, is sovereign. It is not merely the common good of a voluntary association of rational individuals, nor yet is it the recognition by each individual of his rights and duties in society. It is the Will of the Community as a whole, in which every individual takes part (except recalcitrant minorities) and which is yet something other than the will of individuals. This Will Rousseau endows with a sovereignty as absolute as that of the Leviathan. Since it is always good, opposition to it is always wrong, he declares, and thereby places himself in opposition both to the absolute monarchy and to its individualistic critics, such as Voltaire and Diderot. For he feels that true freedom is not to be found either under despotism, or in a system of legalistic and inviolable natural rights, but in a community acting together with one single purpose. For him the Whig oligarchy was a social order almost as rigid and confining as Absolutism ;

the benevolent despotism of the Physiocrats merely another form of prison for the free spirit. He had no preference for one form of government over another, because he judged the state not by its constitution but by the spirit which pervades it; and it was for the sovereignty of the free spirit of " togetherness " that he pleaded, in urging the central importance of the General Will.

This appeal for a sense of community arose in part from a longing for an aspect of life which had disappeared with the Middle Ages. Rousseau sensed that bourgeois civilization would destroy the social organism and atomize society into a collection of propertied individuals. By demanding rights without submitting to obligations, by elevating reason and frowning on " enthusiasm ", by preaching self-interest and decrying love, it would free men from despotism only to enslave them to a new and heartless system. Feeling all this, Rousseau fought for a new recognition of the social bond and made his battle-cry the sovereignty of the General Will. But he was so inconsistent about this central principle of his system that it is impossible to give it any precise meaning : indeed its interpretation has varied with every successive school of readers. Democrats have called it " the will of the people ", Marxists " the interest of the proletariat ", Nazis the spirit of the *Volk*. Everyone has sanctified the group in which he was predominantly interested with a claim to sovereignty and to infallibility and argued that it really voiced the general will. One advantage of Romantic philosophy is the elasticity of interpretation which it permits.

Those parts of the *Social Contract* which follow the

18th-century tradition need not detain us long. In them (like his contemporaries) Rousseau pleads for the recognition of the right of property and for civil government on the lines of Locke, and the General Will is whittled down to a recognition of these natural rights. But such theorizing is an unimportant part of Rousseau's message. His praise of patriotism and his identification of the true community with the State became the gospel of the popular movement, which won the revolution and yet felt that the bourgeois state did not satisfy its dreams. When the Revolution was over and Robespierre, Rousseau's finest pupil had fallen, France accepted not a stable system of representative institutions on the American model, but the empire of Napoleon. In a very real sense Napoleon represented the General Will of Rousseau's dreams. The people under arms fought for the glory of France and felt a patriotism and an exaltation unknown in the days of mercenaries and professional soldiers. Just as the Revolution was completed by the *levée en masse* which saved it from defeat by Germany and Austria, so the Napoleonic armies, inspired by their mission of liberation, represented the new popular force in European politics, no less popular because its political institutions were highly autocratic. In his early days at least Napoleon was the incarnation of the French sense of community ; and the chances of advancement which a military career opened to the humblest soldier gave a new feeling of social equality and of freedom, undiminished by the political tyranny under which France was to live. Where the bourgeois politicians failed to give the masses a sense of participation in the new state or in its philosophy, Napoleon's army succeeded beyond expectation ; and when the wars were over and constitutional monarchy had been restored, it was found that the Napoleonic episode had created a mystique of national unity and of social equality strong enough to bind the people into allegiance to a new capitalist society which had few benefits to offer them. Of this deep unity between nationalism and 19th-century democracy, between the sense of freedom and national service, Rousseau was the incoherent and unwitting prophet. In the General Will he had found the communal emotion which would bind classes with conflicting interests into the service of the nation, a divinity in which each individual had his part ; and by asserting that the right of the community overruled every private interest he satisfied those feelings of self-sacrifice and adoration which, for all their irrationality, are an ineradicable part of human nature. In brief, though he detested bourgeois society and sought to escape from it, Rousseau formulated the myth which was to give it authority over the masses and so to enchant their emotions that they sometimes forgot self-interest altogether. From now on the rational system of representative institutions was to be built on the irrational and romantic basis of nationalism and of the general will.

IV. THOMAS PAINE. 1737-1809

If Rousseau was the prophet of the French Revolution, Paine was its ablest pamphleteer ; and his views are far more representative of revolutionary radical thought than anything Rousseau wrote. Though a less profound, he was a far more influential writer.

The son of a Norfolk farmer, Paine became an excise officer of the English Government. In this invidious trade he showed no more honesty than was usual and a good deal less tact. For both reasons he was forced to leave the service, and arrived in America in 1774. On the outbreak of the revolution he sided with the Patriots, and in a brilliant series of pamphlets rallied the flagging spirits of Washington's men. Revolutionary war suited Paine down to the ground and he excelled both as an officer in command of irregulars and as a newspaperman. With the coming of peace however his radical views fell more and more into disfavour and he began to turn to his other hobby, mechanical invention. In 1787 he sailed for England with plans for a new type of bridge in his pocket, leaving the framing of the Constitution to others less impatient than himself.

In 1789 Paine sided passionately with the revolutionaries. Full of his American experiences, he saw in the fall of the Bastille the beginning of the new era of European freedom, and imagined that the revolution would develop strictly on American lines. In this spirit he penned *The Rights of Man* in 1790 as a reply to Burke's *Reflections on the French Revolution*. *The Rights of Man* was not only a defence of the French revolutionaries but a direct attack on the British oligarchy, and, when in 1792 the second part was published, he was forced to fly for his life. Its success in England indicated that there was plenty of tinder there for the French spark to light; and its suppression initiated a lengthy period of reactionary government. The Press was muzzled, trade unions were suppressed and Jacobinism was suspected everywhere.

This period lasted till the end of the Napoleonic wars and was only brought to its final close by the Reform Bill of 1832.

Meanwhile Paine was elected a member of the French Convention. Lionized as the hero of the American Revolution, he still waited for the peace, prosperity and security which the destruction of despotism should bring. But instead the revolution moved to the left. In 1793 Paine had the courage to vote against the execution of the king, and was imprisoned until the Directorate restored bourgeois law and order. From now on he was to be a disappointed man ; not even Napoleon's flattery could convince him that all was well with the Revolution and in 1802 he returned to America, where a cool reception awaited him. The rationalism of his *Age of Reason* (1793), his denunciations of slavery (and his vanity and bad temper) did not endear him to the sober conservative rulers of the new America. He died in 1809 in poverty and bitterness.

The Rights of Man is, for the English reader, the finest example of the spirit of the actual Revolution and its contemporary supporters. Like most Frenchmen, Paine viewed the fall of the Bastille as the beginning of the Americanization of European politics. The ideas of the new world were infecting the old and would in a few years sweep away the litter of privilege, feudalism and corruption with which it was encumbered. Paine did not notice that the forces in America, which had won the war, had lost the battle of the Constitution. He did not study the class-structure of the two countries or observe the anti-democratic forces which were giving America her social stability. In this defect he was typical of his own and the succeeding age, which were to see in political institutions the complete and radical solution of all the world's evils. Given a constitution based on the rights of man, given political equality and freedom, then, on his view, the millennium had been achieved.

On page 106 we analysed the three evils in France which cried for reform. Paine saw these evils not only in France but in England—and every other country except America; and his remedies were direct and simple.

1. The privileges of monarchy, aristocracy and the Church were to be abolished outright.

2. The State machinery, which was used only for the private good of those who ran it, was to be cut down to a bare minimum and put under the sole charge of representatives of the nation. When this was done, wars and empires would immediately disappear, since the people did not want them, and taxation could be decreased correspondingly.

3. There must be complete toleration of all religious views, and freedom of private enterprise. If this were achieved, man's innate common sense would prevail and world peace would be secured. For the futile conflict of nations would be substituted the free competition of reasonable and industrious men.

Paine's political theory is based on these practical proposals.[1] He finds the sovereign power in the nation, acting through its written constitution, and regards the Government as the servant of this sovereign power. The state is therefore brought into being by the vote of a national assembly approving the constitution, and, until this has been done, there is no legitimate authority whatsoever. Once a people has set up its constitution,

[1] See *Rights of Man*, Part II, sections 3 and 4.

duly based on the rights of man, it can elect representatives and give them the job of legislating in accordance
with it. It need have no fear of counter-revolution,
because revolution is an act of imparting knowledge of
truth and " it has never yet been discovered how to
make a man *unknow* his knowledge, or *unthink* his
thoughts."

Paine's whole theory was as directly derived from
American experience as Locke's had been from English.
In spite of this limitation, however, the *Rights of Man*
represents very fairly both the practical programme and
the philosophy of revolutionary democracy in most of
the countries of Europe where feudal privilege still
reigned ; although where bourgeois institutions had been
established democratic theory was already taking a
different course. It is worth while therefore to analyse
his ideas rather more closely.

1. *Economics.* Tom Paine, like the physiocrats,
still regarded agriculture as the basic industry. " When
the valleys laugh and sing it is not the farmer but all
creation that rejoices. It is a prosperity that excludes
all envy ; that cannot be said of anything else." He
argued, as they did, for laisser-faire, freedom of contract,
and abolition of primogeniture as steps towards the
destruction of the large estates and the strengthening of
an independent yeomanry. But the new industries
interested him too. Himself an amateur engineer, he
saw the early stages of the industrial revolution and
welcomed it as contributing a sturdy body of independent *entrepreneurs* to strengthen the basis of democracy.
True to the American tradition, he still believed that a
just social order could be established on the basis of
private property.

For this reason his thought leads straight on to 19th-century Liberalism. The chief aim of the democrat is, on his view, to abolish privilege and reduce taxation. In Chapter V of Part II of the *Rights of Man* he lists his proposals for England. They include a graduated property tax to relieve the poor of the burden of taxation ; the abolition of the monarchy and all other sinecures, the reduction of the army and navy, combined with better conditions for the men, and the disestablishment of the Church. The resulting savings in overhead expenditure would, he believed, make possible a vast reduction in taxation while leaving funds for a scheme of social services to supersede poor law relief. His proposals under this head are astonishingly modern, including free education, old age pensions and family allowances. In this chapter in fact we find nothing less than the programme of Liberal reform of our own generation. It is based on two pillars, the complete freedom of private enterprise and the right of the whole nation to the fruits of taxation, or, to put it in other words, the free development of capitalism combined with social reform.

2. *Politics*. The instrument of these reforms is representative institutions. These should be, according to Paine, the modern form of Greek democracy and they are useless unless they truly express the national will. Throughout the *Rights of Man*, the word nation has a new significance not known before the American Revolution. It means the whole people without distinction of class or quality, and with its use Paine steps into the ranks of modern democrats, as the first writer who instinctively felt the meaning of social equality. His economic theory has shown us that he assumed

the nation to be predominantly composed of farmers and independent craftsmen, but it is highly significant that he asserts that the aged poor have a *right* to old age pensions because they have paid taxes. Every working man on his view is a full citizen, every child has a right to education. The nation is simply the total number of working people in any country, and representative institutions are the machinery which enables them to secure their interests.

Such a view implied revolution in every European country, and Paine accepted this with equanimity because of his optimism about the character of mankind. Men on his view are naturally sensible, honest and law-abiding; but their decency has been stunted and perverted by the institutions of oligarchy. Once these are cleared away, education will present no problems : there will be no fundamental division of interests, but men will be able to govern themselves in harmony and peace.

Paine displays neither the sentimental romanticism of Rousseau nor yet the intellectualism of the Encyclopædists. Though he is a hard-headed rationalist, he has a heart : though he has a heart, he shows the plain business sense which was soon to put the Anglo-Saxon industrialist into the seats of the mighty. For him the world seems to open limitless prospects of peaceful expansion, once the common people can cast out the privileged, and, declaring once for all the rights of man, set up a constitution based upon them.

The Constitution is the centre of his system. Based upon common interest and justice, it must be acceptable to all, since all, save the privileged, are men of goodwill. Spellbound by that static view of society, which we have noticed in all his predecessors, he prepares to meet the gigantic changes of the 19th century with the constitution as his shield and the convention as his spear. Nor can we blame him for this when we remember that, until the Communist Manifesto in 1848, no one realized the revolution which capitalism would produce, or foresaw that " the people " would be riven into two conflicting nations. Had it not been for the industrial revolution Tom Paine's might well have remained the philosophy of the European working class, as it did remain, for special reasons, that of the American until the Great Depression of the nineteen-thirties.

3. *International Relations*. Here too Paine saw in the political revolution and the sovereignty of the nation the cure for all evils. An alliance of a revolutionary France with revolutionary America and England would obviate the need for armaments, and such an alliance would be produced by the common interest of the three nations. Wars, he held, were the hobbies of privilege and despotism : commerce the business of nations. Democracy, free trade, and the retrenchment of government would substitute the latter for the former, and, once war was abolished, nations could increase their wealth without hindrance. There was only one war to be fought, the war for independence against privilege and class-distinction. In considering this aspect of Paine's thought it is once more important to remember the period in which Paine lived. If his dream of static agrarian democracies could have been achieved, there was indeed no reason why war should not have disappeared. Paine's view is probably not far different from that of a farmer in the Middle West to-day, or even from that of an enthusiastic supporter of

the British League of Nations Union in 1928. The abolition of war seemed to him as to them chiefly a question of turning out the old gang of politicians and letting the man in the street have his way. In 1791 there was far more justification for this view than there is to-day.

V. ACHIEVEMENTS OF NAPOLEON

When we turn from the ideas to a consideration of the results of the French Revolution we are presented with a different and more modest picture. The revolution had swept France in a series of waves. In the first place there was the united attack of the whole people, bourgeoisie, peasants and workmen against the corruption of the *ancien régime*. This first wave did its work thoroughly. In a period of a few months the peasants and farmers had won possession of the land, and the privileges of the nobility, the clergy, and the local corporations had been abolished. Then came the period for construction, and here two new factors intervened, the disagreements among the revolutionaries themselves and the threat of foreign intervention on behalf of the émigrés. The second of these two factors demanded centralized control if France was to be saved ; but the only idea common to the revolutionaries was precisely the destruction of centralized despotism. In this situation, as in Russia 125 years later, there was inevitably a swing to the left. A new and intensely-felt patriotism demanded the defence of France not only from external but from internal dangers, and preached a crusade of liberation for the oppressed peoples of

Europe. In foreign policy this movement, by over-running the Netherlands, gave the Tory Government of England reasons of state to back its ideological dislike of the Revolution, and left France isolated in a hostile Europe. At home it resulted in a fierce wave of anti-clericalism and the dictatorship of the Committee of Public Safety under Robespierre (1793-4).

We saw how in the American Revolution the attempt to maintain civil liberty upon a basis of radical democracy quietly petered out after eight years of public uncertainty, and was succeeded by the return of Conservatives to influence in the construction of the Constitution. France was not permitted so easy a solution of her problems. For here federalism was impossible and, since the *ancien régime* had not per-mitted any independent organs of local government, the social structure had to be rebuilt once more from the centre. To succeed in this task and simultaneously to retain the confidence of the masses in the war-fever which then gripped them was something no conservative could accomplish. The new democratic patriotism sensed treachery in any negotiations with the powers of reaction, and a people under arms saw in external compromises the signs of treason to the revolution. Thus the pendulum was bound to swing to the extreme left until the absurdity happened of a radical government exercising all the autocratic terror of centralized despotism in the name of pure democracy. This tendency was accentuated by the peculiar importance of Paris, the one great city in the country which could virtually dictate to any government. Paris was far more revolutionary than the provinces,

and some of its proletarian leaders were already dreaming socialist dreams remote from the wishes of the
peasant and the provincial merchant. The predominance of the capital pushed the revolution even further
to the left and gave it a far more modern tone than
the facts warranted. The extreme Jacobinism of
Robespierre is the first of those Parisian revolutionary
movements which in the name of the French people
was to impose on the provinces ideas and institutions
which deeply shocked their conservative temper.

It is not a mere fantastic speculation to enquire
why, where Lenin succeeded, Robespierre, the extreme
Jacobin, failed ; for the answer to this question discloses the fundamental weakness of revolutionary
democracy. Robespierre was the incarnation of " The
Rights of Man ", although, under his regime, its author
languished in prison. He made deism the official
religion of France, used his terror to suppress counter-
revolution and introduced a paper-constitution of
undiluted democracy. Legislation was to be submitted
to a sort of referendum by primary local assemblies, and
the legislature was to consist of annual delegates from
these assemblies, while all magistrates were to be
elected by a bare majority vote. On the economic
side this constitution was designed to protect the
interests of a society of free property holders such as
Rousseau and Paine had postulated. Unfortunately
this constitution and the Committee which enforced
it appealed neither to the bourgeoisie nor to the
proletariat of Paris. The Paris *commune*, which
originated now, wanted, not security and equality
of property, but fair wages and bread ; and such
demands were voiced by the workers of industrial

Lyons as well. The bourgeoisie, on the other hand, wanted " Law and Order ", and, as the Convention had shown, were opposed to pure democracy. Thus the Jacobins had no solid basis of support, and were forced to rely on the tyranny of the Jacobin Clubs which played the part of the later Bolshevik party. The revolutionary democrats became dictators, and guillotined not only the reactionaries, but the leaders of the *commune* as well.

This problem faced Lenin too and in itself is not a sufficient account of Robespierre's failure. But the fact is that the constitutional and economic aims of the Jacobins were incompatible. Private property and public credit demanded the predominance not of " the people " but of the conservative bourgeoisie. Robespierre, dreaming of a free society of small-scale capitalism, was forced, in order to introduce a paper constitution, to undermine capitalism, and, in order to feed the masses, to inflate the currency ; meanwhile he was fighting the socialistic demands of the *commune* in the interests of the bourgeoisie.

The short-lived dictatorship of the Jacobins proved that, even at this stage of economic development, the attempt to build a government based on popular sovereignty was bound to end in a ruthless dictatorship and to destroy a nation's credit. It demonstrated even more sharply what the eight years before the making of the American constitution had shown, that radical democracy was a Utopian dream. Not till a revolutionary Government was prepared to scrap the ideals of democracy and to rely, not on capitalist credit, but on complete state control of currency and industry, would a revolution succeed in wresting power

from men of property and substance. Even then
the power it assumed would not be handed back once
more to the sovereign people. Lenin succeeded because
he was a Communist in a period when Communism
was a possibility. Robespierre failed because his
ultra-democratic faith was and always would be a
Utopian dream, while an attempt to introduce socialism
such as Babeuf desired would have been doomed to
failure in the rest of France.

So the third wave came, heralded by the directorate of sharp business men and competent soldiers,
and culminating in the Napoleonic Empire. The
gains of the Revolution were consolidated, the confidence of the bourgeoisie was regained, and France
took her place beside England and Aᵣ rica as a modern
bourgeois state, in which authority was tempered by
civil liberty. As in America, the first task of the statesman was to restore the power of the executive and
of the central government against which the zeal of
the revolutionaries had stormed. This task Napoleon
accomplished with rare skill. Democracy was thoroughly
discredited and disappeared unwept. The old provinces
abolished, prefectures were set up in new artificial
departments under strict control from the centre.
Unlike America, France was organized under a single
central government. The second task was the establishment of a system of law suitable to the new order.
This was enshrined in the *Civil Code*, which is perhaps
the most perfect single document of the bourgeois
state. Strictly secular in character—it ordained a
system of civil marriage—it lays down the structure
of a modern society " based on social equality and
religious toleration, on private property and coherent

K

family life ".[1] For France and for Europe as a whole, it was the first complete elaboration in positive detail of those " natural rights " of which Paine had dreamed, and it was advanced enough to be a fitting framework even for a society transformed by the later developments of industrial capitalism. Within the limits of the nation state it offered to the peasant and the *entrepreneur* the civil liberties and the security which had been the goal for two centuries of the progressive movement.

Napoleon's reconstruction of French life was all in the same mould. Higher education was centralized under state control, the metric system was introduced, and a concordat was reached with the Pope which left the Church in France no greater power than Mussolini permits to the Italian clergy to-day. France became at one stride a modern state, far ahead of her British rival. Though her political institutions were despotic, social inequality and feudal anachronisms were vastly fewer. Instead of a privileged aristocracy she possessed in the Legion of Honour an élite of merit ; instead of the traditional values of a monarchy and an established Church, her tradition and her myth was the revolution and the Empire. No hereditary monarch could show so good a title to represent the people's will as the little corporal who had replaced the tyranny of Utopian democrats by the efficient rule of centralized and modern law.

The failure of Napoleon's foreign policy did not undo these domestic triumphs, although it broke up the hereditary Napoleonic empire of which he dreamed. The stability of the structure he built is proved by the

[1] See *History of Europe*, by H. A. L. Fisher, p. 838.

fact that it stood the strain of a Bourbon reaction, a democratic revolution, a Napoleonic adventure and its defeat in 1870, to emerge finally unscathed in the bourgeois democratic constitution of the Third Republic, which still survives—if precariously—to-day. The lesson of the French Revolution will always be the relative unimportance of political institutions compared to the social and civil foundations on which they are built, and consequently the insecurity of political democracy and " constitutional freedom " in a society where these foundations have been undermined. Though the Revolution created the patriotism and ideal of liberty of modern France, it was an autocrat who constructed the administrative and legal structure in which plain men and women could enjoy them.

CHAPTER VI

THE INDUSTRIAL REVOLUTION IN BRITAIN

I. INDUSTRIALISM AND DEMOCRACY

AS we approach the 19th century the straight-
forward story which we have been telling becomes
vastly more complex. Up till now we have traced
the growth of a single political idea, that of representative government in a small group of countries; and
we have watched how its development runs parallel
with that of a common social and economic system. We
have noted differences between the histories of England,
France and America, but we have nevertheless found a
deep affinity between them. They all speak the same
political language, though in different dialects.

This common political language exists to-day in
what we may roughly call the democratic nations,
Scandinavia, Holland, Belgium and the three countries
we have mentioned; and it is highly significant that in
all these countries the affinity goes far back beyond
the French Revolution. It is not merely a resemblance
of political forms or class-structure or even industrial
development, but a tradition common to the Liberal
forces in all of them, which binds them together. For
centuries (ever since the Reformation) progressives in
these countries have fought for the same sort of freedom,
and, though as nations they have frequently fought
against one another, they all feel themselves part and
parcel of Western civilization.

The 19th century seemed to bring with it the adoption of this common language of politics not only by the Liberals of the other countries of Europe, but by the Liberals of every country in the world. National self-determination and democracy became the gospel of the oppressed nations of Central Europe, of South America, of India and even of China. The ideal of freedom worked out by the Western nations seemed to have become the ideal of the whole of mankind. Nor did the growth of working-class movements with new socialist philosophies contradict the view of those optimists who looked forward with confidence to the complete westernization of the globe. For socialism, as we shall later see, was entirely in the Western tradition, and was merely the translation into terms of working class needs of the old bourgeois ideals. Liberals would fiercely oppose it, but they would have to admit that it argued in a common language and demanded for the individual worker the same sort of happiness and freedom for which Liberalism stood.

A third factor, which confirmed the illusion that Western democracy was bound to sweep the world, was the industrial revolution. Whether we consider it from the point of view of the producer or of the consumer, the industrial revolution seemed to standardize the way of life of all humanity. No country in the world could refuse to conquer nature and distance and to accept the necessary changes in its social life. Whether these changes were carried through by foreign capitalists or by domestic industries, railways, posts, telegraph, gas, electricity and " modern conveniences " gave to every country the appearance of belonging to a common civilization. The backward countries exchanged their raw materials in return for finished goods, or were lent money with which to bring themselves up to date and thus make themselves potential consumers; and even if they wished to resist, they soon found that resistance was impossible without the armaments which Western civilization alone could provide. [Within one hundred years the world had become not only economically interdependent, but the imperial domain of Western ideas.] The same feature is found if we consider the fate of the producer. Wherever industrialism came, it brought urbanization and the factory system on the one hand, on the other modern techniques for the exploitation of raw materials; everywhere the old agrarian self-sufficiency was uprooted or subordinated to the needs of the West. Western factories needed copra: they got it from Melanesia, and incidentally destroyed an ancient and peaceful civilization. They needed markets and found them in China with the same results. With unheard-of energy and with complete self-certainty the missionaries of civilization voyaged the world not to satisfy *felt* needs, but to impose *Western* needs upon all mankind. And in their ships they brought not only capitalist economics but Christianity and representative institutions. The world was to become not only a single vast source of supply and market, but also the universal territory of Western ideas. King Amanullah should not only sell his goods and buy machine-guns with them: he must also become a Westerner. So too with the Indian coolie or the Chinese peasant: they were to become factory workers on the European model.

We have seen in previous chapters that really influential political ideas are rarely the product of a directing brain. They spring instead out of the actual struggle

for existence, and any ready-made idea which we seek
to impose on others will be deeply modified before it
is accepted as an article of faith. As for its realization in the form of concrete institutions, that depends
once more on a host of conditioning factors. We shall
not therefore be surprised to find that the acceptance
of Western ideas was only skin-deep outside those
few countries where they had been slowly developing
ever since the Reformation. Even in those very countries to-day the Liberal tradition has by no means
conquered. In France and England and America there
are millions for whom political democracy and socialism
are virtually without meaning, and it is only a small
minority who use the currency of political ideas at all.
In the rest of the world there are even fewer.

The 19th century did not westernize the *mind* of
man ; it only imposed upon him certain economic
and military methods of action and enabled him to
utilize natural forces for the service of his wishes.
While the applied sciences have progressed and spread
at an incredible speed, their impact on every variety of
social system has stimulated reactions which are largely
dependent on the prevailing social tradition. In nearly
every country it is the conservative forces which have
exploited science and capitalism for their needs, not
science and capitalism which have converted the country
to Liberalism. Democracy has only survived the shocks
of applied science and industrialism in precisely those
countries where the growth of the bourgeoisie preceded
the changes in the technique of production and where
bourgeois ideals were themselves a conservative force
in the 19th century.

Our story divides therefore into three parts. (1) The

history of the impact of industrialism upon those
countries where already the bourgeois tradition was
strongly entrenched ; (2) The history of the impact of
bourgeois ideas and industrialism upon those countries
which became nation states after the break-up of the
Middle Ages but had not by the beginning of the 19th
century developed a national unity on bourgeois lines.
Such countries were Germany, Russia, Spain and
Italy ; (3) The history of the impact of bourgeois ideas
and industrialism on countries which had no share in
the European mediæval tradition. Such countries are
Turkey, China, Japan. In each of these types we shall
find entirely different lines of development and kinds of
political ideas. In the first there is a fairly continuous
growth in which democratic ideas just manage still to
survive the social convulsions ; in the second some form
of totalitarian state and anti-democratic creed has
gained the ascendancy ; about the third, since it con-
sists of countries with every variety of social tradition,
it is impossible to generalize. Moreover, they are
beyond the scope of the present study.

II.   THE SOCIAL REVOLUTION

The defeat of Napoleon found the forces of democracy
exhausted and disillusioned in Europe. The French
crusade of liberation had ended in a futile attempt at
European hegemony, defeated by the English coalition ;
and the Congress of Vienna had tried by every means in
its power to restore the *ancien régime* throughout the
West. The dream, that the peoples had but to summon
a national convention in order to break their chains,

had been rudely broken, and revolutionary democracy on the Jacobin model was a thing of the past.

Meanwhile economic factors were working fast to destroy the Tory reaction which had been supreme in England for so many years. What pamphlets and theories could not do, was accomplished by unknown engineers in Lancashire and Yorkshire; in the course of a generation Liberalism was to become not the defender of a united working people against oppression, but the protagonist of a new method of production and a new class of industrial *entrepreneurs* against the methods and traditions of the British oligarchy.

The industrial revolution has been too often conceived as a sudden isolated upheaval. Really it was one stage in that development of modern capitalism which we have traced from the Tudor epoch and even earlier, and it had been preceded by a financial and agricultural revolution of equal significance. Nor did it come by any means as a sudden change. Starting early in the 18th century, it was completed in the middle of the 19th century, and was succeeded by further transformations. Seen in its proper perspective therefore it can be described as the *coal and iron* epoch and contrasted with the *electricity and steel* epoch which followed it.

This transformation of England has been usually regarded as the type of all future industrial changes in other countries. But the English development was unique precisely because it was the first to occur. For in the first place it gave England a monopoly of manufactured goods which no other country was to enjoy; and in the second place, once England had given a lead, other countries, which entered the race late, would be able to skip the coal and iron period and develop straight away the capitalism of a later age. Thus the industrialization of Japan and Soviet Russia and even of Germany ran along very different lines from that of England. They never experienced many of the special characteristics which we think of in speaking of " The Industrial Revolution ".

It will be convenient to summarize these features in so far as they affect the growth of political ideas under four heads.

1. *Urbanization*. The most obvious result of the change was the collection of large sections of the population into new towns, and the sharp segregation of the agricultural and manufacturing interests. These new urban districts in Lancashire (cotton), in Yorkshire (woollens), in Birmingham and the Black Country (machinery and finished goods), on the Clyde and Tyneside (ship-building), in the Potteries and in the coal and iron districts of South Wales, Durham, Scotland, etc., were not towns or cities in the old sense of the word. They were neither market nor Church nor governmental centres, but merely collections of factories or mills or mines with the workers' houses crowded round them. Instead of an agricultural community, with a small-scale craft and industry scattered among it, England was sharply divided into two nations, one inhabiting the vast area of the countryside, the other a few square miles of blackened towns.

2. *The Birth-rate*. This shift of population was accompanied by an enormous increase in its size, caused not only by an increase in children born but by the reduction of infant mortality. The industrial revolution was accompanied by a scientific revolution in matters

of health; and the "natural losses", which had kept
the increase within moderate limits, were now gradually
removed. Malthus' (1766-1834) laws indeed were
being rendered invalid even at the time they were
made, and, until in the 90's birth-control methods
became widely known, it looked as though the age of
progress and wealth was also to be the age of a well-
nigh limitless population. Bad as industrial conditions
were, they were healthier than the life of the 18th-century
countryside, judged by infant mortality rates.

3. *Political Consciousness*. The new multitudes of
town-dwellers, uprooted from the soil, stripped of all
the community values of the village and the Church,
were forced to search for new values and a new pattern
of daily life. The established order of Church and
State, the fine distinction between a Whig and Tory
Cabinet, the natural rights of property, could have no
meaning for the Manchester spinner, nor yet for the
mill-owner who himself often enough had risen from the
ranks. More than anything else the new crowded-
ness of factory and urban life produced a political
consciousness, previously limited to the London mob;
and at first this consciousness was a feeling of unity
between all those who worked in industry (employer
and employee alike) against the old agrarian interests
which controlled Church and State. Just as in the
Civil Wars non-conformity and the merchant interests
combined against the "old order" so now once again
19th-century Liberalism was born out of the marriage
of the chapel and the mill. The united will of the people
to abolish privilege and power, which had inspired Paine
and the leaders of the French Revolution, was destroyed : the alliance of farmer and merchant, on which

the Physiocrats had built, was broken, and a new struggle between the interests of industrial capitalism and those of tradition and agriculture took their place.

Moreover, within the new industrial order another conflict was slowly emerging between the interests of capital and labour. As the independent craftsman was gradually replaced by the mechanic working in the factory, a new class made its appearance, the proletariat " which had nothing to sell but its labour " and was interested therefore in selling that labour at its highest price. The old Mercantilism of the Tudors, which fixed wages and prices by royal decree, had long since fallen into desuetude ; now the guilds too were to disappear and new proletarian organizations, Trade Unions and Co-operatives, were to fight their way to recognition. Inevitably in his new urban conditions, the industrial worker felt a solidarity unknown before, and was forced to wage a double battle, on the one side industrial war against the capitalist, on the other a battle against the old " feudal order " which, by opposing the free development of British capitalism and safeguarding agriculture, refused him the cheap food which his meagre wages demanded. Only after 1890 when the industrialists were firmly in the saddle would the halt of capitalist advance, caused by foreign competition, bring into being an independent political movement of the industrial workers. Till then they would fight the employer in industry and support him in politics.

4. *Politics and Economics.* Meanwhile the industrial revolution had entirely changed the problems of government. Since 1688 the British tradition of freedom had

opposed centralized control and prevented the formation of an administrative bureaucracy. The voluntary
service of the squirearchy acting as Justices of the Peace,
and of the Anglican parsons, had provided a rough
and ready local government. A standing army and an
efficient police force had been regarded as infringements
of British liberty, and, as Tom Paine had explained,
the executive branch of the Government seemed solely
concerned with excise and wars of prestige. But though
Liberalism might wish to destroy the last traces of
mercantilism and restriction on capitalist enterprise,
a whole host of new problems emerged which could
only be solved by action on the part of the central
government. At a minimum the new urban areas
demanded efficient police and public health services as
well as poor law relief. If the central government was
not to provide them, an entirely new system of local
administration must be invented. But industrial
capitalism needed education as well, both for the higher
and the lower orders. The new worker must be able
to read and write, the new technicians must have a
sound scientific training, and these services could only
be provided with the assistance of the central government. Thus legislation was compelled to concern itself
more and more with the new economic order, and to
provide not only a legal structure to legitimate the
financial and industrial operations now necessary, but
also supervision of factories and mines, and the social
services rendered necessary by the new mode of life.
" Laisser-faire " was a fine dissolvent of the old order,
but it gave no guidance for the building of the new.
In spite of its own dogma the new Liberalism, which
had joined battle with the state for interfering with

economics, was forced to construct a new state, vastly more complex in character, to guide and direct the development of capitalism.

III. JEREMY BENTHAM AND JAMES MILL

In a society so deeply disturbed and divided it was impossible to expect any new synthesis of ideas to replace the individualism of Natural Rights. Instead, political theory became once more the instrument of faction, subordinated to political and economic interests. The Philosophic Radicals, who developed the new philosophy of Utilitarianism, in spite of their high-sounding name, were far better pamphleteers than they were analysts either of human nature or of economic law. But the importance of Jeremy Bentham (1748-1832), James Mill (1773-1836), Ricardo (1772-1823) and John Stuart Mill (1806-73) is inestimable. Not only in England but throughout the world, their philosophy of life was accepted both by its protagonists and by its opponents as *the* philosophy of the industrial revolution. Under this banner, the attack upon the old order was launched, and upon them and their theory of capitalism the new Marxist creed was to make its fiercest assaults. Once again we find that the influence of political ideas seems to be in inverse proportion to their philosophic value.

Utilitarianism was an unoriginal and inconsistent theory, held together not by its own inner coherence, but by the political needs of its middle-class supporters. It was influential just so long as it was useful to the new industrialism in its attack on the landed aristocracy ;

but as soon as free trade had been achieved and the
new middle classes had won the day, it was discarded
by politicians and academics alike. Thus the Utilitarians played the part of the French Physiocrats in
the peaceful revolution of British life. They undermined the old order and left it to others to build a
new one.

We have seen already how Hume and Burke had
attacked the theory of natural law and natural rights
upon which 17th-century individualism had been built.
Bentham continued the work, choosing as his weapon the
association-psychology which we first met in the *Leviathan*. Logically, but quite unscientifically, he developed
a mechanistic view of the mind and repeated Hume's
argument that the principle of Utility would prove as
universal a law for human nature as the principle of
gravity had proved for the material world. In the first
section of his *Principles of Morals and Legislation* he
formulated his theory as follows :—

Nature has placed mankind under the governance of
two sovereign masters, *pain* and *pleasure*. It is for them
alone to point out what we ought to do, as well as to determine what we shall do. On the one hand the standard of
right and wrong, on the other the chain of causes and
effects, are fastened to their throne. They govern us in all
we do, in all we say, in all we think : every effort we can
make to throw off our subjection, will serve but to demon-
strate and confirm it. In words a man may pretend to
abjure their empire : but in reality he will remain subject
to it all the while. The *principle of utility* recognizes this
subjection, and assumes it for the foundation of that system,
the object of which is to rear the fabric of felicity by the
hands of reason and of law. Systems which attempt to
question it, deal in sounds instead of sense, in caprice
instead of reason, in darkness instead of light.

Thus the problems of conduct were narrowed to a single question, how to minimize pain and maximize pleasure ; and law and morality and religion were viewed merely as social instruments, useful or destructive to the individual's happiness. Bentham assumed that pleasures and pains, like the mass of material objects, could be reduced to a lowest common denominator and then summed. Life was composed of a series of experiences, in each of which a definite quantity of pleasure or pain (or both) was felt. Once the psychologist had classified these experiences, and found how much pleasure or pain they contained, he could work out a formula of greatest happiness ; and could then review the laws and morality of any country and measure how far they contributed to the happiness of the individual. A moral rule is useful if it makes us avoid pain ; and even if it inflicts a small pain upon us, that is useful if, by so doing, it enables us to avoid a greater.

Such a philosophy is materialist in the worst sense of that word. It treats happiness as though it were a collection of goods or coins of fixed value, and assumes that reason dictates to us that we should amass the greatest amount of this psychological wealth. But the Utilitarians were not pure hedonists ; they did not follow Hobbes the whole way. The world, on their view, is so arranged that the greatest happiness of the greatest number is also my happiness. Reason therefore demands not that I should make an exclusive cache of psychological wealth, but that I should seek a distribution of happiness such that I, and as many others as possible, can be happy. This strange conclusion they backed by the argument of " diminishing returns ". If I, with 2,000 units, add one more, I am not so much

happier as a man with only two who gets one more.
Ergo he should have the extra unit and not I. This
argument, which implies some principle of "fair distribution" or "natural rights" or "equality", was
one that no logical Hobbesean could use. Once you
have laid down the rule of individual self-seeking, you
cannot consistently maintain that it is *better* for the
individual with two than for the individual with 2,000
to have the extra unit.

Partly for this reason, yet another inconsistent
theory was thrown in, this time borrowed from the
Physiocrats. It was argued that, by a natural dispensation, individual self-seeking *did* promote the general
happiness and that, if all men intelligently pursued their
own maximum pleasure, then the maximum general
pleasure would also be achieved. The Utilitarians
tried to have it both ways, by asserting first that men
should (if they were prudent) seek the greatest happiness
of the greatest number ; and secondly that men *did*
in fact, by pursuing their own happiness, achieve the
good of others ; and by these inconsistencies they
avoided the unpleasant conclusion of Hobbes that
human nature needed a Leviathan.

These inconsistencies were not apparent to Bentham
and his followers owing to their artificial separation of
politics and economics. Their economic theory was
physiocratic, and from it they could deduce the corollary
of *laisser-faire* and unrestricted competition. But when
they turned to government and considered the principles
of sound legislation, they unconsciously shifted their
ground from the *natural* identity of interest assumed in
their economics, and held that it was the legislator's
task to create an artificial identity of interest by

ʟ

distributing pleasures and pains on the principle of the greatest happiness of the greatest number.

In all this they tacitly assumed the sovereignty of enlightened self-interest which would, if all restrictions were removed, develop a code of law, based on the calculus of pleasure and pain, and thus ensure to all citizens maximum happiness. But the contradiction between the ideal of a state enforcing a comprehensive Utilitarian scheme of life and a natural economic order freed from all state interference runs through the whole of Bentham's writings. This confusion was made worse confounded by the new economic theories of Ricardo. The Physiocrats had dreamt of agrarian liberalism and regarded commerce as of secondary importance. Ricardo was pleading the cause of industrial capitalism against agrarian interests and working-class agitation, and was anxious to prove that both were a burden on capitalist development. For this purpose he resurrected Locke's theory of " Labour value ",[1] and in his *Principles of Political Economy* (1817) expounded the thesis that value is proportional to the amount of labour expended in production. From this principle he drew two important conclusions. In the first place, in the celebrated " iron law of wages ", denounced so vehemently by Marx and Lassalle, he concluded that in a free market the proper wage of the labourer would be the maximum which the capitalist was prepared to pay for his labour. More he could not ask for without upsetting the laws of supply and demand, and these laws it was not to his interest to upset since they were the eternal verities of liberal economics. *Ergo* the labourer, if he was reasonable, would accept the laws of supply

[1] See page 73.

and demand without protest; and the state, if it was
Utilitarian, would forcibly prevent the formation of
Trade Unions. For such combinations would upset
the free operation of the market and win for the labourer
more wages than the labour he put in.

In his second conclusion Ricardo deals with the
agrarian interests. His theory of rent is directed to
showing that " the interest of the landlord is always
opposed to every other interest in the community ".
What he takes in rent does not increase the wealth of
the people, but deprives the tenant of the profits of his
labour. The more productive a farm is, the more rent
he demands, and thus the earnings both of the farmer
and of the labourer suffer while prosperity redounds
only to the landlord. This remarkable theory, which
admits a class-conflict between landlords on the one
side and tenants and labourers on the other, was of
course quite inconsistent with the " natural identity
of interest " which the iron law of wages assumed. It
was going to be fatally easy for Marx to show that the
conflict between landlord and tenant was paralleled by
that between capitalist and proletariat, and that if the
landlord stole the rent, the capitalist stole in his profits
the labour-value of his workers. But such awkward
developments did not occur to the Utilitarians. Their
new science had provided the industrialists with a
fine theoretical justification for their attack on the
agrarian oligarchy, for the abolition of the old poor law
relief, for the suppression of trade unions and for keeping wages low.

But what has all this to do with democracy? It
is indeed at first sight somewhat surprising that the
Utilitarians should have found it necessary to include

a theory of political democracy in their programme. How could they conceive that a people, equipped with the weapon of the ballot-box, would tolerate for a moment the ruthless " laws of capitalism " ?   The answer is again to be found in the political exigencies of the moment.   Not one of the philosophic radicals was a democrat such as Robespierre or Paine or even Rousseau. They did not believe in the voice of the people, or the general will or the rights of man.   On the contrary, they denounced such ideas as fiercely and with the same arguments as David Hume, the sceptical conservative ; and they would no doubt have preferred an enlightened despotism guided by the advice of the middle class.   But of this there seemed no possibility in England between 1800 and 1832.   Somehow, somewhere a lever had to be found with which to shift the landed oligarchy.   Neither the King nor the Lords nor the Commons were suited for this function, and an extension of the franchise was therefore the only conceivable method.

That this was really the reason for their " conversion " to democracy is shown by the career of Bentham. By profession a lawyer, he began his writings as an advocate of legal reform.   In the tortuous ramifications of British civil and criminal law he saw something which was of benefit to no one except " Judge and Co.", i.e. the legal profession.   As we have seen, he conceived of law as an instrument for facilitating the private happiness of the individuals who make up the nation ; and he spent much time and labour preparing schemes of prison and legal reform, and drafting a rational code of law.   It was only when his schemes aroused no interest (except hostility) in the ruling oligarchy that he began to develop a political theory. His own experience had shown him that the Utilitarian legislator was thwarted by one thing and one thing alone—the sinister interest. Since all men were self-interested, Judge and Co. could not be blamed for perpetuating a legal system which benefited no one except themselves. His own psychology taught that power would always be exploited by the powerful for the benefit of their own kind.

Thus the problem of government for Bentham was how to expel the sinister interest and to replace it by the greatest good of the greatest number. And here the way seemed clear. Since all privilege and power would be abused, then all privilege and power must be abolished. Every institution which could be exploited in the interests of a group must disappear, and be replaced by institutions which really represented the interests of all. The practical consequence was inevitable : the monarchy and the Lords were doomed, and the House of Commons must be so reformed that it really represented the interests of the nation. Universal suffrage by secret ballot would ensure that the representatives were the resultant of the total self-interested wishes of the nation. Annual elections would prevent the Commons themselves becoming a vested interest exploiting the community for its own profit. In future M.P.s should be not representatives but delegates from and servants of the nation. And since all men were rational and self-interested, such a delegate assembly would be bound to pass the legislation and accept the legal code which Utilitarian philosophy had proved would maximize happiness and minimize pain.

Bentham himself was a diffuse and clumsy writer,

but his follower James Mill has left us in his article on government for the *Encyclopaedia Britannica* a summary of his political theory which concentrates in a few pages the essence of Philosophic Radicalism. It is one of the ablest and most perverse pieces of argument in the English language.

" The aim of government," he writes,

is to insure to every man the greatest possible quantity of the fruits of his labour and this object can best be attained when a great number of men combine and delegate to a small number the power necessary for protecting them all. This is Government . . . all the difficult questions of government relate to the means of restraining those, in whose hands are lodged the powers necessary for the protection of all, from making a bad use of it.

In this passage it is noticeable how small is the difference between the objectives of Locke and Mill. The only distinction lies in the fact that Locke was concerned with checking the power of the King, Mill of Parliament. But the fundamental aim, the preservation of exclusive property rights, was the same for both.

Mill then goes on to expound the deficiencies of direct democracy on the Greek model, aristocracy and monarchy. The first is unbusinesslike, the second and third vicious, since they entrust power to a group or a single man in spite of what Mill regards as the law of human nature, that the strong will oppress the weak as much as they are able, and that those with power will satisfy their own desires at the expense of others who have no defence against their rapacity.

It is upon this lurid " law " that Mill bases his theory of representative government. Man : selfish, and

lusts for power over others as the instrument of his
pleasure. Mutual exploitation is inherent in human
society, and there is no limit to our desire to bring
our fellow creatures under our domination. Somehow
then we must construct a system of government which
will bring the interests of the rulers (who hold power)
into conformity with those of the community. We
cannot tempt them with pleasant bribes " since pleasure
appears to be a feeble instrument of obedience in comparison with pain . . . terror is the grand instrument "
The argument in full is as follows :

If Government is founded upon this, as a law of human
nature, that a man , if able, will take from others any thing
which they have and he desires, it is sufficiently evident
that when a man is called a King, it does not change his
nature ; so that when he has got power to enable him to
take from every man what he pleases, he will take whatever
he pleases. To suppose that he will not, is to affirm that
Government is unnecessary ; and that human beings will
abstain from injuring one another of their own accord.

It is very evident that this reasoning extends to every
modification of the smaller number. Whenever the powers
of the Government are placed in any hands other than those
of the community, whether those of one man, of a few, or
of several, those principles of human nature which imply
that Government is at all necessary, imply that those
persons will make use of them to defeat the very end for
which Government exists.

Thus our task is to check the representative, while yet
giving him scope to do his job. Annual elections will
ensure that " directly his constituents suspect him, that
moment they can turn him out ".

Mill then considers to whom suffrage shall be granted.
Women and children he excludes as having interests
identical with those of their husbands and fathers.

Then, after a great deal of hesitation, he decides on universal manhood suffrage without property qualification, but limited to those of forty and over. A high property qualification, he argues, would create an aristocracy and a low one would only cause annoyance to the few excluded. Faced by the argument that the people are uneducated, he replies that it is easier to educate a people than to prevent an aristocracy from enslaving its subjects. And, anyway, if Protestant England holds that the common man can understand the Bible " the majority of the people may be supposed less capable of deriving correct opinions from the Bible than of judging who is the best man to act as their Representative ".

Such in brief was the theory of government propounded by James Mill. As a piece of reasoning it is on a level with his economic and psychological theories. Cold, dogmatic, and devoid of all understanding of human nature, it proposes representative democracy as the surest safeguard of the freedom of capitalist enterprise. Of the need for social services and of the obligations of citizenship it takes no notice whatsoever. Its England is a nation devoted to the pursuit of wealth, a collection of selfish and almost sadistic power-seekers, and this savage breed is to be tamed and held in restraint by the single political device of representative institutions. If a middle-class Englishman could describe his fellows in such terms as these, we cannot be surprised that Marx borrowed the description and turned it against the upholders of capitalism. He had no need to invent " class-war " : he found it in the writings of his opponents.

The clue to the real significance of Mill's Essay, however, is to be found in the concluding pages. The passage must be quoted in full.

It is to be observed, that the class which is universally described as both the most wise and the most virtuous part of the community, the middle rank, are wholly included in that part of the community which is not Aristocratical. It is also not disputed, that in Great Britain the middle rank are numerous, and form a large proportion of the whole body of the people. Another proposition may be stated, with a perfect confidence of the concurrence of all those men who have attentively considered the formations of opinions in the great body of society, or, indeed, the principles of human nature in general. It is, that the opinions of that class of the people, who are below the middle rank, are formed, and their minds are directed by that intelligent and virtuous rank, who come most immediately in contact with them, who are in the constant habit of intimate communication with them, to whom they fly for advice and assistance in all their numerous difficulties, upon whom they feel an immediate and daily dependence, in health and in sickness, in infancy and in old age ; to whom their children look up as models for their imitation, whose opinions they hear daily repeated, and account it their honour to adopt. There can be no doubt that the middle rank, which gives to science, to art and to legislation itself, their most distinguished ornaments, the chief source of all that has exalted and refined human nature, is that portion of the community of which, if the basis of Representation were ever so far extended, the opinion would ultimately decide. Of the people beneath them, a vast majority would be sure to be guided by their advice and example.

Here at last we find the practical purpose of Liberal Democracy, according to James Mill. It was not to give power to the people but to the middle class, and it was only because and in so far as it did so that he prized it so highly. As his economics was special pleading for industrialism, so his politics was special

pleading for the middle classes. Directly either of
them became inopportune for these interests, it would
be scrapped and replaced by a more convenient weapon.
Marginal Utility would take the place of Labour Value,
and idealism would wave Utility into the limbo of
forgotten creeds. Unfortunately, however, the harm
would have been done, and the doctrines which Liberals
wished forgotten would be made the centre of a new
revolutionary socialist creed.

IV. RELIGION AND CAPITALISM

Meanwhile public opinion was moving along very
different lines. The urban middle classes, which gained
political power in 1832, were composed of devout and
simple men. Many of them had been far more deeply
affected by the Wesleyan revival than by Bentham's
theories ; and the chief immediate result of the shift of
power was the reconversion of the ruling classes to
godliness and piety. In the course of a generation
the cynical brilliance of aristocratic British life was
pushed into the background, the gay clothes disappeared
and the earnest sobriety of Victoria and Albert replaced the dissipations of the court of George IV. Disraeli, the budding politician, wore flowing curls and kept
a mistress ; as the first minister of Queen Victoria,
clothed in discreet black, he went solemnly to church at
Hughenden. The classical elegance of Georgian mansions
was transformed into the baronial gloom of the Gothic
revival ; and while industrial capitalism ousted the old
economic order, middle-class respectability was achieving
a far more spectacular success in the social field.

Lately it has been the fashion to decry the intense moral seriousness of the Victorian age, and to expose its " hypocrisy ". But such an attitude is both un-historical and psychologically unsound. British history, as we have seen, has been determined ever since the Reformation by the interests and ideas of the middle class. Although this middle class has time after time become the upper class and even the aristocracy, in the course of the change it has never completely for-gotten its bourgeois origins ; and each succeeding wave of political emancipation has resulted in a victory for the ideas of the lower over the upper order. Victorian-ism was the supreme instance of such a victory. In fashions, in sexual morality, in business methods, in art and literature, it reflected the ideals of the small number of electors enfranchised by the reform of 1832. James Mill's panegyric on the middle classes had a sound basis in fact. But they were supreme not only over the work-ing people but over the court and aristocracy as well.

Unlike the Utilitarian theorists, the Victorian busi-ness man based his politics upon a foundation of religion. He detested the oligarchy not only for its defence of the landlord, but also for its flagrant disregard of moral principle. Imbued with the Calvinist spirit of Cromwell's army, he preached thrift, work and charity as the moral basis of the new capitalism, and amassed his wealth not from a Utilitarian desire to maximize his pleasure, but from a stern sense of duty. Seeing in the new industrialism a vast potential weapon of social good, he felt that the development of his business was a divine vocation, and that the sufferings of his workers were part of an irrevocable plan, and their hardships only to be allayed by Christian charity.

It was the theological setting of capitalist economics which gave them their irresistible force in British life. The progress of industrialism displayed at the Great Exhibition of 1851 was taken as a token of God's mercy to the faithful, not as a proof of the Englishman's success in maximizing his pleasure. Precisely because economics and politics were not the centre of his spiritual life but sciences subsidiary to a religious ideal, the British industrialist could accept their conclusions without difficulty, in spite of their disastrous social repercussions. For him capitalism was the indisputable framework provided by God for the self-improvement of the human race. Evil and pain had always been part of the mysterious plan of the Deity ; they must be accepted, and softened by Christian charity. But any attempt to remove them by reconstructing the economic system was not only a violation of property but of divine commands. If Burke was the conservative prophet of the settlement of 1688, British Liberalism was not less conservative in its defence of the new industrial dispensation.

Thus the intellectual energy of the Victorian age was directed not to a critique of Utilitarian economics, but to theological speculation. It was Darwin's *Origin of Species* not Marx's *Capital* which really disturbed the British middle classes ; the Oxford Movement and the Ritualistic controversy into which the activity of its ablest minds were thrown.[1] Gladstone genuinely felt that politics was a second best in comparison with taking orders.

The enormous moral stability and self-confidence of

[1] For a fine description of this moral struggle, read *Father and Son* by Edmund Gosse.

19th-century England can only be explained if we give proper weight to this religious faith. The increase of wealth, the expansion of the empire and even the increase of the population were felt by their contemporaries to be the blessings of a merciful Lord. " God had set his rainbow in the sky and the colours, truly read, spelt competition." England, mercifully redeemed from the immorality of a degenerate aristocracy, could now look forward confidently to a limitless progress of Christian prosperity.

The belief in progress, strengthened by entirely fallacious deductions from evolutionary theory, was indeed the centre of the Victorian creed. Intellectuals like Matthew Arnold and Carlyle might throw their doubts upon it, and thereby win considerable circulation for their writings, but the middle classes believed in free trade and peaceful competition as eternal verities, and regarded their task not as the construction of a new world, but as the purging of the new dispensation from a few trifling survivals of the past. History, they felt, was on their side and it was only left for man to perfect the edifice.

So the full force of the evangelical fervour was directed to the furtherance of good works, and the cruel economics of capitalism were mitigated by a new humanitarian philosophy, which believed that Christian love and generosity alone were needed to turn capitalism into the Kingdom of God. The abolition of slavery, the revival of the missionary crusade, the attack on child labour, the spread of public education, and dozens of other movements sprang not from a political faith but from the Christian conscience of the community. Wilberforce and Howard, Lord Shaftesbury and Charles

Kingsley, Livingstone and Florence Nightingale were not political reformers or critics of the economic system. They were social reformers in a new sense of that word; disinterested humanitarians, who, accepting the new dispensation, sought within its framework to humanize its working. Most of the great 19th-century movements of reform were derived from this source, and only after they had fired the popular imagination did they become part of the programme of politicians. When they did, it was largely a matter of chance and opportunity which of the two great parties carried them through.

It is only on this background of religious conviction and social reform that a true portrait of British political ideas can be painted. On fundamentals the nation was united, as never before, and the political conflict, though intense, was wholly subsidiary to the unity of religious fervour and economic optimism. This conflict moreover was less one of ideas than of interests and of personalities. Until the '90's Liberalism was the party of industrialism and non-conformity, Conservatism of the landed interest and the established Church. But with the abolition of the Corn Laws (1846), this conflict became far less intense. For a generation British agriculture and industry flourished simultaneously, and free trade became almost an agreed policy, while neither party stood clearly for a programme of social reform. The industrialist, freely accepted into the ruling class, felt himself at liberty to join either party; and the stage was set for a new play of personalities within a new and balanced equilibrium. More and more Disraeli and Gladstone became the incarnations of the two opposing forces. Once more a period of social revolution had closed with the accession of a new class to a share of power ; but no revolutionary change had been made in the constitution of the country, which was still based on the principles of John Locke. Once the prosperity of the '50's had dissipated the last vestiges of Chartism, England could safely affirm that she had escaped unscathed from the revolutionary ferment of the French Revolution, by a moderate and timely enlargement of the social oligarchy.

V.　JOHN STUART MILL

The moment had arrived for a fresh synthesis of British political ideas. With the middle classes firmly in power, with a working arrangement between agriculture and industry, and a compromise between the old oligarchy and the new business men, the inconsistencies and deficiencies of Utilitarianism became more and more obvious. It was John Stuart Mill who first began to question his father's articles of faith and to grope for a new philosophy of freedom.

The theories of the younger Mill are unintelligible save in the light of his *Autobiography*, one of the most revealing documents of political philosophy. Confused, timid, and doctrinaire, yet displaying an intellectual integrity and humanity far greater than that of any of his predecessors, his work was of the highest importance in the history of political thought. Mill was educated by his father from his earliest years to be the paragon of Philosophic Radicalism, and its principles were so firmly stamped on his infant mind that they became rather unconscious reflexes than intellectual theories.

But even an education as fanatical as his could not destroy the sensitivity of his nature ; and, as he grew up, while his mind remained Utilitarian, his spirit hungered for a more humane creed. For this reason, in tracing the intellectual development of the younger Mill, we can discover the forces which broke the supremacy of Benthamite theory. His spiritual crisis was the crisis of Victorian politics.

Mill was disturbed not by the inconsistencies in Benthamite theory but by its soullessness. Point by point, his own natural emotions forced him, while retaining the general framework, to make concessions in matters of detail, until, unaware that the whole philosophy had been exploded, he himself was left in a tangle of inconsistencies worse even than those of his father. Like other great philosophers, he showed his greatness most of all in the daring with which he permitted his native sense to modify " self-evident " propositions. Though he could never free himself from the shackles of the system imposed on him in childhood, his heroic efforts to do so made it easy for successors, less inhibited than he, to build a new system upon firmer foundations.

Mill's intellectual conscience was tormented by three problems. The first arose from moral theory and needs only a brief attention here. In the first place he felt that there must be a distinction between higher and lower pleasures ; a lump sum of happiness could not be the aim of any sensitive soul. Bentham had declared push pin to be as good as poetry if you liked it as well, but Mill retorted with the aphorism " Better to be Socrates unsatisfied than a fool satisfied," and with this single sentence brought the whole structure of Utilitarian ethics tumbling to the ground. For once pleasures were distinguished in quality, they could be no longer summed ; and " the greatest happiness of the greatest number " became a useless formula for the benevolent legislator of Bentham's dreams. Out of this wreckage —for Mill clung desperately to the calculus of pleasure— emerged his passion for the disinterested judgment of social problems and for the sense of social obligation without which he foresaw that capitalism was bound to kindle the flames of class war. Utilitarianism had ridiculed just these two notions ; it had denied the possibility of an unselfish action or the need for a sense of community in modern society, and had preached that a clear-cut self-interest would replace such old-fashioned sentimentality. Now the last member of the school was to attempt to argue that in the Ethics of the New Testament the principle of Utility had first been proclaimed. Alas ! Though James Mill possessed virtues, they were not those of Nazareth, and not even his son could successfully reconcile the ferocious rationalism of the Essay on Government with the Sermon on the Mount. The effort to do so was the last spasm of a dying creed.

As a result of this attempt to soften the asperities of his father's teachings, Mill became increasingly aware that Utilitarianism left no room for real liberty. Laisser-faire and its industrial consequences had handed the future of the country over to a devout and industrious middle class ; but the theory that universal suffrage would produce a House of Commons ready to serve the interests of the community had encouraged the working classes to demand the vote. Mill felt himself sailing between the Scylla of a selfish

M

capitalism and the Charybdis of mob-rule. To preserve
the former involved the sacrifice of the workers to
new sinister interests ; to enfranchise the latter, the
destruction of disinterested leadership and impartial
legislation. Uncertainly he began to fumble towards
the idea that good government could not be achieved by
the simple device of substituting the clash of interests
for the rule of an élite. If there were higher and lower
pleasures, there were also distinctions of quality between
individual men, and the future of the country depended
on the facilities it offered to the gifted few to develop
their talents in the service of their fellow men.

And here a personal crisis in the life of John Stuart
Mill became a crisis of political theory. The cold discipline
of his early education, its mechanistic dogmas and its
crude atomism revolted the young poet, who had found
in Wordsworth a " culture of the feelings " strangely
at variance with his philosophical principles.[1]   He
began to feel that free personal development was incompatible with such an education, that the individual spirit
must be allowed to develop along its own peculiar lines
and be permitted food for its æsthetic sensibilities.
Precisely those things of which he had been deprived
in his youth became the centre of the new philosophy
of freedom which he developed in *Liberty*.

Thus a personal reaction against the tyranny of Benthamite discipline was extended to the field of social
relations. Here too Mill felt that a Benthamite society
could never produce free and noble citizens. If the
nation's life was to consist solely of an attempt to maximize its worldly goods, if each individual was to be
encouraged to disregard his social feelings and " make

[1] For this crisis see *Autobiography*, Chapter V.

his pile ", and if representative government was to become merely the executive committee of a wealth-getting association, then the common good would be blotted out of existence. In 1861 he completed *Representative Government*, and once again unwittingly undermined the Utilitarianism which he preached.

Representative Government, published just before Disraeli's extension of the franchise, marks the moment when [British Liberalism had begun to feel the awkwardness of the theories with which it had ousted the landed oligarchy.] The vested interests which it disliked had been abolished or checked, its economic demands had been adopted and its ideals accepted as the national philosophy of life. Bentham's tirades against oligarchy and his desire to turn M.P.'s into delegates of the popular will sounded differently to a class in power ; and in this book Mill moves back towards a defence of oligarchy tempered by democratic safeguards, closely similar to that of the 17th-century Whigs. Defending the right of the representative against the mandate of his constituents, he repeats the arguments of Edmund Burke ; fearing the tyranny of the majority, he invokes proportional representation and plural voting as methods of giving more weight to the opinions of the enlightened minority. Once again, as in his moral theory, his belief that [quality must not be sacrificed to quantity] that [leadership must not be degraded into demagogy] make him willy-nilly a traitor to Benthamite theory. Terrified of the masses, whose plight he dimly feels is the result of industrialism, he moves towards the Platonic view that a country can only be saved by a breed of philosopher kings and seeks to achieve this end through modifications of the suffrage.

This tendency increased in later years. With added sympathy for " socialist ideas ", his last published work (1873) was a claim that the state should control the unearned increment on land, an idea which was to be popularized later in the works of Henry George. Favouring Trade Unionism and Co-operation, he also saw in the tendency to monopolistic organization a factor which could be used for achieving real co-operation between capital and labour, and envisaged the future of the country in a way not wholly unlike that of the later Fabian Socialists. Capitalism, under the guidance of disinterested statesmen might yet, he dreamed, become the economic basis of a united nation working for the common good.

Mill's writings are important not because of any originality in his ideas, but owing to their sensitivity to the needs of the age. In each of his spiritual crises he reflected a real problem of English life, and even his notorious friendship with Mrs. Taylor was to rouse him to a defence of women's rights, which in due course issued in the women's suffrage movement. The colossal effort, by which the protagonists of the iron law of wages were to transform their country into a social service state, was reflected in his struggle to turn Utilitarianism into a social gospel. His appeal for disinterestedness and objetivity in government found realization in the growth of a great national and local service of administrators who more and more assumed the functions of government. His desire for a free and undogmatic education was at least partially achieved by the transformation of the Universities and Public Schools and the construction of a national education system. Even his view of the duties of Trade Unions and Employers'

Federations was to be justified by the actual developments of later years. In all these ways Mill was the
prophet of a new Liberalism which was the perquisite
of no party and still dominates the minds both of
statesmen, and of the non-political Englishman in 1938.

Mill could not foresee how these changes would
come. His Benthamite upbringing caused him to
concentrate his attention too closely on politics, in the
narrow sense of the word, and to give to the House of
Commons and to universal suffrage a significance they
did not possess. Within a few years Joseph Chamberlain, by the invention of the party-machine, was to
ensure that democracy brought, not the tyranny of
the majority, but its political subordination to a
hierarchy of officials and an élite of leaders ; the M.P.
became not the delegate of the people but the servant
of the Party Executive, and the popular mandate was
virtually controlled by a machine far safer and more
effective than proportional representation. So too with
the Civil Service. This again was to remove from
" politics " a larger and larger share of government and
to mitigate the ignorance and narrow-mindedness of
the politician by its impartial machinery of administration. Of all this, as of the sedative effect of the
20th-century Press, cinema and wireless, Mill could
know nothing. He could only paint the ideals and
objectives of the new National Liberalism : others,
less philosophic than he, were to develop the institutions
by which the equilibrium of social forces was to be
maintained.

CHAPTER VII

NATIONAL LIBERALISM AND IMPERIALISM

I. CONTINENTAL LIBERALISM

WE have indicated already the peculiar character of British and French developments in the 19th century. In both of these countries, the industrial revolution, when it came, found a stable structure of bourgeois law and order and a national tradition of individualism; for this reason they were able to weather the storm and to adapt their institutions to the new conditions. England became a great manufacturing nation, but admitted only so much of democracy as was compatible with representative government on the Lockean model, only that amount of capitalist individualism which could be reconciled with the growing demands of the industrial worker. France, in spite of a series of revolutions, retained the Napoleonic structure of civil life, an economy rooted in agriculture, and political institutions which, through all their changes, always relied on the support of the small farmer and the small investor.

But other countries were not so fortunate. In 1840 Germany, Italy and Austria-Hungary were still states governed on the old despotic lines, in which neither nationalist nor democratic nor yet industrial aspirations could gain satisfaction. And the complete failure of the 1848 revolutions in every country proved that

bourgeois revolution on the French model was a thing
of the past. For this reason Liberalism in these countries developed along quite different lines and was
faced with problems unknown to the bourgeois movements of the West. These differences will be clearer
if we summarize the chief characteristics which we
group under the name of Liberal.

We have seen that from the Renaissance onwards a
new and individualistic concept of the rights of property
and private enterprise had been gaining ground all over
Europe, and brought with it the economic institutions
of international banking, large-scale farming and merchant enterprise. One element in nineteenth-century
Liberalism was the desire to continue this development
to the stage of industrial capitalism, as England had done.
But this could, it was thought, only be achieved if it
was accompanied in the political sphere by the substitution for the " old order " of representative institutions and a modern system of law ; and this political
aspect of Liberalism was closely connected with two
other movements, the one for national self-determination,
the other for the abolition of clerical supremacy over
education, science and the arts. Anti-clericalism,
democracy, nationalism and industrialism were the
four strands which were woven into the intricate and
varied web of European Liberalism. Yet a fifth com-
plication was introduced by the growth of anarchist
and socialist movements, which, even before the bourgeois state had been established, were struggling to
convert the working classes to their extreme creeds.

We have seen moreover that the weakest side of
English, French and American Liberalism was their
political theory. In all these countries Liberals had

wished to weaken the central government, and were inclined to rely on the suffrage not as a method of selecting the government, but as a substitute for government itself. Liberalism was an excellent weapon for an attack on a strongly entrenched system of law and order ; it could mitigate its tyrannies and purify it of many of its privileges and corruptions : but it had never shown itself able to build a new democratic system without the help of some at least of those forces which it denounced. But outside France, England and the Netherlands there were no such forces on which it could safely rely. If, for instance, the absolutism of the Hapsburgs was demolished, a great empire would be broken up into an anarchy of warring minorities, since here the nation state was not coterminous with nationalist aspirations. Such a prospect could have but little appeal to the merchant or to the peasant, who, if he wanted freedom, wanted security even more. Again the dominant position of the Church in Spain, Italy, Austria and Russia made it inevitable that Liberalism in these countries should either assume an extreme rationalism or else come to terms with the old absolutist state. Since the Catholic Church was both fiercely anti-Liberal and also enjoyed great privileges under the status quo, Liberals were usually bitterly anti-clerical, and thus alienated the sympathies of the rural areas where the vast majority of the population lived. This resulted in a peculiarly close connection between Liberalism and the bourgeois society of the towns, and this again had as its consequence that the Liberals were fighting not only the established order and the peasantry, but also the growing Socialist movements as well. Broadly speaking therefore, the political

parties in these countries were divided into three groups :
(1) the Conservative agrarian clerical interests ; (2) the
Liberal urban bourgeoisie ; (3) the Socialist organizations of the workers which grew rapidly after 1848.

Comparing this analysis with that of England, we
are immediately struck by four facts. In the first place
British democracy evolved within the firm framework of
national unity, and British Liberals could demand
freedom without any fear of disrupting the nation
into nationalistic minorities. They could lay down with
confidence, the proposition that man is a narrowly
self-interested individual because the Englishman
was nothing of the sort. They could speculatively
atomize English society precisely because it was *not*
atomic, but a community inspired by the deepest of
common feelings—patriotism. Such feelings were so
strong and so habitual that reformers could simply
assume them, and disregard them in their theories
altogether. But Liberals in Spain and Germany could
not. Spanish unity was threatened already by demands for autonomy by Catalans and Basques, while
Germans. divided into countless petty states, were
faced by a Catholic Emperor in Vienna and a Protestant
King in Prussia and must, before they dreamt of a
democratic republic, decide on its boundaries and its
religion. Whatever form the national democracy of
Germany assumed, it would be bound to arouse passionate antagonism in the hearts of Germans, and might
well include within it Slav minorities which desired
their own self-determination.

In the second place, British democracy had been
closely connected with the fight for religious freedom.
Since the Elizabethan settlement, Catholicism had not

been a serious political problem, so that the struggle could take place once again within the limits of national unity, and be viewed merely as the effort of British citizens to gain their rights against the established Churches of the country. Thus the religious motive, in its primitive Christian form, could be harnessed to the service of democracy, and the triumph of Liberalism could bring a religious revival to Victorian England. Nowhere else, save in America, was this possible. Loyalty to Catholicism in Protestant Prussia could be fairly construed as an act of political disloyalty : Protestantism in Spain or Italy was closely allied to treason. In England and America non-conformity was essentially national ; in the rest of the world it implied conformity with the dogmas of churches whose existence might endanger the unity of the nation.

For this reason European Liberalism found its prophet in Rousseau. Unable to appeal directly to the religious motive, it sought to canalize it into the secular religion of humanism and the worship of political institutions. It was anti-clerical not only in the sense of hating the privileges accorded to the Established Church, but also because it sought to substitute for organized religion organized politics as the fulfilment of man's needs. Gladstone was as much a churchman as he was a statesman, but for German and Italian Liberals, progress, the nation and democracy were the objects of a secular worship. If the Church made a totalitarian claim for obedience on its members and sought to ordain their political opinions, Liberalism, inspired by Rousseau, was equally totalitarian in its claims. The devout Catholic was bound to feel that an unbridgeable gulf divided the religion of Christ and the religion of progress : the devout Liberal that clerical domination of the spirit was incompatible with freedom and democracy.

In the third place, the economic theories of the British Liberals were firmly based on British facts. Laisser-faire had indeed been of benefit to the country, and by 1860 Free Trade had made England the workshop of the world. But a policy of benefit to the first industrial country might not benefit the second or the third. To build up industries in Germany or France, or even America, not Free Trade but Protective Tariffs were needed. Sheltering behind these from British competition, and subsidized by the state, the industrialists might well hope to break the monopoly of British manufacturers. *Manchestertum*, to borrow the German word, might be the gospel of merchants and ship-owners, but it could never be a gospel to unite business interests in an attack on the old order. Moreover, nationalism (which was the burning fire of the 19th century) favoured a *national* economy and made a breach between National Liberals who found their inspiration in imperialism, and Free Trade Liberals who conceived of liberty on true Utilitarian lines. As a result, in Germany for instance, industrialization was pushed through under the old autocratic dispensation, and the industrialist was easily tempted to sacrifice democracy and align himself with the agrarian interests. The same thing was to occur in even more striking form in Japan, where a nation passed direct from a feudal economy to the highest form of monopoly capitalism.

Fourthly, it must not be forgotten that the social effects of industrialization varied according to the date at which it took place. In Britain it had been part of a

Liberal movement and individualistic in character.
Industrialism had meant the right of the small *entre-preneur* to stake everything on the success of his mill,
his factory or his mine, and had been often animated
by hostility to the old merchant companies and the
well-established banks.   The new capitalists in fact
rebelled against the restrictions of the old merchant
capitalism, and it was not till the middle of the century
that British Company Law was overhauled and the
legality of the Joint Stock Company was established.
To a great extent the new industries were financed
locally : Lancashire cotton for instance remained till
after the Great War outside the control of London.
The industrial revolution therefore brought not only the
enrichment of a new social class in new areas, but a
decentralization of the control of British capital.   Birmingham, Manchester and Glasgow became not only great
manufacturing towns, but capitals of business enterprise,
whose Liberal politics were animated by a deep hostility
to the supremacy of London and the old ruling class.

This centrifugal tendency in the industrial revolution (although after the turn of the century it was
completely counteracted by a new concentration of the
control of capital) reflected an essential feature of British
Liberalism, which would not be repeated in countries
where industrialization was from the start under central
control.   Once again we find the contrast in Germany,
which, forcibly united by Bismarck, built up its heavy
industries not by local private enterprise but under the
guidance of the central banks and in a system of cartels
and trusts which transgressed every law of utilitarian
economics.   Germany, in fact, because she delayed it
till the '80's, missed the centrifugal stage altogether and

was thus deprived of the industrial basis for an individu-alistic Liberal movement.

This difference is repeated in the Labour Movements. The typical working-class organization of Great Britain was the craft union and the local Co-operative Society. From 1850 to 1900 the increasing prosperity of the country permitted the workman to retain his old political allegiances, while building his own multifarious com-binations in the industrial field. Thus the British Labour Movement, when it finally achieved unity in the Trade Union Congress and in the Labour Party, became a loose federation of autonomous societies and has remained so to this day ; whereas in Germany and in Austria, where the political movement preceded the indus-trial, the dogmatic discipline of Marxism was centrally enforced upon a united working-class party, and, when in the nineties Trade Unionism did begin, it immediately developed a centralized bureaucracy in accord with the structure of German and Austrian industry.

Although therefore to-day the prevailing form of industrial organization in all countries is the cartel and the combine, and a highly centralized financial oligarchy, there is a marked difference between those countries which passed through the centrifugal stage and those which did not. This difference is displayed in political organization and in the reactions of public opinion to continued concentration of control. In America and England widespread opposition can be aroused in all classes, in countries such as Germany it is only felt among the petit bourgeoisie. Fascism occurs precisely in those countries where the centrifugal liberal tenden-cies found no industrial basis in the economic develop-ment of the 19th century.

II. FAÇADE OF ITALIAN LIBERALISM

With such profound underlying differences it is not surprising that the ideas of bourgeois democracy underwent a startling transformation in Germany, Italy and Central Europe. Only in Italy was a modern nation state successfully created ; but even here, though national unity was achieved, representative institutions were doomed to failure.

The Italian *Risorgimento* was the greatest triumph of 19th-century Liberalism. A nation parcelled out among the Great powers, petty principalities and the Roman Church, was successfully united under a constitutional monarchy on the English model, true to the principles of free trade and civil liberty. In the course of twelve years (1859 to 1870) a modern nation state was formed in spite of the opposition of the Church and the Austrian Emperor, and the people's acclamation manifested in a series of plebiscites. Clericalism had been defeated in its very home. But on closer observation the unification of Italy discloses several features disturbing to the adherents of the Liberal creed. In the first place it was only made possible by Cavour's manipulation of the European balance of power. French support was obtained for the first campaign against Austria ; Venetia was won not by Italian arms, but by Bismarck's victory at Sadowa in 1866, and the Papal States were the fruits of yet another victory of Bismarck, that of 1870 over the French. All the idealism of Garibaldi and Mazzini could have availed nothing without the assistance of Great Powers, and the passive connivance of an England interested in the possibility of railway and other contracts. From now on it was clear that the right of self-determination for oppressed peoples would be circumscribed and conditioned by the interests of existing nation states, whatever their political principles.

The early Liberals had believed that the disappearance of the old despotic order would usher in an era of peace and goodwill. Once these obstructions to the general will were removed, each people could choose its own government and live at amity with its neighbours. England, France and America seemed to have proved this simple theorem, and bourgeois Liberals the world over believed that international relations would offer no fundamental problems in the new age. America, by the declaration of President Monroe in 1822, had established the principle of America for the Americans and the right of self-determination for its southern republics [1]; British Liberals, hating war and denouncing the Empire as an unnecessary and burdensome expense, were pouring out their sympathy for the oppressed peoples of Europe and looking forward to the day when universal democracy would break all trade barriers and substitute the peaceful competition of business for the futile wars of despots.

These high ideals, which were to find their supreme apostle in President Wilson, were little regarded in the formation of the Italian nation. Already by 1860 it was clear that representative institutions in no way affected the external policy of nation states, and that

[1] But the refusal by the U.S.A. to permit European interference in South America did not mean that the U.S.A. itself would refrain from ' dollar diplomacy '.

the theories of Hobbes in this sphere had a closer relation to reality than the rhapsodies of Tom Paine. The
Liberal might realize some of his ideals at home ; abroad
force and fraud would remain the dominant forces
so long as national sovereignty was unchecked by any
higher coercive power. This fact, which no continental
Liberal could fail to grasp, was not so obvious to the
Anglo-Saxon peoples. Owing to the unusual security of
their positions, American and English public opinion
could remain blind to the real forces at work, and,
leaving diplomacy to the trained expert, limit themselves to a high-minded form of moralizing. On the
Continent, however, the Liberals and even the general
public were forced to face the new facts and consequently
found themselves more and more widely separated from
the lofty idealism of British and American progressive
thought.

The Liberalism therefore which triumphed in Italy
seemed in its later developments positively Machiavellian to the remoter admirers of Garibaldi and Mazzini.
They were shocked to see the adroitness with which the
statesman of the new Italian nation played the dip-
lomatic game, and, by skilful bargaining, managed to
ensure that even a second-class power should achieve
its share of Empire and a place in the sun. They failed
to realize that the new Italy, which was largely a product
of " power politics ", could only survive and increase
its strength by a strict adherence to the rules of diplomacy which had remained unchanged since the
Renaissance. Internal freedom could only be achieved
on a basis of external security : external security for
a second-class state necessitated a calculated policy of
playing off one great power against another.

The Machiavellian character of Italian diplomacy was also reflected in the domestic politics of the new state. Italy was sharply divided into three parts, the prosperous North, Rome, and the poverty-stricken agricultural districts of the South. It was the North which had unified the country and introduced the ideas and institutions of democracy, but the North remained a minority of the population, and the bitter hostility of the Church to the new state [1] confined political education to Rome and the northern towns. The vast mass of the people remained entirely passive or hostile to democracy. Industrialism and civil liberty could offer nothing to the poor peasant whose only hope lay in the formation of peasants' co-operatives, while the worker was soon organized into a Marxist Labour Movement which showed little inclination to collaborate in government. Without any mass-basis, Italian democracy soon floundered into a bog of petty intrigue. Thus the only really compelling factor in Italian Liberalism was its nationalism. Everything else was shoddy and unreal, but the unification of the nation and its later imperial efforts became the myth of the New Italy, and all active political forces were soon canalized either into the effort to strengthen a second-rate nation or to overthrow it by revolutionary activity. The compelling ideas of Liberalism were Machiavellian ideas of Empire, the compelling ideas of the Labour Movement were Machiavellian ideas of violent revolution. Italy had not yet suffered that dose of Napoleonic discipline which gave fibre and stability to the French Revolution. It was a Liberal state without that Conservative

---

[1] Including an official ban on political activity.

tradition of government which we have found so vital to the prosperity of the western democratic powers.

III. THE PROBLEM OF GERMAN UNITY

In Italy the national revolution resulted at least in an immediate success, but this was not the case in the rest of Europe. Germany, Austria and Russia remained until the Great War autocratic nation states on the old model, in which the middle classes were subservient to the old order. The failure of Russian Liberalism resulted in the Communist revolution of 1917, that of the Germans and Austrians at long last in the National Socialist revolution which transformed the balance of post-war power.

The German people never fully recovered from the effects of the Thirty Years' War. This great religious struggle had ended in a peace of exhaustion, which left Germany proper a collection of petty principalities, while Austria remained a vast bureaucratic state, sprawling over Northern Italy and Central Europe, and deeply influenced by papal policy. The old Austria was not a national state like England or France or even Spain, but a supra-national empire in which German culture and the German minority were predominant. Heirs to the Holy Roman Empire, the Hapsburgs, until the Napoleonic period, still laid claim to the hegemony of Europe and directed their policy not to the strengthening of German interests, but to the maintenance of Catholicism and of their semi-feudal dominion over non-German peoples. Only in 18th-century Prussia was there to be found a truly German state, and even this was under the sway of French culture.

Thus, when the French Revolution came, there was no natural rallying point for German nationalism. The German people were divided, and the one German idea, the Holy Roman Empire, was attached to an institution resolutely opposed to change. Napoleon found it easy to divide up Germany as he pleased, to defeat and cripple Austria, and even to remove from Prussia her Westphalian and Polish provinces. In so doing he did not offend the feelings of German progressives. On the contrary, Goethe and Heine welcomed his coming. For the great literary and musical movement, which at the end of the 18th century put the German people at the head of contemporary culture, sprang not from the soil of a united nation, but from a race which had attained its cultural emancipation without any political unity at all; the Germany which Goethe and Herder, Lessing and Kant represented was a people without a state. In the modern world Germans and Jews are the only two races which have contributed greatly to mankind on a basis not of national but of cultural unity. Perhaps this is a reason for the deep antipathy between them

The Napoleonic Wars are the dividing line in the history of Germanism. Even while the literary and musical giants of cultural Germany were still alive, a new political consciousness was capturing the younger generation and expressing itself in the wars of Liberation. Goethe, the prophet of non-political individualism, was in Weimar when Fichte in Berlin wrote his *Addresses to the German Nation*, and the young poets of nationalism were stirring the students of the universities into a deep impatience with the calm impartiality of the German professor.

The political centre of the new nationalism was Protestant Prussia. Here the Liberals could count on a fine military tradition, and here Hardenberg and Stein carried through a sort of military bourgeois revolution. But Prussia in 1813 was not strong enough to oppose Napoleon alone. Forced to seek the friendship of Austria, her nationalists unwillingly gave up the idea of a single German nation state and permitted Metternich to carry through a policy not of national unity, but of Austrian conservatism. When the Congress of Vienna met in 1815, it was dominated by the single motive of repressing those dangerous nationalist forces which had alone made possible the defeat of Napoleon. Austria became the head of a new and deliberately vague Confederation of German states.

The failure of the Germans to achieve unity in the Napoleonic era was of tragic importance for Europe. For as industrialism developed in the 19th century and the new nation state began to take form, the shape of Central Europe seemed more and more anachronistic, and yet more and more difficult to recast without upsetting the balance of power. Italy could be unified in the sixties with the connivance of the Great Powers, but a unified German nation, ruling possibly over millions of Slavs and Magyars, would endanger the security of France and England and Russia. The nationalist interests of Germany ran counter to the national interests of the Western bourgeois states; and so German nationalism was now alienated from the democratic ideals of the French and American Revolution.

But there were internal difficulties too. Once the Congress of Vienna had strengthened the position of Austria, the Germans themselves found it difficult to envisage the frontiers or the capital of a united Germany. Catholics looked to Vienna, Protestants to Berlin, while Republican Liberals sought for some centre which would not offend religious susceptibilities, and would still be strong enough to hold Germany together. Their difficulties were aggravated by the foreign policy of England and by internal developments in Prussia. Castlereagh, determined to prevent a repetition of Bonapartism in France, in 1815 joined the Concert of Russia, Austria and Prussia which imposed on all Europe a régime of extreme reaction. For seven years, until in 1822 he was succeeded by the more liberal Canning, Conservatism was permitted to consolidate its position. Those years of British compliance were as fateful as the years which succeeded the Treaty of Versailles, one hundred years later. After the great convulsion which could have issued in progress and reform, all such movements were repressed until it was too late for them to be effective. In Prussia moreover the Liberal activities of Stein and Hardenberg were succeeded by a period of frustration. Encouraged by England, the feudal nobility (or Junkers) prevented the development both of Parliamentary institutions and of industrialism, and succeeded in exploiting the liberation of the peasants for the enlargement of their estates. Church and state were united into a single force for the suppression of political freedom, while the bureaucracy, efficient, nationalistic and shrewd, permitted enough intellectual liberty to keep the bourgeoisie quiet. The undeniable capacity of the

Prussian ruling class only added to the difficulties of the progressives.

Great hopes had been felt of the young prince who in 1840 became Friedrich Wilhelm IV of Prussia. But instead of inaugurating a period of reform, this romantic monarch tried to move back beyond enlightened despotism to a pseudo-mediævalism even more reactionary than the policy of his predecessor.

At last the outbreak of revolution in Paris in 1848 seemed to offer the chance for which Europe had been waiting. A democratic Government was set up in Vienna, Hungary claimed her independence, and an all-Austrian Parliament was summoned. Meanwhile throughout Germany proper National Liberalism prevailed, and on May the 18th a National Assembly met at Frankfurt to work out a unified system of central government.

Once again an attempt was made by prudent lawyers and business men to frame a constitution for a whole people. The Frankfurt Parliament was the last effort of revolutionary democracy on the American model. That it failed was not due to the faults of its members but to the differences in the situation of the American colonies and the German states. Of these there were thirty-eight, excluding Austria.

The first disagreement arose between the adherents of Greater and Little Germany. The Radicals and the Catholics wished to include the German provinces of Austria as a make-weight to the Protestant military power of Prussia. The Protestants and the Prussians feared the clerical influence of Vienna and were jealous of its imperial pretensions. For five long months the delegates argued, and avoided this major question. The second disagreement arose out of the nature of the parliament. Must the new constitution be ratified by each of the Governments or no ? Finally, by a narrow majority, it was decided to back the power of Parliament with the sword of Prussia, and the romantic reactionary Wilhelm IV was offered the imperial crown of the new democratic Germany.

But by this time the revolutionary tide had subsided. The Austrian movement, which had in the first few weeks eliminated many feudal privileges in the German provinces, had been shattered by racial rivalries. The Sudeten Germans were terrified by a Panslavonic movement for the liberation of oppressed races. The Croats, fearful of Magyar supremacy in the new régime at Budapest, were induced to follow a Croatian general and to smash Kossuth and his democratic army with horrible cruelty. The Czechs were defeated in Prague, the Germans in Vienna, and the old Empire was successfully restored, though Hungary retained a measure of independence. Within a year emancipated Liberalism was chained once more in the Imperial mill. It was only necessary for Friedrich Wilhelm to refuse the offer of the Frankfurt Parliament to complete the catastrophe. Not till 1918 would the German people once more have the chance of building a free democratic society. By then it was too late.

After 1848 German Liberalism was compelled to work within the old order both in Germany and Austria. The latter retained her supra-national structure and, during the long reign of Franz Josef which lasted till the Great War, the Empire tried to accommodate itself to the new nationalism by increasing concessions to the non-German minorities. As a result, Austrian

Liberalism became more and more concerned not for the private rights of the individual against the old feudal order, but for the rights of the national minority against rival minorities. Moreover, the progressive forces were hampered by the backward nature of Central European economy. Except for the fringes of Bohemia, inhabited by the Sudeten Germans, and Vienna itself, the country was almost entirely agricultural, and remained so until the Great War. Democratic movements therefore could only assume a Jeffersonian agrarian form, but in so doing they ran counter to the interests of nationalism. If a peasant wanted home-rule for Hungary he could not attack the Hungarian landed aristocracy. And, on the other hand, the emperor could not abolish privilege without undermining his own imperial power. The Austrian Empire was doomed to stagnate, because any change would disrupt it altogether. Liberalism was bound to be unconstructive because it could find no basis on which to unite the warring minorities.

On the other hand the bourgeoisie, whatever its race, could not afford to break up the empire. The few who were interested in industry needed a market for their goods and feared very properly the consequences of dismembering the body of Imperial Austria, while the majority found their livelihood in the imperial bureaucracy, which was recruited, as the century progressed, from all the minorities. The Liberals therefore once more divided into those concerned to maximize their privileges under the old régime, and those other Utopians who were prepared to annihilate it without very much regard for the new system which was to replace it.

In this confused atmosphere, German Liberalism in Austria developed along peculiar lines. The working classes in Vienna were, after the failure of 1848, converted to Marxism and fell into uncompromising hostility to the Church and the peasants. The German bourgeoisie however was deeply divided. In Bohemia it fought Czech nationalism, while importing cheap Czech labour in order to break the German Trade Unions. It opposed every concession by the Central Government to racial minorities, yet could not afford, for industrial reasons, to advocate the break-up of the empire, since that would make it a minority itself. In Vienna, where industrialization had been carried through almost entirely by Jews, the Germans were mostly servants of the state and petit bourgeois. Liberalism therefore on the French model became " Jewish " and anti-German, and the German middle classes either remained staunchly Conservative, or were swung into a Catholic Anti-Semitic movement. Racialism, which is the central doctrine of National Socialism, arose out of the peculiar conditions of 19th-century Vienna. It is the Nationalism of a privileged bourgeois minority, excluded from the advantages of the industrial revolution.

Meanwhile in Germany the inevitable happened. The unity which the Liberals had failed to win was imposed by Prussia, and a German Empire was constructed by Bismarck upon the basis not of the national will but of a federal arrangement with the princes. The democratic tradition of South Germany was suppressed by a Germanism which was Prussian in all but name, and Germany proclaimed her political unity by the defeat of France in 1870. A new great power had emerged as the result not of a spontaneous democratic movement but of the power politics of a Prussian Junker. From now on the leadership of the German people passed from aged Vienna, with its mediæval notions of Roman Empire, to a modernized Prussia, fiercely nationalist and resolutely anti-democratic. And it was under this military leadership that the industrial revolution was carried through.

IV.   ROMANTICS AND DEMOCRATS IN PRE-WAR
GERMANY

Bismarck's solution of the national problem was highly artificial, and could give little satisfaction to the aspirations of 19th-century progressive thought. By defeating Austria and yet permitting her to survive, he secured an ally for the German Empire. But this ally was so infirm that she could not outlast the world war. By constructing the German Empire under Prussian leadership, while leaving the states and their princes considerable federal freedom, he created a new nation. But this nation had never experienced the national revolution. It had been unified from above, not from below, and remained a Bismarckian artifice, dependent on the skill of its founder for its strength and coherence. The common man had no share in its making or in its government which retained most of the features of 17th-century autocracy. In brief, the modernization of Germany was the superficial work of a single man.

This superficial character of the German victory was felt by many but especially by Nietzsche, (1844-1900).

For all his hatred of democracy and humanism, he was no supporter of the Wilhelmian *Kultur*. He knew that the brand-new German nation was a vulgar shoddy affair. In 1873 he published the following remarkable prophecy :

A great victory is a great danger : human nature stands victory worse than it stands defeat. Indeed it seems easier to win such a triumph than to prevent it resulting in worse defeats. Of all the consequences of our victory over the French, the worst is the illusion, which seems to be almost universal in Germany to-day,. that German Culture was also victorious at Sedan and so should be decorated with the wreaths which such a triumph deserves. Such nonsense is poisonous, not because it is nonsense (there are mistakes which bring with them the blessings of health) but because it can transform our victory into utter defeat, the defeat and extirpation of the German spirit for the sake of the German Empire.[1]

Nietzsche knew that the new Germany had no inner life of her own : it was an affair of bricks and mortar, of iron and steel, of technical efficiency and military skill, but it lacked the cultural tradition which France and England possessed, and which the German people even in the time of their abasement could proudly claim.

Because he was an inconsistent, emotional, unpolitical thinker Nietzsche expressed that feeling of deep dissatisfaction and self-mortification which was to shadow the German Empire even in its greatest triumphs. Between 1870 and 1914 Germany became one of the great manufacturing nations of the world, and the most splendid military power. Her industry was more highly organized

[1] From introduction to *Unzeitmässige Betrachtungen*.

than that of any country : her Labour Movement excelled all others. Germans were the best capitalists and the best socialists in the world. But below the display of self-assurance, there lurked a sense of inferiority : below the outward unity, a terrifying capacity for mutual destruction. Just because the new Germany was an artificial construction, the natural sense of national unity was perverted and suppressed. Having no outlet in action, it expressed itself only in philosophy, speculation and mystical movements.

Through the latter part of the 19th century, German thought was divided into two parts. There was the busy activity of administration and every-day work on the one hand, and on the other the tortured striving for a way of life which did not fit into any of the existing forms. A nation state, yet not a nation, Germans dreamt of a *Volk*, which should not obey Bismarck's commands, but express the German spirit ; of a *Gemeinschaft* or community which really expressed their inner nature. German culture seemed at variance with German politics, the German soul with the German mind.

This undercurrent of discontent was not fully reflected in philosophical speculations or in political life. Here, swayed by the colossal material success of the new empire, the ideas expressed were respectable and " western ". Imperialism and Liberalism, Conservatism and Socialism fought their correct battles in the press and the lecture-room, but all the while the revolutionary force of these new ideas was quietly moving the German mind away from the bourgeois ideas of France and England into a national romanticism which would conceive of revolution not as a step towards the fulfilment of the bourgeois state but as the destruction of bourgeois reason and bourgeois " rights " and the creation of a new and unique German state, with its own German reason and German justice and German community. Once more Rousseau's theory of the General Will would suffer a transformation into the *Volksgemeinschaft* of Möller van den Bruck and Adolf Hitler.

But for fifty years after the Franco-Prussian war this movement was subterranean or purely cultural. The German Liberals, faced by Bismarck's *fait accompli*, were easily persuaded to give up their hope of democracy in return for national unity and international power. With him they waged the *Kulturkampf* against the Catholic south whose loyalty to the empire was doubtful; and when, their services rendered, Bismarck discarded them, it was far too late to resist. The German middle classes had accepted the political leadership of the Prussian Junkers, had swallowed their ideology of power and carried through the industrial revolution under their control.

The new Germany became a vast bureaucracy. The Reichstag, with no control over the fighting services or foreign policy, was impotent. Without the bother of cabinet responsibility, the Chancellor and the Kaiser were supreme. Granting all the trappings of universal suffrage (except in the Prussian Landtag) Bismarck retained all power in the hands of a ruling clique steeped in the military tradition of Prussian Junkerdom. Against this autocratic state, which was supported by the Catholic Church once its rights had been established, there grew up a democratic Liberal opposition. The Liberals of the southern states, with their tradition of constitutional monarchy, joined the Social Democrats, who controlled the votes of the organized workers, and dreamt of a constitutional government on the English model. Ardent supporters of the new Germany and of industrialism, deeply interested in Germany's foreign trade, they were in no sense revolutionary, but wished quite simply to humanize the existing German empire by introducing parliamentary control of foreign policy and of the fighting services, and by winning for the Prussian Landtag universal suffrage. These reforms they felt were all that was necessary to transform Germany into a progressive state. Many of the Marxists believed that, granted these changes, Socialism would develop of its own accord.

The temper of this Liberal parliamentary opposition was not dissimilar from that of the opposition in the epoch before the French Revolution. Its ideas were based upon conscientious research into economic and political theory but, like their French predecessors, the German opposition was ignorant both of the responsibilities and of the art of government. They were decent law-abiding citizens who longed for civil liberty, peace and prosperity : with no desire for power, they had a wildly exaggerated respect for parliamentary institutions and were blinded by the delusion that others were as decent and law-abiding as they were. Whether they called themselves Democrats or Liberals or Marxists, almost all of them were inspired by the same liberal ideals of progress, law and order, and unconsciously became a permanent opposition, satisfied to criticize, unwilling and unable to rule.

Such an outlook was defensible in countries where the bourgeois revolution had established the principle of representative government. There at least it was possible to believe that the tradition of toleration and compromise had been assimilated by the old ruling classes. Even in America and England this had not been accomplished without violence, but the violence had been forgotten. In Germany however the old order had never been successfully challenged : on the contrary it had defeated the revolution of 1848 and strengthened its position by modern industrial organization. Against the age-old claims of the Prussian bureaucracy it was madness to believe that the mild weapons of constitutional government would prove effective. Without a victory to its credit, tolerated contemptuously by the ruling class, the German democrats might organize millions of voters, but they would find it hard in the hour of crisis to take over the reins of government and to give orders to that class whose obsequious critics they had been.

Until the Russian Revolution lit a spark of revolutionary spirit in the German workers, it can safely be said that, in spite of Marx, the German Left had no revolutionary tradition. 1848 was a catastrophe of which it was difficult to be proud ; Bismarck's persecution of the Socialists had aroused a spirit of tenacious resistance, but not of revolution, while the programme of State-Socialism which he initiated had taken the sting out of Marxist propaganda. How could a workman ruthlessly oppose the state which led the world in social reform, in industrial activity and in military glory ? From 1890 onwards the Social Democratic party became a sober reformist party theoretically opposing and practically co-operating with the state.

Thus the seeds of National Revolution which should

have developed on normal democratic lines sprang up into the tangled growth of cultural and political romanticism to which we referred at the beginning of this section. The worker accepted the new order of centralized industrialism and listened obediently but without enthusiasm to his Social Democratic leaders. The peasant, retaining his religious orthodoxy, was content to accept the leadership of the great landowners in return for the protection of his livelihood. Only in the middle classes were there signs of a spirit of rebellion against the Wilhelmian system. Anti-Semitism and racialism flourished from the '80's onwards, and the Youth Movement in the new century grew rapidly and absorbed the energies of thousands into a cultural revolt. The finest minds among the bourgeoisie, too honest, to believe in the placid optimism of the democrats, became infected with romantic longings for a new unbourgeois Germany and began to preach a creed of the German super-man which was best expressed in the music of Wagner, the poems of Stefan George's school and the literary criticism of Gundolf. Before 1914 this movement was politically insignificant, but its mere existence showed that if the Empire were to collapse, the democratic opposition's dreams of a Germany dominated by respect for bourgeois law and order might be rudely shattered, not merely by the forces of reaction but by the enthusiasms of youth.

V.   IDEALISM AND METAPOLITICS

In tracing the peculiar development of Italian and German Liberalism, we have carried our story forward into the 20th century. We must now retrace our steps and very briefly summarize the changes in other countries, and in particular in France and England.

We have seen how in both countries the period of liberation from the old order was followed by a new stage of construction and of centralization. Almost before they were perfected, the political theories of the early Liberals were outmoded and a new state made its appearance, more bureaucratic, more powerful and more intrusive than the despotism or oligarchy of the old order. The same occurred in economics. Though England retained free trade till 1931, the rest of the world competed to enlarge its tariff walls; though Liberalism denounced combinations of employers and employees, by 1900 the Cartel, the Trust and the Trade Unions were the chief features of industrial life. Everywhere, before the age of free and unrestricted private enterprise had really begun, it was succeeded by a new age whose practices contradicted at almost every point the principles laid down by the early democrats and the protagonists of industrialism.

The sphere of international relations shows an especially striking contrast between the principles of the national democrats and the practice of national democracies. At the beginning of the 19th century it was the middle classes who were denouncing the expensive futility of colonial enterprise and of the armed forces necessary to protect them. Seventy years later Liberal Governments in France and England were competing madly in the scramble for colonies and for commercial privileges in China and other undeveloped countries. The necessity for raw materials and for markets could not be gainsaid, and every country, whatever its political complexion, which wanted to rank as a major power, was bound to enter the race and stake out its imperial claims. The Liberal revolution, instead of abolishing national rivalries, intensified them and extended them over the whole globe until the European struggle for power was felt on every continent and over every ocean ; instead of crying for the abolition of useless navies, big business at the end of the century was demanding increased armaments, in order that the benevolent shelter of the new state might protect its enterprises overseas.

These new developments had an important effect upon political thought. The idea of National Democracy which had inspired the French Revolution had always, even in the days of the Terror, been based on the essential brotherhood of man, and summoned the oppressed individual to break his chains. The Democrats had believed in universal reason and in the equality of all rational beings, and their nationalism was the expression of these equalitarian beliefs. Now both in domestic and international politics a split occurred. On the one side the new classes which rose to power found themselves separated by social and class distinctions from the working people and brought into contact with the old ruling classes. In this process, although as we have seen they gave much, they received much in return. Hostile to state interference, they saw that it was increasingly necessary if the industrial system was not to be destroyed by class-war ; and they began to apply to the state the administrative and organizing ability which they had developed in industry. Government and business imperceptibly drew together, and instead of equality, social service became the guiding notion of middle-class democracy. Representative institutions were less and less regarded as the organ for the destruction of vested interest and privilege, more and more as the instrument for smoothing out social frictions and for providing those services which efficient business required. Parliament in fact became the machinery for the representation of interests, and democrats envisaged an ideal state in which a just equilibrium between these various interests would be reached within the capitalist system.

This notion of a just equilibrium between the demands of capital and labour was really a return to Burke's notion of providential inequality. The status of rich and poor, of *entrepreneur* and wage-labourer, was assumed as a permanent factor in the social order, and the dream of an equalitarian society of small *entrepreneurs* was quietly forgotten. It was felt that industrial capitalism brought material benefits greater than any abstract political idea, and that if the business man became aware of the full responsibilities of his position, and the working man made only reasonable demands, then society as a whole would achieve its common good. What was needed was to destroy ruthless competition and self-interest, and to substitute for them a sense of civic responsibility.

The state therefore on this new theory was not a necessary evil, nor yet a policeman to protect the natural rights of property, but an *instrument of positive good*, essential to the lives of its members. Through its educational and social services it would become the vital unifying centre of national life, and a real freedom could only be found within the framework of goodwill which it provided.

This theory of the state is best exemplified in the writings of T. H. Green and the later British Idealists. Green, an Oxford Don and a member of the City Council, completed the task begun by J. S. Mill. Under his hand, Liberalism lost its radical ferocity and became the benevolent gospel of a responsible ruling class. Gone is the urgency for universal suffrage and the belief in a freely elected parliament as the cure for all evils. Green was not really interested in party politics, or the machinery of government, nor was he a convinced supporter of any economic or psychological dogma. Utilitarianism in his eyes was a narrow, selfish creed, scientifically wrong and ethically unsound. Turning his back therefore on the individualism and materialism of the British philosophers from Hobbes to Bentham, Green found new inspiration in Rousseau's general will, in Kant's moral conscience and above all in the works of Plato. There in the community of the free Greek state, in Plato's rule of philosopher kings and definition of justice, he found a moral attitude to politics which British Liberal thought had hitherto lacked.

Green's philosophy, like Plato's, expresses a noble ideal. The notion of a community ruled by a mutual respect for personality and limiting its freedom in order to achieve a real co-operative life, is a fine one ; and it is a noble thought that the state, that ugly instrument of torture and oppression, should become the central instrument for its achievement. That a nation would be better if all its rulers acted on this creed is unquestionable, but, when this is admitted, it still remains to ask how we can attain it. Plato's answer had been simple. Educate a new ruling class, he said, and impose it upon your city. Such revolutionary doctrines however did not suit Oxford. Instead of keeping ideal and facts carefully distinguished, Green from the first confused the two, and, having sketched the former, proceeded to find it present in the institutions of his own country. The Utilitarians had said, " Since this is right, let us abolish what is wrong." Green replied, " Since this is right, it must in some sense be here already."

In brief, he hitched his idealism to the sure star of progress. Seeing in history the slow development of universal reason in concrete form, he was able to explain that any imperfections which existed were due to our being still at a stage of imperfect development. Society must, he felt, be organized on the right lines, and our duty was to accept the pattern of the historical process, and give our aid to universal reason in its unfolding of the millennium. God was not an angry deity in heaven above, but the spirit moving and realizing himself in the solemn process of history.

Although Green himself retained a strong Radical fervour for social reform, his ideas as they were developed by his followers like Bernard Bosanquet became deeply conservative in character. Bosanquet's philosophy is but an academic rationalization of Burke's belief in providence. It accepted the new industrial state as a stage in the march towards perfection, the new economic order as the only possible basis for social justice. Instead of encouraging a radical criticism of existing institutions, it gave excellent reasons for believing that all fundamental criticism of them must be morally wrong. It was man's duty to promote goodwill, not to stir up warfare and sectional strife. Wrongs there were to be righted, but the best way to go about the job was to enlighten public opinion, arouse the public conscience, and spread the light of education to all. Green's teaching did much to educate the middle classes to the responsibilities of their new political and social power. He stirred the social conscience to see that individual charity and private movements for social reform were not sufficient, and that the state could and should become the active promoter of such ideals. But Bosanquet was even less democratic than J. S. Mill, even clearer that the crude voice of the mob must be purified before the words of Reason could be discovered. Accepting the existing structure of British society as fundamentally sound, he was quite unable to undertake those radical analyses of economics and politics, those exposures of sinister interests and exploitation and privilege, which the spokesmen of the oppressed and the defenders of freedom had made in the past.

It was, however, in relation to international affairs that Idealism displayed its gravest defects. The tradition of European bourgeois thought had always maintained a deep suspicion of the state, and of the despotic central power. Every progressive thinker had tried to tear away the mystery surrounding sovereignty and to display government as a piece of machinery made by human beings for human use. The idealists unfortunately reversed the process. Decrying the materialism of the Utilitarians, they robed the state once more in a mystique of *meta-politics*, and showed it as an emanation of universal reason. For the divine right of kings, they substituted the divine nature of the State and degraded the individual into an effluence of this *Civitas Dei*. Thus they developed that secular

- IMPERIDUSM -

religion of politics, which we discovered in Rousseau, and made the government and administration the exponents of a divine reason, worthy of an obedience not dictated by self-interest or by a social contract, but by the intrinsic merits of the state itself.

Such a view was bound to contribute to the decay of international democracy, and to harden the demands of absolute national sovereignty. If the national state was the supreme expression of the human spirit, then attempts to look outside it or beyond it were almost treasonable. At a period when economic and industrial interests were exploiting the idea of Empire for the furtherance of their aims, Idealism gave a veil of decency to these pretensions. Economic imperialism could be so easily disguised as the extension of the state's benevolent power, and native exploitation as the shouldering by an educated community of the " white man's burden ". By the turn of the century, Nationalism had ceased to be a democratic movement against the old oligarchy and in France and England, as in Germany, had become the blind sense of subordination to the demands of the nation state.

This explains why, when war broke out in 1914, every European nation reacted in the same way. The nation state retained the unswerving obedience of the vast mass of its population, in particular of the upper classes. Few democratic voices were heard questioning the validity of its claims or the justice of its cause. Each nation fought strictly in self-defence, and, even more significantly, accused its enemies of moral guilt in doing the same. Churchmen and politicians alike were able with the approval of their listeners to talk of the nation state as a person, endowed

with its own life and character, with superhuman
needs, and a superhuman code of morals. The personification of the nation state gave a moral justification to warfare which had previously been lacking.
The wars of the 17th century were wars of religion,
those of the 18th century wars of national prestige
or the disputes of hereditary monarchs. The American and French Revolutions had given rise to wars
of liberation against the forces of reaction. But the
Great War of 1914-18 was a war for survival between
gigantic industrial states striving for their livelihood
in the markets of the world. For the first time in
history whole peoples fought one another and served
willingly not their religion nor their prince, nor yet
the cause of freedom, but the mysterious entity—
the Nation. In the age when publicists were announ-
cing the triumph of democracy, Leviathan had established himself as an object of humble worship in the
mind of Western man. Shrewdly enough he had taught
his subjects that his self-interest was their moral duty;
and the Idealists had provided him with the arguments
for this strange conclusion.

The movement from Utilitarianism to Idealism is
paralleled in practical politics by the development of the
greatest British statesman of the period. Joseph
Chamberlain (1836-1914) was no philosopher, but he
was endowed with a natural intuition which enabled
him to feel, without fully comprehending, the historical
forces at work. Son of a Unitarian business man, he
built up his business in Birmingham at the period of
most intense competition and expansion, and there, for
six years from 1870-5, devoted his business capacity
to the construction of an efficient local government

service.   At this period, he was the typical representative of the industrial Liberalism of the provinces.
A non-conformist and therefore a passionate advocate
of universal undenominational education, he organized the National Education League as a weapon
against the Church of England, and denounced the
monarchy and the House of Lords.   The first politician
to seek explicitly the support of the working classes,
he found himself urging the need for social reform
in opposition to Mr. Gladstone and the Whig leadership
of the Liberal Party.   Advocating a further extension
of the suffrage and at the same time constructing a
modern party-machine, he reorganized the Liberal
Party as a weapon with which to enforce his own radical
leadership upon the old parliamentarians.   His programme, a skilful mixture of agrarian and industrial
democracy, became the banner of the new war upon the
ruling oligarchy.   But from his earliest years Chamberlain had combined with his radicalism a dislike of the
sentimentality of Liberalism in foreign affairs.   He saw
that British industry would depend for its expansion,
now that the period of monopoly was over, upon diplomacy and naval strength, and that the prosperity of
the working classes was bound up with our imperial
policy.   Social reform in his view was only possible if
British trade under government protection could continue to outstrip its rivals and secure both markets and
raw materials.

Chamberlain's radical imperialism was not a contradiction.   On the contrary, it was a realistic development of Liberal theory.   The competition of German
technique demanded a new educational system, of
German social legislation the development of social

services. The new factories of Germany and America and the new scramble for colonies meant that we must re-align our foreign policy and reorganize our empire. Chamberlain believed that this reconstruction of the nation should be carried through, not dictatorially from above, but by a great democratic movement of the people.

The personality of Gladstone and the chances of the Home Rule controversy prevented the fulfilment of this policy. Forced into the Conservative camp, the Radical Imperialist became more and more purely imperialist, while his ideas of social reform were allowed quietly to die. Only between 1906 and 1914 was this part of Chamberlainism to be realized by a ·Liberal Party led by another radical, Lloyd George, and under the pressure of a new Labour Party. It is significant that Lloyd George was later to become as resolute a defender of the imperial position as his predecessor.

Had Chamberlain remained a Liberal, it is probable that the Conservative Party would have shrunk to a tiny rump and that the growth of the Labour Movement would have been considerably delayed. Merely an accident of history prevented this happening, and produced and split the Liberal Movement into two sections : one, the Unionists, adopting imperialism ; the other social reform. Fiercely though the two fought they were essentially complementary features of that single philosophy of Liberal Imperialism which controlled the policy of England till 1914.

VI.   PROGRESS—WHITHER ?

When we try to draw together the tangled threads of 19th-century Liberalism, we are struck by two facts In the first place economic developments took place despite every idea and political institution. The first stage of individualistic capitalism was succeeded by a second stage of monopoly and control ; the movement for the suppression of state interference, by the erection in every country affected by industrialism of the social service state ; the wars of liberation by new imperial rivalries. Ideas, instead of controlling and directing progress, seem in the 19th century to have been chiefly the product of industrial development. Statesmen, in spite of their impassioned controversies, hardly altered the process by which the human race was given a new environment, new work and new pleasures. In the 17th and 18th centuries man had conceived himself as a creature, uniquely endowed with reason, able to understand the workings of a mechanical universe and to settle his problems by sober discussion. He was above the animal and material order, almost above the process of history itself, a creature sovereign over a universe which he could easily understand.

In the 19th century this estimate of man's nature was no longer tenable. The process set in motion by his inventive genius was not understood by the statesmen who controlled his destinies. His theories of economics and of politics were disproved time after time by the acts they tried to explain : the institutions he set up were, by an ironic twist of history, converted to opposite uses. For all his energy and skill, Frankenstein had pro-

duced a monster which took hold of his creator and
pushed him whither he knew not. Despite vastly increased control of nature, better communications, and
enlarged political organization, Western man was more
insecure in the control of his destiny by 1914 than he
was in 1700.

Moreover, the foundations of his faith had been
undermined. Everywhere, even in England and America,
religion, which had provided the structure of his social
and private life, was on the wane. The inspiration of
Anglo-Saxon democracy departed almost before democracy was born, and left it to a Liberal Humanism to
direct the passions of the race. The secular religion of
Nationalism and Progress, of which Paine and Franklin
had dreamt, was now the established Church in most
civilized countries ; and, as we have seen, it was singularly unable to shape the process of history. In the
Middle Ages the Christian creed, for good or ill, had
dominated political and economic life. Ideas for centuries
had controlled matter.   Now the great liberation begun
in the Renaissance had accomplished not the freeing of
mankind from superstition (the belief in progress was
no less superstitious than that in transubstantiation)
but the freeing of material forces from social control,
and the subjection of political institutions to economic
change.

Nineteenth-century Liberalism swam desperately
with this tide, and found it hard to keep up.   Instead of
advancing to a new stage of universal freedom, it only
succeeded in retaining freedom in those countries where
it existed before the coming of industrialism. Elsewhere
capitalism and " progress " were harnessed to the
chariot of the old absolutist order, and the fight for

freedom was waged by young socialist revolutionaries with all the enthusiasm of the democrats one hundred years before. Though the world was prosperous and economically interdependent as never before, it was also rent by class-divisions and by national rivalries which surpassed in intensity those of every previous age.

CHAPTER VIII

SOCIALISM AND THE RUSSIAN REVOLUTION

I   SOCIALISM AND THE BRITISH LABOUR PARTY

IN the preceding chapters we have traced the development of the ideas of Liberal democracy and seen how they were moulded to the needs of the industrial nation state. We must now turn to a new set of ideas whose growth coincided with that of the industrial proletariat. Socialism, Anarchism and Communism are the names under which we group a confusing variety of programmes and philosophies held together by the single fact that they grew out of the social conditions produced by the industrial revolution. Though the men and women who worked them out were often of middle-class origin, these ideas are as closely connected with the struggles of the working class, as Liberal democracy is with that of the bourgeoisie. Where the interests of the working class seem to coincide with those of the rest of the community, Socialism remains essentially Liberal and democratic, as in England, or hardly makes an appearance, as in America. Where, however, a conflict arises, there Socialism assumes a new and revolutionary form, either as Anarchism or as Communism.

It is chiefly with this latter type that we shall be concerned in this chapter. British Socialism, though it is in itself a fascinating study, is so deeply imbued with

Liberal philosophy and springs so directly from the
religious tradition of non-conformity that it has not
produced any ideas peculiar to itself. Accepting the
state as an instrument of positive good and parliamentary institutions as the instrument of political power,
it has been chiefly concerned to accelerate a process of
social amelioration and class-conciliation whose beginnings are found in the thought of J. S. Mill. Its demands
for the nationalization of certain major industries, for
an enlargement of social services, for the public control
of finance, and for the redistribution of income by means
of taxation, are only an enlargement of the Liberal programme of 1906. Partly because its claims have been
so modest, partly owing to the peculiar advantages
enjoyed till recently by British industry, Liberal Socialist
ideas in Britain have been singularly successful in
winning concrete benefits for the mass of the people, and
in converting the ruling classes to a conciliatory social
policy, until Fabianism has become not the battle-cry of a
party but the accepted philosophy of British government.

For this reason, at least till 1931, British politics were
divided not so much by ideas as by interest. In the
middle nineteenth century, Conservatism stood for the
Church and the landed interest, Liberalism for Non-
conformity and industry. By the end of the century,
however, a new division had arisen between those industries which favoured tariffs and those which favoured
free trade, and the Liberal Party became the spokesman
of the latter, retaining its non-conformist tradition, and
adding a programme of social reform abhorrent to the
old Gladstonian Liberals. The war brought a coalition of
all parties, including Labour, which since 1906 had grown
up as the special political representative of Trade-

Union interests ; and demonstrated conclusively the
underlying agreement among all sections of the community. In 1914 Liberal Imperialism was the creed
accepted by all except a tiny pacifist section of the
Socialist Movement. After the war, the vagaries of
Lloyd George and the growing strength of Trade
Unionism destroyed . the Liberal Party, and it was
replaced by the Labour Party (now officially Socialist)
as the official opponent of Conservatism. But as Conservatism, under Baldwin, absorbed most of the Liberal
creed, and the Labour Party's Socialism was, merely
an extension of the Liberal programme, once again
the two political parties were divided on the basis not
of ideas but of the interests behind them. The electoral
support of both was predominantly working class, but
now the one depended on big business, the other on the
Trade Unions for its finances, while the leadership
was similarly divided on a class basis. The religious
issue having now disappeared, class-interests were
paramount, only concealed in the case of the Labour
Party by a smattering of middle-class leaders, whose
Socialism had little influence on the blunt Trade-Union
policy of the party-machine.

In brief, the peculiar good fortune of British industrial and imperial development after 1850 prevented
the growth among British industrial workers of a revolutionary political tradition. Instead the Labour leaders,
like their German equivalents, became even more deeply
imbued with the ideals of bourgeois Liberalism than the
middle classes, since they believed that under an expanding capitalism they could gain more through
constitutional democracy than through the revolutionary
struggle for a new idea and a new society. Since 1931

the Trade-Union leaders, who control most of the Labour Party's financial support, have adopted an extremely cautious policy, struggling to repel the violence of Fascism on the right, and of an imaginary Communist danger on the left ; imaginary, because, as we shall see, Communism has also become a strenuous defender of bourgeois liberties.

The new ideas of Socialism therefore were developed not by Englishmen or for English organizations, but in countries where the class conflict was more open and more acute. In these industrially backward countries, Socialism was bound to replace Liberalism as the revolutionary force simply because after 1848 the latter seemed to have no chance of success. When once the impotence of Liberalism in the face of autocracy was proven, the Liberal Movement divided into two parts ; one accommodated itself to the status quo, the other, carrying with it the bulk of the industrial workers, developed out of Liberalism a new philosophy which challenged at the same time Liberal economics and the autocracy of Church and State.

This movement from Liberalism to Socialism took place not because any philosopher wished it but through the sheer compulsion of events. The harshness of capitalist conditions, contrasted with the ideals of the French Revolution, forced the industrial worker to find salvation in his own strength, and to look for a new theory of life which should give him some hope of liberation. This theory was provided by Karl Marx (1818-1883) and Friedrich Engels (1820-1895). They did not invent Socialism, but they did work out an analysis of capitalism and a theory of the state precisely suited to the situation of the industrial worker in these countries.

P

Paradoxically, they evolved their theory out of a study of the conditions of the British working classes, and of British liberal economics. It was the Anglo-Saxon countries, in which they were to find no response to their appeals, which they regarded (quite wrongly) as typical of the new age. Engels from his experience on the Manchester Stock Exchange (he was a wealthy business man) and Marx in the reading-room of the British Museum, where he worked from 1849 till his death in 1883, produced together a monumental analysis of British capitalism which is still the Bible of the Labour Movement outside the Anglo-Saxon countries. Even Englishmen and Americans, who have never read their works, cannot avoid being deeply influenced by them. More than Locke or any other Liberal, they set their stamp upon their movement and upon its opponents. Socialism without them is like *Hamlet* without the Prince of Denmark

II.   HEGEL'S DIALECTIC

Unfortunately it is impossible to understand their writings without some consideration of contemporary German philosophy and in particular of Friedrich Hegel. Hegel (1770-1831), whose influence on British Idealism is often stressed, would have had relatively little importance in the history of political ideas, had Marx not been his pupil. Indeed it can safely be said that he would have been read only by academic metaphysicians and logicians ; while the British Idealists, without reading a word of him, could have evolved the main tenets of their creed. His real significance can only be appreciated when we view the philosophy which he began in the complete version which Marxism presents. Together he and Marx achieved a real revolution in the sphere of political ideas.

This revolution, which entailed the transformation of the postulates of Liberal, rationalistic philosophy, is centred in a new attitude to history and to the place of man in the historical process. We have seen how, from the earliest days, the bourgeois movement had viewed man as the centre of the universe. His reason was capable not only of understanding the laws of nature but of grasping the *natural laws* of society, whether these laws were viewed as a system of moral rights, or as the economic laws of utility. Politics was regarded as an applied science, whose principles could be deduced from a pure science of ethics or economics, as eternal and changeless as the laws of Euclidean geometry. Against this view of man as a rational creature and of society as a construction made by the wit of rational man, Hegel evolved his *historical relativism*. Morality, religion and the principles of political science, are not clear-cut rational concepts evolved by the free spirit of man, but fragments of a great historical movement and can be understood only if we study them in their place in the historical process. The Ten Commandments, for instance, are not eternal laws but expressions of morality at the Mosaic stage of development. No human thought or action can be hauled before an impartial conscience outside history and then evaluated; it can only be considered in relation to its own cultural epoch. Liberalism itself is merely a stage in the process, a fragmentary and one-sided aspect of truth with its limited place in the great historical pattern.

This historical view we have already found vaguely outlined in the writings of Burke (pages 84 *ff.*) ; its cogency was to be greatly enhanced by Darwinism which enlarged still further the historical perspective and made politics a subordinate branch of a great biological science of animal life. But Hegel was not content to preach historical relativism. Such a doctrine, he saw, would lead to a purely determinist and mechanistic view of history. Looking at the great pageant of human society, he felt sure that there must be some key to its enigmas and some pattern in what seemed to be its aimless play of chance and accident. This pattern he found, strangely enough, in Logic, and enunciated the theory that human history was simply the articulation and the clothing in concrete form of a developing system of pure reason. As a mind would develop from abstract clashing principles a coherent logical system, so in history human society undergoes a development from warring opposites to a synthesis in which those contradictions are taken up and harmonized at a higher level.

There are two important innovations in this theory. Montesquieu had analysed the social organism as a finely adjusted equilibrium of forces. But he had viewed this equilibrium as a *static equilibrium.* King, Lords and Commons balance and check each other : each without the other would be tyrannous, and each is opposed to the others ; but, by adjusting them one against the other, we create a harmony out of conflict. This was the theory of the founders of the American constitution. Hegel saw history however as a piece not of political *statics*, but of political *dynamics* in which the equilibrium is reached through a process

of conflict. The unity of Tudor despotism breaks down
into the thesis and antithesis of Cavaliers and Roundheads. The *thesis* is both a social group, the King and
the great landlords, and a principle, the Divine Right
of Kings ; the *antithesis* is not only the Roundheads,
but also the principle of parliamentary control over
the executive. During the Civil Wars thesis and antithesis are mutually exclusive. Each can produce
satisfactory political arguments to justify its actions,
and there are two logical systems current between
which understanding cannot decide. *No human mind
can stand above the warring systems and judge between
them,* because at this stage both of logic and of history,
there is a sheer incompatibility such as we found in
Hobbes' *Leviathan* (see page 66). But then comes the
stage of synthesis ; out of the contradictions a new
social order is produced which does harmonize the
principles of central state authority and individual
liberty, and unifies the policies of both factions. As a
result we get both the historical equilibrium of British
Society in the 18th century, and the Lockean synthesis
of *Civil Government.*

But history does not stand still ; the new synthesis
soon produces a new conflict. Thesis and antithesis
now stand once again opposed, this time at a higher
level of articulation. On the one side the old order
defended by Burke, on the other the demands of the
people whose principles are promulgated by Paine.
Once again no human being can mediate between the
two contradictory systems, but once again history
produces her synthesis in the National Liberal State of
the 1850's, and the Idealism of T. H. Green.

To illustrate the Hegelian system, I have purposely

selected an example from this book and not one of
Hegel's own, because it is vital to see his theory of
Dialectic not as a clever dodge but as the pattern of
a historical development of which we have some knowledge.   There is so much profound truth in the theory
that we cannot afford to " disprove " it by picking out
a few inconsistencies.   On the contrary, we must realize
that it stands with Newton's Gravitation and Darwin's
Evolution as one of the discoveries which has moulded
not only our intellectual outlook but our morality and
institutions as well.   Hegel showed in brief that special
political theories, like the rest of our ideas, are always
incomplete manifestations of truth, and have relevance
only to a limited epoch.   He destroyed the notion that
science and religion could discover natural laws or
eternal truths or self-evident principles upon which
they could base an absolute theology or a final science of
society.   His philosophy of the state is an attempt to
show that no philosophy of the state is possible and to
replace it with an historical understanding of the
relativity of political concepts.   That he was false to
his own principles and misinterpreted by later idealists
does not detract from his greatness.

Hegel gave the names Reason and Idea to the whole
objective reality, distinguishing them sharply from
human reason, human ideas and human understanding.
Mankind, he believed, could never completely understand its own destiny, because it could not climb out of
history and view it objectively from a timeless standpoint.   We are creatures not creators of time, and our
reason is the sport of Reason, not its overlord.   During
the crisis, our understanding is conditioned by the
conflict and enslaved to one side or other in the war

of ideologies. Whichever side we are on, we fight for principles which will never be realized in the form we cherish them. History twists even our proud human minds to her tricksy ways, and decrees that the wicked man shall produce what is ultimately beneficial, that the moral man's morality leads to disaster, and that the " objectivity " of him who believes himself an impartial mediator or a mere spectator shall redound to the advantage of one side. Only when the conflict is over and the synthesis arrived at, can impartiality begin. Philosophical analysis and true understanding come after the period of decision and can pass only a melancholy and inactive judgment on past events.

" Philosophy comes too late to teach the world what it should be. . . . When it paints its grey upon grey, a form of life has already become old ; and in grey and grey it can no longer be made young again but only understood. The owl of Minerva begins its flight when the shades of night have already fallen." This sombre judgment on the ability of human reason to mould history to its will was in startling contrast to the optimism of the Liberals. They saw the state as a machine invented and run by human ingenuity ; Hegel saw it as one feature of a swiftly changing social process beyond scientific control. They believed their political theories were demonstrable truth, Hegel regarded them as neither right nor wrong, but aspects of a truth relative to the historical situation.

But Hegel himself was influenced by his environment, and accepted much more of Liberalism than he himself knew. He assumed that the nation state was the final form of historical evolution, and that individual freedom of thought was a value which must be recognized and aided by the state. Apparently he believed the dialectical process had reached fulfilment in his own life-time and that human self-realization was achieved in the Prussian autocracy of the 1830's. Despising the political Liberals and feeling the need for strong central authority, his practical proposals for the establishment of individual liberty were limited to a monarchy, a strong bureaucracy and parliament as the mouthpiece of public opinion. In brief, in terms of current politics he was a liberal nationalist of a very timid type, whose nationalism was a great deal stronger than his trust in human nature. Moreover, the actual pattern which he discovered in history was not really derived from logic : on the contrary, it was already in his mind before he developed his logical system, and this system became a very cumbersome framework into which his personal view of history was forced. Hegel's special interpretation of history and theory of the nation state are therefore of little interest ; his importance lies not in any particular discoveries he made, but in his revolutionary effort to admit the temporal " conditioned-ness " of thought without denying its objectivity. For anyone who had studied him deeply, it would be impossible in future to accept a static view of society or to admit that the forms of thought which are so useful in science apply equally well to the actual process of human history.

III.   MARX AND HEGEL

Long before Marx began his study of economics and his analysis of capitalist organization, he had developed his version of Hegelian philosophy. His socialism was

originally derived not from sympathy with the workers'
lot or from experience of industrial conditions, but
from a radical criticism of Hegel in terms of Hegelianism.
Hegel had seen world-history as the slow self-develop-
ment of Reason in human history and had sometimes
permitted his metaphor of the *World-spirit* brooding
over the process to lead him into a teleological philosophy of emergent evolution.   Such a philosophy, in
Marx's view, was reactionary.   Removing from humanity
its freedom of choice, it left us the passive instruments
of a Calvinist predestination.   Somehow freedom must
be real, and man must be able to fashion his own world.
On this point Marx agreed with the Liberals in condemning the fatalism and pessimism of his master.   And
yet he saw the truth in Hegel's Dialectic.   History did
seem to be the product of forces outside man's control ;
morals, religion, politics and culture were intelligible
only in their historical environment and relative to
their epoch.   The synthesis exhibited by periods of
equilibrium did appear to be the resultant of contradictory theories and conflicting interests.

How then was he to retain freedom of the will,
without falling into the Liberal fallacy of regarding
human reason as the timeless legislator ?   How was
he to square his Hegelian concept of the historical process with his belief in freedom ?   Out of this tremendous
antinomy Marx evolved his theory of Dialectical Materialism.   Freedom was only possible, he declared, if the
historical dialectic was not the emergence of an idea,
but the conflict of social and economic forces, directed
by no World-spirit, but operating according to laws
discoverable by social science.   History then would be
not a metaphysical mystery, but data for the science

of the future, a science which would not apply mechanical laws of cause and effect but seek out new types of
uniformity peculiar to the social organism. If the
dialectic was in this sense *material*, not ideal, man would
become free by discovering the laws of social development and controlling his destiny. Man, self-conscious
of his material conditions, would then be the creator
of his own history.

The true Liberal, or emancipator, therefore, was the
social scientist, who guided his actions not by looking
inward to his own conscience or upward to a trans-
cendental God, but outward to the facts of his social
environment. Once he could grasp the pattern of the
historical process from conflict to harmony, from
harmony to conflict and so on, he would be able to base
his political programme on sound scientific ground.
Although mechanical causation could not be operative
in the social process, since human freedom left always
an unknown, the new science should enable him to
predict the general trend of events and to foresee the
various possibilities with which he would have to
reckon.

With these assumptions, Marx viewed the conflicts
of history in a new perspective. From the Stone Age
to his own time, he saw only one factor which had
remained fairly constant throughout change. Cultures
had risen and fallen, whole civilizations had flourished
and disappeared, but through all this man had slowly
evolved an increasing power over nature. His language,
his tools, his methods of communication, his memory
inherited from generation to generation, had served him
instead of brute force in the struggle for survival ; and
enabled him to live in society, to increase the fruits

of the field, to tame the animals to his use, and to harness the forces of nature to his purposes. The history of man, the tool-using animal, was the history of scientific prediction and control. It was this faculty which had enabled *homo sapiens* to flout the laws of natural evolution and to produce a social evolution, caused not simply by biological, geographical or climatic factors such as natural science studies, but also and predominantly by peculiar social factors for whose study a new science must be elaborated.

Disregarding therefore the natural factors (earthquakes, heredity, disease, etc.) Marx sought for a specifically social cause of historical change, and found it in those changes in the technique of production and distribution which increasing control of nature had produced. The wheel, the plough, currency and the factory system, each, in its time, had by its invention upset long-standing habits, moral laws, religious and political systems. It was the development of the science of warfare, of communication, of farming, industry and finance which had really changed our ways of life and thought. These *changes in the technique of production and distribution* were the primary factors in the dialectic of history ; the principles of legislators and the whims of princes could delay or accelerate change but they were secondary to the basic economic forces which controlled the process.

In stressing the importance of social and economic causation, Marx was deeply influenced by the Physiocrats and the Utilitarians. But once more (like Hegel) he turned social statics into social dynamics. His predecessors had pictured the economic system operating by natural laws as immutable as the laws of gravity.

Against this economic determinism he rebelled as he rebelled against the teleological determinism of Hegel's *Weltgeist*. Economics, he felt, was not the study of unchanging natural laws but of the methods of exchange current in a particular *mode of production and distribution*. In destroying mediæval society and discrediting its political and economic theories, the European bourgeoisie had not conquered falsehood and replaced it by eternal truth ; on the contrary, they had substituted one productive system for another, and there was no reason why their system should not be replaced by yet a third. Indeed, this was bound to happen, when once technical developments demanded it.

Thus Marx regarded bourgeois society and its capitalist economics merely as a stage in historical development. The elaborate structure of 18th-century rationalism, its self-evident concepts and natural rights and laws of nature were for him the instruments with which the bourgeoisie had moulded society to their needs. They were true only if you accepted the view that everything must be sacrificed to the development of capitalism ; they would remain the principles of morals and legislation only so long as they were compatible with the technique and mode of production. If these were changed radically, then a new economics and new principles of morals and legislation would inevitably oust them from supremacy, just as they in their time had been rendered possible by those changes in the technique of production and distribution which undermined the mediæval system.

In his criticism of bourgeois economics, psychology and political theory Marx was not concerned to prove that his predecessors were wrong absolutely, but only to show that their conclusions were relative to a passing phase of history. Far from being a materialist in the common sense of the word, he denounced the mechanism and materialism of Liberal thinkers who gave the name of social science to their free-trade booklets. Welcoming the industrial revolution as a triumph of applied science, he freely admitted that capitalism, private enterprise and *laisser-faire* were the best weapons for destroying feudalism and revolutionizing the forces of production. Capitalism, he thought, and with it the Liberal national revolution, were, by their very ruthlessness, shortening the period of misery which any social revolution must bring. Without them, humanity could never have advanced to a stage where nature was forced to yield an abundance of its riches sufficient to free millions from bondage to the soil. What Marx hated was not capitalism, but the assumption that capitalism and Liberal Nationalism were the final stage of evolution and that the principles of bourgeois society were absolute; what he fought was not merely the low wages paid, but the view that those low wages were for ever justified by Ricardo's laws of economics. Such a view, he argued, was materialist in the worst sense of the word, since it implied that humanity must remain the passive slave of capitalism.

IV. THE CLASS WAR

If we admit that capitalism is merely a stage in human evolution, a new problem arises : " What is to follow it ? " In answering this question, Marx enunciated his second principle, *the class war*. If the cause of social change is scientific invention, the way in which it proceeds is through the struggle for political power between those who control and benefit by the older system and those who are seeking to change it. Every system of production and distribution has its own peculiar institutions, churches, forms of government, etc., but the fundamental institution is property —the control of the means of production. Law, morality and religion are all harnessed in any state to the preservation of the existing property system, and that system is in its turn determined by the technique of production and distribution prevailing at the time. Private property (in the bourgeois sense of exclusive ownership without social obligation) is not therefore a natural right but a peculiar characteristic of bourgeois society. To establish the claim to it, the bourgeoisie was compelled to break up the social organism of mediæval society, and since the 14th century had been in conflict with the beneficiaries of the old feudal order. This conflict was an instance of the class-war, which always arises when human inventiveness has discovered new techniques whose exploitation will upset the established social system and its beneficiaries. Only through class-war is it possible to adapt institutions to new social needs, and to advance towards the emancipation of humanity from its bondage to nature.

The clash between two classes and two modes of production was reflected, according to Marx, in a conflict of *Ideologies*. The bourgeoisie, in its struggle against feudalism, had been compelled to elaborate its individualistic theory of natural rights and to champion the cause of reason against mysticism and of science against superstition. This conflict had generated a new philosophy

of life and a new culture which Liberals had sought
to realize in concrete political and social institutions.
But Marx saw that the new ideology was not merely a
reflection of the class-war and an instrument of propaganda. Human thought develops independently of the
social struggle, though its postulates are always derived
from it, and builds a rational structure of theory which
may come into conflict with class needs. Thus Liberalism had been logically compelled to evolve a theory of
political equality and representative democracy which
was incompatible with the needs of the bourgeoisie,
once it had attained power. The ideals of Liberal democrats, however sincerely held, were inherently contradictory to the demands of industrial capitalism ; and
it was out of this philosophical antinomy that the
theory of Socialism was bound to arise. Socialism
alone could expound the principles of an economic
system in which individual freedom and equality could
find realization. The dialectic of ideas, advancing
beyond the actual historical situation, pointed the way
to the new historical synthesis. Man was not the
slave of a tricksy *Weltgeist* ; he could solve the class-
struggle *in theory*, and thus harness the Liberal will to
freedom to the concrete needs of the only social class
which could build a free society.

By analyzing modern history as the struggle of the
bourgeoisie against the feudal order, Marx was enabled
to argue that directly the bourgeoisie had emancipated
itself and established capitalism and private property,
a new conflict would begin. Feudal society had nur-
tured the bourgeois class which was to destroy it : so
too bourgeois society, as it developed, would bring into
being a new class essential to its needs, and this new

class would undermine the structure of capitalism and finally overthrow it. The advance of those very techniques, to which capitalism owed its triumphs, would in the end make capitalism an obstruction in the path of progress.

This new class was the industrial proletariat. Torn from their ancestral homes, and herded into factory towns, the proletariat provided the labour for bourgeois prosperity. With only their labour to sell, they became the human cogs in the capitalist machine, ruled by the iron law of wages. Capitalism, since it needed minimum wages and maximum profits, would be compelled by an inner necessity constantly to increase this mass of propertyless labourers ; on the other hand, by another inner necessity, the desire for safe profits would tend to monopoly and the concentration of capital into fewer and fewer hands. Thus the Liberal state would be divided into two classes, a diminishing number of owners of the means of production, and an increasing number of increasingly poor workers. In spite of the power, which capitalism provided, of maximizing the output of wealth, the wealth would be enjoyed by fewer and fewer people. Moreover, since on the one hand profits can only increase when there are consumers to buy, and on the other hand, the purchasing power of the masses was falling, capitalism would be liable to slumps of increasing severity as it advanced to monopoly capitalism. The market would be even more frequently glutted with unwanted goods, and profits would be possible only in shorter and shorter booms. This inherent contradiction of the system (its failure to find a market for its goods, while it must constantly expand production) would finally lead to its downfall. The dictatorship of the proletariat would replace the bourgeois régime and Socialist production for use would take the place of capitalist production for profit.

The theory of class-war here outlined is a direct descendant of the Dialectic. The stable harmony of mediæval society splits into the thesis and antithesis of feudal Cavaliers and bourgeois Roundheads; from the conflict arises 18th-century bourgeois England with its private property and mechanical inventions. These advances in the technique of producing wealth precipitate industrialism, the new transition stage with its thesis of capitalist and capitalism and its antithesis of proletariat and socialism. Out of their clash arises the new class-less society, the final equilibrium in which, exploitation abolished, human nature is free to develop itself without economic conflicts.

Marx's attitude to capitalism was deeply Hegelian. He could not condemn a period of history outright (such moralizing was meaningless) but viewed it instead as an unpleasant but necessary transition stage which every nation must go through on the way to "health, work and happiness". Socialists who dreamed of a workers' state to be established immediately in the France and Germany of 1848 he regarded as Utopians, since Socialism was a phase of history only possible *after* a bourgeois revolution. In the capitalist transition, the manufacturers and their Liberal ideology must be dominant, and the proletariat could only arise through their activities, and achieve consciousness of its objective in the class struggle of industrialism. When the 1848 revolution broke out, he appealed to the workers of the world, in the Communist Manifesto, to support the bourgeois revolution and to agitate for democracy:

then, when the middle classes were in power, the contradictions of capitalism would soon produce a revolutionary situation in which the workers should destroy
their former allies and seize the means of production
for themselves.

Scientific Socialism therefore was distinct both from
Liberalism and from Utopian Socialism, since it alone
claimed to discover the historical moment when revolution was practicable. Marx labelled " Idealist " any
thinker or statesman who believed that, to achieve his
ideals, only will power and political reform were necessary. History, he argued, moves along lines broadly
determined not by legislators or philosophers but by
social and economic conditions. Only if the statesman
understands these forces and adapts his ideals to them,
will he be able to influence history. To control our
destiny, we must be aware of the narrow limits within
which our freedom of choice is confined. Human reason
is not presented, by a benevolent deity, with a mechanical
universe which it can operate as it pleases ; nor is it
enslaved on the other hand to unchanging laws of
society. The truth lies between these poles of Liber-
tarianism and Determinism, and can be grasped only if
we see history as a dynamic process of change which
gives us scope for action, and only at the precise moment
when the social conflict has produced a revolutionary
situation. Such a moment may be long delayed, but
the scientific socialist will know how to wait and to
restrain the Utopian from futile ventures. Capitalism
may last ten, twenty, a hundred years ; but until
it manifests its inherent contradictions, the scientific
socialist will be content to spend his time training that
small élite of class-conscious collaborators who will be

indispensable in the crisis. Then, when the moment comes, philosophy will show that it can not only understand the world but change it.

V. THE DICTATORSHIP OF THE PROLETARIAT

Dialectical materialism, though a direct development of Hegel's thought, completely reversed his theory of the state. Hegel had regarded the state as the supreme expression of human reason and the end of the dialectical process of history ; Marx maintained that it was an instrument of coercion, which, though inevitable so long as class-conflict continued, would disappear when once the dictatorship of the proletariat had abolished classes. Then oppression would be replaced by co-operation and politics by Communist society.

Here again Marx remained true to the old Liberal tradition which, until the period of T. H. Green, had conceived of the state as a necessary evil, with which we would all of us prefer to dispense. He simply took the theories of Locke and the Utilitarians and adapted them to the theory of class struggle. They had affirmed that government's chief function was the securing of property rights and private enterprise. Marx agreed, but argued that this meant increasing oppression of the working class. Out of their own mouths, he demonstrated to the Utilitarians the futility of combining a theory of democracy with the iron law of wages. A community in which the greatest good of the greatest number prevails must be a community with an economic identity of interest. But capitalism had torn the social organism asunder and fixed a gulf between employer and

employee : in such a society, whatever principles were
enunciated, the government must maintain the owners of
the means of production in their supremacy and the
proletariat in its bondage. Bourgeois politicians were
simply the executive committee of the ruling class.

From this Marx concluded that, where class conflict
exists, government will always be a coercive force for
the imposition of class dictatorship. In periods of
equilibrium or of economic expansion, the dictatorship
may be mild and even constitutional, but, whenever
the property system is threatened, it will shrink from
nothing to maintain itself in power. A bourgeois democracy may discard all its principles, if (as the Chartists
did) the workers begin to demand universal suffrage
in their own interests. Governmental forms are determined not by fair play or natural rights or utility, but
by the development of the class war ; and, though
individuals will protest on principle, ideals will often
be scrapped when they come into conflict with the interests of the class in power.

This view of the state which makes politics a super-
structure and political ideas ideologies, is not specifically
Marxian but derived from the Liberal tradition. Marx's
economic and political theories are indeed the weakest
part of his system precisely because they are so obviously
a *tour de force* which accepts the Liberal analysis and
turns it against the Liberals. Point for point he refutes
them out of their own mouths and shows that if capitalism and democracy are as they describe them, they must
finally break down by their own intrinsic contradictions.
His argument is dialectical not in the Hegelian sense of
the word, but in the old Aristotelian sense of refuting an
opponent on his own ground. By adopting this method

Marx was able to produce a series of political pamphlets more corrosive even than those of the Utilitarians, and to build up an overwhelming case against his opponents. In so doing however, he forgot to enquire whether the postulates were sound upon which he and his opponents were both agreed.

From this principle that every state must be a coercive authority working in the interests of the dominant class, Marx deduced his theory of Socialist revolution. Since constitutional democracy was the mode of the dictatorship of the bourgeoisie, it could only be overthrown by erecting a *dictatorship of the proletariat*, in which the coercive authority of the state would be used to carry through the socialization of the means of production. This period of proletarian dictatorship would be no more controlled by all the proletariat than democracy was controlled by all the bourgeoisie. It would be managed, he envisaged, by a trained élite of revolutionary Marxists, but it would be managed in the interests of the proletariat; and it would last until the old property relations had been finally destroyed.

The dictatorship of the proletariat, however, and the erection of the Socialist State was only a step towards the realization of a free Communist Society in which the state would wither away. Since the state was evil, the Socialist State could only be justified if it abolished that class-conflict which rendered oppression inevitable. It would be a transition stage like the transition stage of capitalism, and its statesmen would be forced to employ methods no less ruthless than those of the early capitalists to achieve their ideal of human emancipation. But once the socialist surgeons had performed their grand operation upon the body of human society, it would be restored to a permanent good health in which the medicines of politics would be wholly unnecessary.

Marx and Engels were so busy analysing the diseases of society and preparing it for the operation, that they had little to say about the organization of the Socialist State and even less about the Communist millennium. They were, however, clear both that political democracy must be abolished and that independent nation states must disappear. A Socialist revolution in one country would be useless unless it was the beginning of a *world-revolution* which would overthrow capitalism in every country and make the world a Union of Socialist Republics. Only if this happened could Socialism lead on to Communism ; for, if the leaders of the proletariat were successful in one country only, they would have to maintain the apparatus of state power not only to liquidate their own bourgeoisie, but also to defend their Republic against foreign aggression. For this reason, the chief slogan which Engels gave to the *Second International*, the federation of Social Democratic parties which he formed in 1889, was " Workers of the World Unite ". For the success of the cause depended not merely on the success of the well-organized parties of France and Germany, but of the proletariat all over the globe.

This vision of a world-revolution was as inspiring as it was vague. Because he was so certain of the inner contradictions of capitalism and of its inevitable collapse, Marx did not trouble to elaborate it. Because he was convinced that the period of Socialist dictatorship would be as short as it was sharp, he did not con-

cern himself about its methods or feel any conscientious
scruples about its destruction of human liberty. For
him, as for the Liberal optimists, the state was merely
a phase in human development, and it was because he
believed that the Socialist state would be the last and
briefest phase of government that he accepted its totalitarian tyranny without qualms.

Marx's philosophy in fact was as deeply conditioned
by its environment as any other. He was a product of
the 19th century in Europe, and he viewed the whole
history of humanity from this perspective. As passionate a believer in the power of applied science to solve
the problems of society as the Utilitarians, he shared with
them their exclusive interest in economic problems
and in economic freedom, and their optimistic belief
in human nature. They defended the property-system :
he denounced it. They thought bourgeois democracy
would bring universal happiness : he proved that it
could not. But both agreed that human nature would
progressively emancipate itself from the state and enjoy
the fruits of applied science in non-political co-operative
society.

This Liberal treatment of politics as fundamentally
concerned with property-relations led Marx to subordinate every other function of it and every other notion
of humanity to the class war. Religion, nationalism,
ambition, and humanity were all in his eyes genuine
motives of action, values for which mankind would
strive disinterestedly : but none of them could stand
against the dynamic of economic change. It was almost
inevitable that Marx should hold this view. The whole
history of Europe since the 14th century seemed to
support it ; for 450 years economic interests had fought

tradition and religion and conquered them or twisted
them to their convenience; and the history of the
Greek city state seemed to confirm the view. Obsessed
by these two instances, Marx generalized them into a
philosophy of history which included all human experience past, present and to come.

To-day with a far wider knowledge of anthropology
and a larger experience of capitalism, we can see the
dangers of this generalization. What was really a unique
phenomenon (the rise of capitalism) was made the
standard by which all history was measured, at precisely the moment when, the Liberal period of economic
emancipation over, the older forces of tradition were
once more asserting themselves. These elements of
tradition, which Marx and every progressive believed
would disappear as rational man outgrew his super-
stitions, reasserted themselves and decisively influenced
economic developments at the end of the 19th century.

That this should happen is perfectly consistent
with Marx' theory of dialectical change, and indicates
a deep contradiction between his philosophy and his
special theories of economics. Marxian economics and
politics were really mechanistic in their analysis and
forecast of the development of capitalism. Instead of
discarding the laws of nature of the Physiocrats, they
utilized those laws to argue the case for Socialism.
Such a procedure was justifiable, so long as Marx and
his followers treated these laws as truths relative only
to a single phase of development and were prepared to
modify them radically, when the facts they analyzed
had disappeared. So too with his treatment of the
state and of the class-structure of society. Granted
that these were accurate diagnoses of conditions between

(say) 1840 and 1860, they were to become increasingly irrelevant as the 20th century developed. Most of his followers were unable to grasp this, and retained the whole Marxian analysis as their holy writ long after its practical applicability had disappeared. For this the later writings of Marx himself were partly to blame. Once he had worked his method out, he found it increasingly difficult to modify it.

This contrast between the extreme relativism of his philosophy and the mechanism of his economics indicates a real difficulty of social science. Any science must abstract certain features from the welter of events and predict their regular recurrence in terms of a general law. But if Marx and Hegel were right in asserting that the historical dialectic produced new syntheses unintelligible in the categories of the previous epoch, then no special theory of social science can for long give safe grounds of prediction. Moreover, any particular interpretation of history, such as Marx provided, will itself go out of date as history develops. Marx believed that history had only one more lap to go before Socialism ushered in the class-less society and for that reason assumed that his analysis of capitalism would hold good for the duration of the class-struggle. His Liberal optimism deluded him, and deluded his followers still worse. For though Lenin did introduce important modifications and in particular produced a masterly theory of imperialism, he still retained the view that the needs of capitalist development would be the fundamental explanation of every development in the historical process. Instead of undertaking a fresh study of the historical process, and assessing the various factors anew in the light of modern conditions (the task which

Marx undertook in 1848) Marxism has tried to adapt the old analysis to new circumstances and has frequently succeeded merely in omitting from consideration those factors inconvenient to the theory.

These criticisms however do not detract from the gigantic achievement of Marx himself. As Engels said at his grave, " Just as Darwin discovered the law of evolution, so Marx discovered the law of evolution in human history. . . . Marx also discovered the special law of motion governing the present-day capitalist method of production and the bourgeois society that this method has created." Engels' comparison of Marx with Darwin is fully justified. They were the greatest of all the Victorians. Both of them revolutionized men's outlook on life and set science upon a new path. But just as Darwinism has been modified later, so Marx's special law which dealt with history in the making needed revision. Those who grasped Marx's philosophy felt unable to remain loyal Marxists, while the Marxists, by turning his theories into dogmas, lost the power of self-modification which is essential to science but so awkward for politicians.

VI. MARXISTS AND MARXISM

Marx never believed that his philosophy could be widely understood. Essential to any *leadership,* which was not to fall into Utopianism, it could only be made palatable to the masses in a vulgarized form. As a serious revolutionary, he was not disturbed by this. The proletariat was the lever which the skilled scientist would use to overthrow capitalism, not the oracle of

truth ; and he was prepared, as Lenin after him was
prepared, to discard the orthodox theories and practice
of democracy and to substitute for them a democratic
centralism which was dictatorship in all but name. Here
he parted company with the Liberals and with most of
the Socialist leaders in Europe. They were still dis-
ciples of Rousseau ; conceiving of humanity as essentially rational, they hoped to convert the masses to
Marxism and enable the man in the street to fulfil his
own destiny by the right of his own reason. He believed
that, until the revolution was over and the economic
conditions of freedom were established, understanding
and therefore leadership must remain in the hands of a
tiny minority.

In a great democratic working-class movement this
was impossible. The trained Marxist was not always
the most popular or most persuasive politician, and it
soon became clear that scientific socialist leadership
was only possible in countries such as Russia where the
masses could not express their wishes and revolutionary
conspiracy was essential. Elsewhere, although Marxist
slogans were accepted, working-class movements fell
under the control of Trade-Union Leaders and Democratic politicians, and Marxism was adapted to the
prevailing mood of Liberal optimism. In Germany it
became, despite the superficial differences of Kautsky
and Bernstein, a reformist philosophy, and scientific
class-consciousness was supplanted by the sentiment
of working-class solidarity. The Great War, which
showed that working-class movements the world over
were as patriotic adherents of democracy and progress
as the Liberals, was the supreme proof of Marx's theory
that Socialism would not come by the education of the

general will, but by a crisis of the system itself which would give an opportunity to a new leadership suddenly to leap into authority and to impose a new order upon the masses.

The tragedy of Marx's life as an émigré in England, peevish, quarrelsome, and self-assertive, was largely caused by his refusal to submit to " working-class leadership ". Like Lenin, he refused absolutely to accept the ideas of bourgeois democracy as proper to a revolutionary party, or to pander to the belief that the worker's opinion was to be respected simply because of its working-class origin. Their philosophy taught them that many ideas were mere ideologies, which reflected social conditions but had no scientific validity. If a Socialist party was to abide by conference decisions and accept the voice of the majority, then it would become, in their opinion, merely an institution within the bourgeois order instead of the instrument of its destruction. Completely convinced of the validity of their diagnosis, neither Marx nor Lenin was willing to have it flouted by a popular vote, and, as a result, their lives became a series of stormy conflicts with confederates who dared to resist their will. Revolutionary socialist organizations split into dozens of " deviations ", each convinced that it alone had the key to truth in its hands.

For this reason we must distinguish sharply the Marxism of the well-organized labour movements and its development as a weapon of revolution. In the former, its analysis of capitalism was misread and only its slogans were adopted. Denouncing imperialism and the class-war, the Marxist Labour Movements encouraged a deep emotional antipathy to the bourgeoisie and often

refused to co-operate with middle-class parties. Thus
they became the class-conscious parties of the industrial proletariat, with no sympathy for the needs of any
other section of the community. And, since within
the Labour Movement itself a complete democratic
organization was evolved, the industrial worker became
even more " constitutional-minded " than the bourgeoisie and tended to picture the coming revolution as
the substitution of working-class democracy for middle-
class democracy. Moreover, since the Marxist politician
in France, Germany and Italy was condemned to permanent opposition without any of the responsibilities
of government, and was able to criticize the capitalist
order without any fear of having to rule himself, he was
never able to test his principles in action and never
needed to define too accurately his vision of the proletarian state.

The net effect of this degenerate Marxism was
usually disastrous. It isolated the industrial proletariat from the middle classes and from the peasants,
thus weakening the progressive forces. It gave an
appearance and a feeling of revolution to a movement
which was really content to criticize the existing order
and to enjoy its benefits. And, most important of
all, by its self-righteous dogmatism and revolutionary
slogans, it provided the forces of reaction with a
dangerous weapon. If you do not really mean to be
a revolutionary, it is unwise to tell your opponents
that you are one ! From this point of view, the British
Labour Movement was in a far stronger position than
any of its continental critics. By admitting openly
that it was a reformist democratic movement, it prevented the growth of reactionary movements whose

pretext for overthrowing democracy was the danger of proletarian revolution.

The only parties which really continued the revolutionary tradition of Marx were the Anarchists and the Russian Communists. The Anarchists in France and Spain (and to a less extent in America) accepted the analysis of Marx, but concluded from it that the state must be immediately abolished by the proletarian revolution. Since it was simply an instrument of class-coercion, it must be replaced by local units of labour organization both in the village and in the factory, and all the paraphernalia of centralized bureaucracy and of parliament must vanish overnight. The proletariat must evolve its own form of co-operative society, untainted by bourgeois ideas or institutions.

Anarchism, undoubtedly the noblest and the most futile variant of Marxism, was a direct descendant of the Liberalism of Paine. It offered to the peasant an easily intelligible creed of direct action and united his interests with those of the industrial worker as the early Liberals had tried to do. It was in fact the Liberalism of the suffering and oppressed and its democratic belief in equality and spiritual emancipation was far more sincere than the formal democracy of the official Marxist Labour Movements. Its incapacity however to achieve its aims has been proved once for all in modern Spain.

A variant of Anarchism was the philosophy which between 1905 and 1926 aroused the only truly revolutionary movement in Britain since the Chartists. British Syndicalism saw no hope of revolution in the Labour Parliamentarians and conceived of the proletarian revolution in terms of direct action by the Trade

Unions themselves. The strike was their weapon of emancipation, the General Strike their moment of revolution. Recognizing that the Anarchist abolition of central government was Utopian, they conceived of a new type of industrial democracy in which a Parliament representative of the producers should replace the bourgeois House of Commons. "Guild Socialism" was a genuine Trade-Union philosophy and inspired the wave of strikes which swept England between 1910 and 1914. With its main strength in the coal-mining industry, it depended on the peculiar sense of Union-solidarity which that industry demands. But the bulk of the British workers remained true to the individualism of the Liberal tradition, and the failure of the General Strike in 1926 marked the end of the attempt to substitute direct industrial action for the political methods of parliamentary democracy.[1]

VII. THE RUSSIAN REVOLUTION

This brief sketch of the variants of Marxism in-dicates clearly enough that Lenin was the one revolutionary who really understood Marx's theories and developed them on revolutionary lines. It has often been remarked that the Communist revolution occurred in the one country where Marx had not expected it to occur. But in fact, by the beginning of the 20th

---

[1] In France and Italy too there was a Syndicalist movement whose philosopher was Georges Sorel. Its rejection of parliamentary action and its gospel of sheer *violence* deeply influenced Mussolini, whose Fascist corporations still bear some traces of their Syndicalist origins.

century, a revolution such as Marx conceived in 1848 could only begin in Russia or Spain or China. Elsewhere capitalism, as we showed in a previous chapter, had evolved far beyond the stage described in the Communist manifesto and the Liberal revolution had been either so long delayed that it was now impossible, or so long established that it could not be overthrown by a single class.

Marx had conceived of the Socialist revolution as the direct continuation of a bourgeois revolt against feudalism. This conception postulated a rising capitalism thwarted by an *ancien régime*. But in Germany, Italy, and elsewhere, capitalism had come to terms with the Church and the old order. Of all the European countries, only Russia and Spain still retained a despotic alliance of Church and State which forced Liberals and Socialists into an uneasy alliance. Elsewhere, as the Paris Commune had shown, Socialist insurrection would meet with the opposition both of the peasants and of the middle classes and end in futile bloodshed.

Thus the objective conditions in Russia at the beginning of the Great War, precisely because they *were* backward, provided a possibility for a revolution along strictly Marxian lines. The suppression of all Liberal movements, and the ruthlessness with which the 1905 Revolution had been stamped out, had prevented the growth of democratic organizations among the proletariat and had kept the peasants in a condition of such ignorance and poverty that they would offer no resistance to a dictatorship which gave them their land. The very smallness of Russian industry also was of assistance, since, once the workers in a few key towns were won over, power would be in the hands of the revolutionary government. In the western countries, the power of the central government had been enormously strengthened by the bureaucracy of the " Social Service State " ; in Russia it was still as weak as that of England in 1848.

Russia in fact had been kept in cold storage for seventy years, while the rest of Europe advanced. Russian Bolshevism,[1] therefore, which had tenaciously clung to the orthodox creed of Marx, was well adapted for seizing power when the Great War produced a breakdown of the Russian State. Precisely according to plan, a weak democratic government arose, breathing the spirit of nationalism and of freedom, and the bourgeois revolution was followed by a Socialist revolution, which succeeded because its leaders had no doubt what they were going to do. Giving the land to the peasants, they summarily disbanded the Constituent Assembly called by the democrats, and entrusted all power to the workers and soldiers councils (Soviets) which were controlled by Bolsheviks.

The Bolsheviks—or Communists as they now called themselves to show their hostility to the old social democratic parties—succeeded because of the weakness of the state, the backwardness of industry, the absence of democratic tradition, and the genius of Lenin and Trotsky. This success was consolidated by the inter-

[1] In Russia there were as many Socialist sects as elsewhere. Even within the Russian Social Democratic party, which was specifically Marxist and a member of the Second International, there was a cleavage between Mensheviks and Bolsheviks. The Mensheviks (minority) split from the Bolsheviks (majority) in the party congress of 1903. For the differences between them see Rosenberg *History of Bolshevism*, p. 28*ff*. Lenin was the leader of the Bolsheviks ; Trotsky veered between the two factions.

vention first of Germany and then of the Allied Powers
which gave the Bolsheviks, as intervention gave the
French revolutionaries, the rallying cry of nationalism.
Trotsky could call his army a national army defending
Russia from White reactionaries, the agents of greedy
imperialism, and thereby dispel the feeling that Bolshevism was a foreign importation. When the war
was over, the Bolsheviks were so firmly entrenched that
nothing but armed revolution could expel them.

In its early days however Bolshevism was not a
nationalistic movement. True to the Marxist tradition,
it believed that a world revolution must occur before
the socialist state could be transformed into the communist commonwealth. From 1917 to 1920 that dream
seemed likely of accomplishment. War-weary and disillusioned by their home-coming, the industrial workers
were ready for revolution, and the Third International
proclaimed that " the day " was at hand. With Trotsky
at the gates of Warsaw and Germany on the edge of
civil war, the summer of 1920 seemed auspicious.

But the tide of revolution ebbed as quickly as it had
risen. In the west of Europe, the Trade Unions and the
Co-operatives (as well as the Socialist politicians) fought
back against Communist " interference ". Not even the
Great War could alter their belief in ordered progress,
or, more important, could undermine the strength of
the nation state. The overthrow of Czarism had been
feasible ; the destruction of the administrative machinery even of defeated Germany was quite another thing,
and without its destruction a proletarian dictatorship
was impossible. Since the Communist Manifesto, an
entirely new form of political and industrial organization
had been erected, which could neither be controlled nor

overthrown without the active co-operation of the civil servant, the technician and the manager. The political significance of this new administrative class was first proved by the failure of orthodox Marxism, but it was not till 1933 that the orthodox Marxist learnt his lesson. Till then, in spite of his scientific socialism, he remained blind to an obvious factor in the class-struggle.

Among the colonial peoples however and in China, the Bolsheviks came within measurable distance of accomplishing their aims. For here once again capitalism had not developed beyond the Marxian stage. In China the democratic revolution came under Communist influence, and even after their defeat by Chiang Kai-shek, the Communists remain probably the most constructive politicians in China, as well as the most fervent nationalists.

It is impossible to discuss internal developments in Russia in a sketch such as ours. Moreover, such dis cussion is more relevant to the succeeding chapter. Marx had evolved a theory of revolution and an analysis of capitalism, but he had said singularly little about what was to happen once the dictatorship of the proletariat had been achieved ; nor had he foreseen that it would be achieved only in one country. There was no precedent therefore in Marxist theory for the Russian statesman to build on, and discussions whether Stalin or Trotsky is the true disciple are entirely futile. Since the world revolution had not come, it was clear that the state could not wither away and Communism could not be achieved in the near future. The supreme coercive power of government must remain, and Russia must develop as one nation state among others.

This meant that a completely new analysis and tactic must be worked out and that a task must be accomplished of which Marx never dreamt. Though the means of production were now under public control, an increasing amount of labour power must be spent on national defence and every effort must be made in the shortest possible time to bring Russia up to the level of production of its potential enemies. An administrative class and a host of skilled technicians must be drawn from an illiterate proletariat and dreams of social emancipation must be indefinitely postponed. In brief, the Communist revolution could not lead straight to Communism but must undertake the infinitely more difficult task of introducing a planned Socialist economy in a backward country. This effort, however fascinating in itself, could have little relevance to the highly-developed states of Western Europe and of America. In 1921 Russia began a unique period of development which steadily isolated her further and further from the ideas of the West.

In spite of this, the Russian Revolution became a symbol of tremendous significance to Socialist parties all over the world—and to their opponents. Quite irrationally both sides assumed that the success or failure of the Russian experiment would be the supreme test of Socialist theory. Even more disastrous, the extremists in all countries believed that the October revolution had proved the truth of orthodox Marxism, and for fifteen years preached the old dogmatic doctrine of industrial class-consciousness with renewed fervour. Thus the drastic revision of Marx's special theories of economics and politics in the light of modern developments was once more delayed, and the middle classes, repelled by the pseudo-revolutionary obscurantism of the Communists and the staid constitutionalism of the Social Democrats, were ready to look elsewhere for a creed of revolution when the Great Depression hit the world in 1929.

CHAPTER IX

FASCISM

I. THE FAILURE OF THE LEAGUE

IN 1918, when the Great War ended, it was confidently assumed that the world was safe for democracy. America, France and Great Britain had repulsed the attack of the greatest military power in Europe; Russian and Turkish despotism had disappeared, and in Central Europe democratic constitutions were being set up by the oppressed nationalities. More important, the balance of power had been destroyed; there was no nation left strong enough to oppose the will of the victorious democracies. At last it would be possible to show that National Liberalism was a creed capable of bringing peace and security not only to the Western peoples, but to the whole world.

It is both difficult and disconcerting to recall the high hopes which the Armistice brought. Never before had there been so fervid a love of peace, or so bitter a hatred of war, tyranny and injustice. Both among the conquerors and among the conquered there was a universal determination " It shall not happen again ", and a universal willingness to accept new ideas and new institutions which would prevent a repetition of the catastrophe. Especially in Germany and in Austria, pacificism, internationalism and democracy became the creed of the masses.

The democratic statesmen, therefore, who gathered in Paris in the spring of 1919, had perhaps the greatest chance of constructive statesmanship since the collapse of the Roman Empire. With irresistible power at their command, they could fashion the world according to their will, and mould it to their principles. Those principles had been clearly enunciated by Woodrow Wilson in his Fourteen Points and accepted by the Germans as the basis of the Armistice. The American President indeed was the prophet of the new world order. In every country it was felt that only he could lay the foundations of a just peace. On his success or failure depended the future of civilization.

Woodrow Wilson's character was a curious blend of academic pedantry, idealism, shrewdness and vanity. He had risen from a Professorship at Princeton to the leadership of the Democratic party and finally to the Presidency. In the lofty isolation of Presidential power, he had lost none of his idealism or his self-esteem, and he had gained little understanding of European problems. He remained a sectarian Liberal of the old school, and his diagnosis of the ills of Europe was as simple as it was inaccurate. German militarism had violated the rights of small nations and attempted to substitute power for justice as the determinant of world politics. Militarism and secret treaties must therefore be abolished and in their place national self-determination should become the basis of future peace. Trade barriers must disappear, and in the settlement of colonial claims " the interests of the populations concerned must have equal weight with the equitable claims of the Government whose title is to be determined ". Finally, " a general association of nations must be formed under specific covenants for the purpose of affording mutual guarantees of political independence and territorial integrity alike to great and small states ".

Such were the principles upon which the new democratic world-order was to be based, principles not only of the peace settlement but of the League of Nations. It is remarkable that these principles, which were to be imposed on Europe, hardly accorded with American practice. The American Civil War had been fought by the North precisely to prevent the self-determination of the Southern States, and American history had shown the increasing need of a Federal government in the development of the American people. If the states had retained all their rights of self-determination and granted to the Federal Government only those powers enjoyed by the League Council and Assembly, how little of America's greatness would we have known ! Instead of realizing that Europe, in order to destroy trade barriers and gain security, needed a statesmanship like that of the creators of the American Constitution, the President encouraged the forces of disintegration by strict adherence to national sovereignty.

For both the Treaty and the Covenant were a tacit denial of the need to curb the lawlessness of nationalism. They relied upon an inherent harmony of national interests to prevent aggression, and created no central coercive power to impose the Law and Order of which they prated. Although history had proved that even the individual, who is full of kindly emotions, needs force to restrain his baser passions, it was idly supposed that the nations would be able to dispense with these hard necessities of civilization, and that they would spontaneously co-operate, once frontiers had been *nationalism*

rearranged to suit national aspirations. The real weakness of Versailles was not the injustices of the settlement, which were in fact less than those of other settlements, but the principle upon which it was based, that the nation state was the final form of civilized society.

President Wilson and the statesmen of France and England thus sacrificed the universal principle of democracy—the combination of coercive power with individual freedom—to the narrow aspirations of nationalism. Instead of transcending the nation-state, they intensified its nationalism. Even where the Austro-Hungarian empire had offered a possibility of combining cultural autonomy with a supra-national government, they permitted the destruction of a great economic unit and the substitution of nationalistic succession states. Instead of initiating a new democratic world order or European order, they retained the old, with the one change that now France and England enjoyed undisputed mastery. Whereas the Bolsheviks in Russia built up a new continental supra-national state on the theory that national self-determination in cultural affairs is compatible with central planning, none of the western democrats even dared to conceive that such a solution was possible.

Nor did they tackle the colonial question with any greater success. The Japanese suggestion that racial equality was the proper principle of a democratic League was discreetly shelved by the Anglo-Saxons who all had good reason to argue that such ideals were Utopian. Neither the American nation nor the British Empire could stomach the idea. But once this admission was made, it was clear that the League of Nations would guarantee, not equality, but imperial privileges, and, while paying lip-service to the rights of colonial peoples, would ensure to the Western democracies the maintenance and extension of their imperial domination. Instead of inaugurating a new policy and extending the principles of democracy to the colonial field, the Peace-makers sanctified with the fiction of Mandates the claim of Europeans to the exploitation of colonial peoples which could only be based upon a theory of racial superiority.

The principles of Versailles were thus democratic only in the sense that they were principles accepted by the statesmen of the Western democracies. But in truth they were nationalistic and imperialistic, and the Covenant was a vain attempt to veil this fact with a curtain of " International Law ". By adopting an antiquated policy of *laisser-faire*, the peacemakers permitted precisely those forces to rule the world which had been responsible for the catastrophe of 1914. For since they had created no central coercive power, international affairs had necessarily to be shaped by the national policies of the Great Powers. There was no other force to shape them, and the League therefore became the talking house of national statesmen, each anxious to mould policy according to the immediate needs of his own country. The fiction of the equality of nations was annulled by the fact that the Great Powers, in a world of legalized lawlessness, could impose their will upon their weaker neighbours and thus exploit the League machinery, each for its own designs. And the repudiation by America both of its President and of the League, meant that only those national rights would be guaranteed which seemed to be of use to either

France or England. 1918-1933 was the period not of
international law and order, but of the supremacy of
the Versailles powers.

Moreover the Covenant of the League presupposed
a rigid division between politics and economics. The
early Liberal conceived the job of the state to be the
creation of freedom for private enterprise, and Wilson
conceived the League of Nations as a new institution
to complete in the sphere of international affairs the
task of Liberal democracy. Once law and order had
been imposed both internally and externally, the
economic system could be left to work out its own
salvation by its own laws. Under the new world order
of the League, civilized man could achieve that equality
of opportunity and freedom from trade restriction which
he desired. This theory, both of the state and of the
League, was untrue to fact. As we have seen, the
nation-state by 1914 was itself an economic unit in
which politics and economics were inextricably tangled.
Mercantilism had been abolished by the Liberals only
to be replaced by imperialism ; and the restrictions
on trade of the *ancien régime* had been replaced by
an active interference much more far-reaching than anything previously known.

In brief, the attempt to organize the world as a
collection of independent sovereign states was as futile
as the idea that capitalism still meant the free enterprise
of the individual *entrepreneur*. A realistic map of
Europe would have shown not a number of different
political units each with its own frontiers, but a few
great powers each with its zones of influence and satellite
states ; and a true picture of the League would have
portrayed Europe under the military control of France

and the financial control of France, England and America, and, to a lesser extent, of Holland and Switzerland.

Furthermore, it would have shown a division between the political and the financial power. Though the Western democracies had constantly extended the control of the state, they had left foreign trade and investment very largely in the hands of private enterprise or monopoly concerns. Though the state protected its economic interests abroad, and on occasion, particularly in the case of France, guaranteed them for political reasons, there was no state planning of foreign investment and foreign trade. Sometimes, as in the case of the League Loan to Austria, or the Dawes Loan to Germany, the various states of the League would organize assistance to other governments, but the main bulk of international lending was conducted in much the same way as the early bankers conducted it in the 15th century. Neither the American nor the German state controlled or planned the flow of capital into Germany between 1926-29, and out of Germany in the succeeding years. The politicians only intervened after the catastrophe occurred.

In brief, the transition epoch of *laisser-faire* capitalism was at an end and once again finance was regaining control of the productive forces. In many countries it could decide the fate of governments with small regard to political etiquette; and the Great War meant that the financial control of the world was in the hands of people who belonged entirely to the victor powers. In such a situation the political equality of the members of the League was of little significance, especially when the military and naval power was monopolized by France and England. Inevitably countries such as Germany and Italy, which were debtors, felt themselves to be the financial colonies of the Versailles bankers.

II.   THE MYTH OF COLLECTIVE PACIFISM

The post-war epoch is only intelligible when we grasp the moral and spiritual conservatism of the Peace settlement. The attempt to extend democratic principles beyond the shifting confines of the nation state was not made. Instead, the old order of nation states was re-established, the colonial empires enlarged, economic imperialism encouraged and central Europe balkanized. Such a settlement would have been excusable on one condition, that it was recognized for what it was, a temporary expedient hurriedly thrown together by exhausted politicians. But this did not happen. On the contrary, the peace was ushered in with a blowing of moral trumpets unprecedented in history. Wilson, anxious to save his face, argued that the settlement was in accordance with his Fourteen Points, and the peoples of the victor nations were taught to believe that a new era of international order had begun. An old-fashioned treaty was decked out with all the attributes of a new dispensation, and the German nation was denounced as guilty of the world war.

The result was that the peoples of the victorious democracies were lulled into an easy acquiescence. Believing (for men will always believe what they want to believe) that peace and justice had been established, they assumed that no more needed to be done. First the Covenant of the League and disarmament, and then Collective Security, became for the common man the symbols of international righteousness, and a strange new philosophy spread, particularly in England. " Collective Pacifism " sufficiently describes its character.

This theory held that power politics had in fact been abolished and that, since the rule of International Law was an accomplished fact, the peoples of the world could rely upon the Covenant of the League for their security. Now that the civilized nations were united in their abhorrence of aggression, world-wide responsibilities could lightly be undertaken simultaneously with an extensive disarmament. The unpleasant fact that Collective Security might mean British war was discreetly veiled under the name of sanctions, just as the extension of the colonial empires had been disguised as mandates.

The myth of collective security captured the progressive Liberals of England just as the myth of the U.S.S.R. captured the Socialist Left. What actually happened in Russia or Geneva was immaterial to people who desired less to organize peace and justice than to believe that peace and justice were already organized. The trained Marxist and the intelligent Conservative, who ridiculed these airy visions, were regarded as brutal materialists by people whose ignorance of foreign affairs was only matched by their desire for a secular religion to replace the orthodox Christianity which they had mostly lost. Russia and the League became articles of belief for growing sections of public opinion which were able to unite when Russia joined the League in 1934.

This was the first occasion on which the Left in Great Britain had evolved its own foreign policy. Previous to 1914 such matters had remained outside the sphere of party politics because the balance of power had been for so long an undisputed dogma. It is not surprising therefore, that the British Left accepted President Wilson as its prophet and brushed aside all doubts of the new dispensation. Anti-militarism and anti-imperialism had been for generations strong in all classes and had gained added strength since the Boer War. To these negative feelings were now added a positive creed, which satisfied the consciences of democrats who had been vaguely worried by British imperialism.

We have observed previously that political ideas percolate upwards, and that the British middle classes constantly impress their ideology upon the rulers of the country. The post-war period was no exception to this rule. Great Britain was crippled by debts, and soon discovered that she would be unable easily to regain her pre-war trade. Though in the early years the Conservatives preferred isolation and permitted the French to rule Europe, they soon discovered that economic recovery was impossible without a revival of Germany and a restoration of European confidence. This was achieved at Locarno in 1925, and from that year onwards Conservative opinion became gradually converted to League ideals. Since there was no potential aggressor, it seemed easy to accept the Covenant and to relieve taxation by easing the armament programme. Without any immediate sacrifice of imperial interests, Britain was able to accept the League idea.

Seen in retrospect, the period from 1918-1933 is

marked by a growing lethargy in the victor nations. Neither at home nor abroad did democracy undertake a single great constructive enterprise. Victory seemed to have deprived France and Britain of their dynamic : their Conservatives ceased to be ardent imperialists, and their Socialists lost their revolutionary fervour. A spirit of collective pacifism possessed them, and made the peoples content with the lazy approval of high ideals, the verbal condemnation of injustice, chicanery and oppression. Holding all the power, the Western democracies disdained to use it, so long as the status quo was in any way tolerable. The attitude of America was not dissimilar, except that here the League idea was rejected and the Monroe doctrine was still regarded as America's contribution to world peace.

A myth is only justifiable if it stimulates to action. But " Collective Pacifism " was a sedative, not a stimulant. It intoxicated the democracies with a feeling of moral superiority and well-being, while it sapped their sense of responsibility. Gradually statesmen and peoples alike began to believe that the League of Nations was a force able to do the work which previously fell to the various nations. Instead of relying on themselves and on co-operation with their allies, they began to rely on the League to preserve peace. Since the League had no coercive power at its disposal, this trust was wholly unjustified.

No one Party or section of the population can be blamed for this collapse of democratic morale. The great opportunity had been missed in 1918-19 : and it was difficult for the Western democracies to recover from that failure. They had encouraged nationalism as the basis of government ; they had retained economic imperialism and permitted international finance to function independently of government policy. In brief, they had as far as possible returned to pre-war conditions. Having done so, they sought to humanize them. That they failed is an indication that good intentions and kindness, unbacked by resolution and knowledge, may disguise injustices but never eradicate them. Kindness and good-will no doubt console the patient suffering from cancer, but they will not cure the cancer ; and the patient whose practitioner only displays these qualities, may, in his intolerable agonies, turn to a quack and curse the Christian humanity which his practitioner displays.

The growth of Fascism is only intelligible against the background of Collective Pacifism. Though in each case its immediate cause was internal economic distress, both its philosophy and its success are largely due to the international situation produced by the Anglo-French hegemony of the post-war years. Since the Western democracies had so lamentably failed to organize the world for peace, the Fascists have been able without much difficulty to organize it for war. Since France and England were determined at all costs to retain the sovereignty of the nation state, Fascism has mobilized the nation against the League Powers. Since the democratic victors refused to recognize racial equality, Fascism has made racial inequality into a principle of policy. Against democracies too lethargic to end the exploitation of colonial peoples, Fascism has begun a new crusade which openly glorifies imperialism as a national right of the nobler races. In brief, it has selected from Liberal democracy all its nationalism and imperialism, stripped them of their humanitarianism and displayed them to the world in all their nakedness.

But the struggle between the ideas of Liberal Nationalism and the new totalitarian creeds is still unfinished;
and the Fascist state is changing so rapidly that it is
difficult to describe it. For this reason neither dis-
passionate objectivity nor completeness can be expected
in any study of contemporary ideas. In the concluding
sections of this book I have tried to suggest the problems
rather than to give ready-made solutions. More than
this is impossible in a world such as ours.

III. REVOLUTION FROM THE RIGHT : THE FASCIST MYTH

Although it was the wish of the Anglo-Saxon nations
to return to pre-war conditions and to re-establish
" normal " international trade, this objective was
never achieved in the post-war world. The colossal
wastage of the war, the burden of reparations and the
increase of tariff barriers, produced by the Treaty,
resulted in a chronic financial instability. Until the
Great Slump of 1929-32, America fared reasonably
well, but every other country was subjected to acute
depressions which continually threatened to result in
social upheavals.

In the immediate post-war years revolutionary
discontent inevitably took the form of Communist
activity. The Russian Revolution had stirred the
imagination not only of the industrial workers of Europe,
but of the colonial peoples and the nations of the Far
East, and Lenin confidently believed that the world
revolution was at hand. Throughout 1919 and again

in 1920, it seemed possible that the peoples of Germany, Italy and Central Europe would unite with the Russian Communists and so create a Union of Socialist Republics stretching from the North Sea to the Pacific. These hopes were dashed not only by the policy of the Allied Powers, but by the refusal of the organized Labour Movements in most countries to accept Communist control. Though the industrial worker sympathized with Russia and wished her well, he remained for the most part a democrat and a nationalist. The Communist International, instead of rallying the European proletariat to the support of Moscow, only succeeded in splitting it from top to bottom. From 1919 onwards in almost every country there was a Social Democratic Party and a small Communist Party, controlled by the Russians and bitterly opposed to the " traitors " who formed the bulk of the working classes.

This conflict between the Second and- the Third (Communist) International was of the greatest importance. In the first place it weakened the organized Labour Movement and made the Social Democratic leaders even more conservative and " constitutional " than they would otherwise have been ; and, in the second place, it meant that in future Socialist Revolution was inseparably connected with " Internationalism " and with Moscow in the minds of ordinary men and women. Whereas, before the War, the democratic and socialist revolutionaries could claim to be patriots and to speak for their own people, now the Communist Parties in the different countries appeared to be agents of a foreign power, conspiring not only against the capitalist but against the working-class leadership of the Trade Unions, Co-operatives and Social Democratic Parties.

In every revolution the instinct for national self-determination has been a powerful motive ; that motive was now turned against the·Left.

From 1917 to 1920 it was fully justifiable to accept this grave disadvantage. But by the end of 1920 it was clear that world revolution would not come. The Communist armies had been repulsed from Poland, the Social Democrats in Germany, allied with the old officer class, had suppressed the Left with the greatest rigour, and in Italy the occupation of the factories had ignominiously failed. When Lenin introduced the New Economic Policy in March, 1921, it was a signal for a general retreat. This retreat, however, was not accompanied by a decrease in the activity of the Third International. On the contrary, with increased bitterness, the Communist parties in each country attacked their Socialist opponents and these attacks continued unabated until 1934. Although it was clear that a divided working-class movement was weakened in its democratic activity and completely ruled out for any successful revolutionary action, the Third International continued to proclaim its intention of promoting world revolution. Its method of promoting it was to concentrate all its energy on attacking the leadership of the working-class movements.

In the post-war period therefore, we find the paradoxical situation of a Labour Movement incapacitated for any revolutionary action, while the fear of Communist revolution continued to increase. Although the Third International could not achieve a single success, it did succeed in creating a Communist bogey which was to prove invaluable to the Fascists when they made their bid for power. By claiming to save their countries from a Red revolution which existed nowhere outside the manifestos of Communist leaders, they were enabled to carry through a real counter-revolution and to destroy democracy. Staging a sham war between Fascism and Communism, they diverted attention from their real objectives, and succeeded in persuading many law-abiding citizens to consent to the abolition of their democratic rights.

Marx and Lenin had both believed that revolution could only be achieved by the revolutionary activity of the proletariat, but they had perceived that such activity must be stimulated and directed by a small élite of trained revolutionaries. For the masses the simple slogans of popular demagogy should suffice, and the civil liberties afforded by democracy should be exploited by the select leadership for the overthrow of capitalism and the establishment of a totalitarian state. This theory implied a sharp distinction between the self-conscious policy of the leadership and the emotional reaction of the rank and file, or in other words, the distinction of policy and myth. A policy is a plan of action which may never be stated in public ; a myth is an idea or body of ideas which produces loyalty to the leadership. It is accepted not for its truth but because of its emotional value. It may be true, but that is immaterial to its utility.

The crude Communism of the streets was precisely such a myth. But unfortunately the industrial workers were of all classes the least susceptible to myths.[1] With

---

[1] The theory of the Myth, first explicitly developed by George Sorel in *Reflections on Violence*, has been developed into a fully-fledged philosophy by Pareto. For a brief account see *Pareto*, by F. Borkenau.

their considerable experience of democracy inside their own Party and Trade Unions, with their passionate belief in education and reason, they would neither accept a dictatorial leadership nor swallow without question a political myth. The technique of power which Marxism outlined was unacceptable to the very class which it selected as the lever of revolution. Moreover, the social development of Western Europe did not proceed along the lines which Marx had predicted. Capitalism, instead of producing increasing misery, enabled the organized Trade Unions to achieve a certain status within the industrial state, and imperialism gave them a common interest with their employers. The standard of living of the working classes became more and more closely bound up with the maintenance of the strength of the nation. Instead of an international solidarity of the working classes, the 20th century brought an international conflict between the industrial systems of the Great Powers in which defeat meant catastrophe not only for the capitalist but for the worker. German coal miners benefited by the British General Strike, just as British coal miners had benefited in 1923 by the French invasion of the Ruhr; and the struggle of the working classes became a struggle not to overthrow capitalism or the nation state, but to achieve, within the nation state, those democratic rights which would enable them to win a larger share of the national dividend.

Deep divisions also began to appear in the ranks of the working class. Here too, instead of solidarity, a sectional conflict arose. The skilled craftsman soon attained a bourgeois standard of living, but found it threatened when the unskilled machine-tender began to squeeze him out. As a result there came the struggle between craft-Unionism and industrial-Unionism among the workers of America. Again, the recurrence of slumps of ever-increasing intensity brought a deep rift between the employed and the unemployed. The latter became open to revolutionary ideas from any direction, the former, clinging desperately to their jobs, felt that even a reduced wage was a " stake in the country " worth defending. And lastly, the growth of distributive trades and of managerial staff, combined with the spread of secondary education, brought into being a large new class of black-coated workers, who, despite their frequently exiguous salaries, claimed a social superiority to the industrial worker, and sided with the ruling classes in any political crisis. By the end of the war the unity of the working classes had almost entirely disappeared, to be replaced by an intricate network of social loyalties and sectional interests. In so far as the industrial workers were still inspired by a common philosophy, that philosophy was becoming a conservative philosophy of peace, democracy and education.

If, therefore, the democratic state was to be overthrown, a new philosophy must be discovered and a new political army forged. Each in his own way, Hitler and Mussolini performed this task. Instead of assuming that the industrial proletariat must be their chief support, they appealed to those who were really discontented and raised the banner of counter-revolution; and of national unity against foreign foes. Unlike the Communists, they did not believe that economic interest is the only binding force, but discovered a new myth which would unite individuals and classes in spite of their conflicting interests. *national pride*

This myth was the necessity for united action against the internal enemy of anarchy and revolution, and the external enemy of foreign exploitation. Mussolini exposed, very properly, the impotence of a weak Liberal democracy. In Italy this was not difficult to do, where party politics were corrupt and leadership ineffective. He could argue that, if democracy prevents anyone from achieving absolute inescapable power, it also prevents anyone from doing anything at all for the good of the people. An ineffective government might be satisfactory for the wealthy Westerners in England, France and America who merely wanted to keep what they had got ; a poor nation like Italy could not afford such a luxury. Italy, he claimed, needed leadership and discipline such as Liberal politicians and institutions could not provide. And he threatened that, if such leadership were not forthcoming, anarchy would soon follow. Thus the appeal for national unity and authoritarian leadership was made palatable to the middle classes and to the rich by the threat that the alternative to it was revolution. Italian Fascism conquered as a counter-revolution to prevent a worse catastrophe.

But the Communist bogey would not have been a sufficient argument in favour of Fascism had it not been for the aid which Mussolini could draw from the international situation. We have seen how Italian unity had been achieved by an ingenious exploitation of the European balance of power. Italy, for all her nationalist fervour, still felt herself a second-rate nation, and dreamt of Dante and of the Roman Empire. The peace conference seemed to shatter these dreams. It was not merely that Italy won less than her claims, but that she was treated as an inferior nation by the great Western

democracies, which so solemnly proclaimed that all
nations were equal before the Law. Democracy was
damned in Italian eyes, not only for its ineffectiveness in
Italy, but for its effectiveness against Italy. Patriots who
in the days of the Risorgimento had looked to France and
England as deliverers, and even in 1918 had hailed
President Wilson, soon began to feel that Italian self-
determination could only be achieved by the destruction
of Anglo-French hegemony, of the League of Nations
and of democracy itself. Against the military and
naval power of the Western democracies Italy must forge
an Italian militarism, against the philosophy of national
Liberalism, an Italian philosophy of sacred egoism.

Thus Mussolini was able to combine an attack upon
the ineffectiveness of representative institutions and a
defence against Red revolution with an appeal to national
pride. He could appeal to the tradition of National
Liberalism against the Liberal state, and disregard the
opposition of the organized workers, once he had obtained the support of the middle classes and the financial
backing of industry.

But the myth of Fascism was not merely expressed
in words and slogans ; an essential part of it was the
organization of the Party itself. The Fascist squads
with their black shirts and banners, and their assumption that theirs was the obligation to restore law and
order, were themselves part of the myth of Fascism.
They were the incarnation of the new spirit which
challenged the weakness of democracy and once more
claimed that politics were based on organized force.
Mussolini was the first man to see that militarism is a
powerful weapon of political propaganda in a modern
democracy. The Labour Movement made its vast

demonstrations, but those demonstrations were mere crowds of working people. The destruction by Fascist squads of Trade-Union and Socialist newspaper offices was a demonstration not of the general will but of the new state which Fascism was to bring into being. It aroused fear in their opponents and a new sense of disciplined elation amongst their own supporters. Though their fighting powers were questionable, they expressed a fighting spirit and a belief in action which was more effective propaganda than hundreds of speeches.

Italian Fascism was the first mass-movement in Europe which was openly anti-Liberal and anti-Socialist in character. By adopting the technique of the Communists and developing his own myth, Mussolini was able to capture power without disclosing his aims or developing a new philosophy. Displaying a determination to do something, he did not divulge what he would do, except that he would destroy the anarchy of democracy and replace it with discipline and order. To a disillusioned people, leadership seemed preferable to freedom, and the myth of National Action more attractive than class dictatorship. The industrialists were delighted, the Liberal politicians uncertain and the peasants apathetic. In such circumstances it was not difficult for a resolute man at the head of a political army to permit his opponents to defeat themselves by their own impotence and then climb quietly into power.

When we turn to the ideas of Italian Fascism, we are faced by a problem which will confront us also in the case of National Socialism. The idea or myth which inspired Mussolini and his followers differs profoundly, first from the principles of the state which he has built, and secondly from the philosophy which he and others have elaborated to justify it. The basic principle of the Italian Fascist state, the destruction of the Liberal division of political power, we shall discuss in a later section, while the official philosophy of Fascism, best epitomized in Mussolini's own article in the *Enciclopædia*, is a modern version of the Hegelian apotheosis of the state, not dissimilar from the idealism of Bernard Bosanquet, except in its clarity and brevity of expression. "Fascism," writes Mussolini, "is a religious conception in which man is seen in immanent relation to a higher law, an objective Will that transcends the particular individual and raises him to conscious membership of a spiritual society." In this doctrine there is nothing original to note, except that its downright opposition both to democratic individualism and to the Marxist interpretation of history is of great political convenience to a statesman who has been compelled to seek an understanding with the Catholic Church.

When we turn, however, from the academic apologia for Fascism to the ideas which inspire it, there is much which merits our attention. Unlike Hitler, Mussolini sprang from the working classes and received his political education in the revolutionary syndicalist movement. Not only the writings of Sorel, but his own political experience, taught him the futility of orthodox Marxism and the fundamental weakness of the Labour movement. The Left was ready to analyse the economic situation and to build up in the Trade Unions and Co-operatives defensive organizations. It was content to educate and organize its members, but it left the destruction of the existing state to the forces of progress. In spite of its revolutionary slogans, it lacked the will to power and by its stress on " working-class action " destroyed the dynamic of personal leadership which is essential to a revolutionary movement.

Mussolini perceived that a really dynamic leadership must be opposed to the rationalist tradition of nineteenth century progressive thought. Democracy discouraged it, while Marxism sapped its vitality by harping on the *inevitable* collapse of the system. As a Syndicalist he saw that a political system will never be vanquished by the intellectual education of the workers or by their mass organization. Not intellect but courage gives victory in a revolutionary situation ; and courage depends not on systematic analysis but on the personal will to power. The syndicalists and anarchists had stressed this moral aspect of revolution, but, being democrats, proposed to inspire the working classes with their revolutionary ethic ; they sought the spiritual regeneration of the peoples ; Mussolini saw that the will to power and the moral force were only needed in the leader. In 1919 he wrote :

Navigare necesse est . . . against others and against our-selves. . . . We have destroyed every known creed, spat upon every dogma, rejected every paradise, flouted every charlatan—white, black or red—who deals in miraculous drugs for restoring happiness to the human race. We put no faith in any system, nostrum, saint or apostle ; still less do we believe in happiness, salvation or the promised land. . . . Let us get back to the individual. We stand for everything that exalts and ennobles the individual, gives him more comfort, more liberty and a wider life. We fight against everything that restricts and harms the in-dividual. Two religions, one black, one red, are fighting to-day for the mastery of our minds and of the world ; two Vaticans are sending forth their encyclicals, one in Rome and the other in Moscow. We are the heretics of both these religions.

Here we have the essence of Mussolini's revolutionary creed. Economic forces can create a revolutionary situation : only the individual can exploit it. Not reason but will is the determinant in history, and those who wait on progress win no spoils.

The stress on character as against economic forces, on Will against Reason, on the individual against class, on the Leader against the Party machine is not in itself a Fascist doctrine. On the contrary it is common sense. But when these qualities are stressed to the exclusion of their correlatives, and when they are employed to crush the Labour movement, they create a Fascist dictatorship and a Fascist philosophy.

In Italy, however, traces of the old syndicalism survive in the structure of the state. Though it is ostensibly totalitarian, it still contains unresolved the conflict of capital and labour, and both the workers' syndicates and the peasants' co-operatives retain a modicum of independence which has no counterpart in Nazi Germany. Only the personality of Mussolini harmonizes the conflicting elements and bends them to the service of the nation. In a very real sense Fascist Italy is a concrete realization of Mussolini's philosophy of anarchic individualism. But the supreme personality is not the state, but Mussolini himself. Should he die, the totalitarian state will disappear and the battle between syndicalism and the old order will begin anew.

IV. THE NATIONAL SOCIALIST MYTH

In a previous chapter we have seen how the National Liberal movement failed to bring satisfaction to the German peoples. In Austria-Hungary the Germans

felt themselves threatened by the growing demands of
the Slav minorities and retained an uneasy loyalty to
the decrepit imperial régime ; in Germany they had to
accept the nation state created by the statesmanship
of Prussia. The collapse of the Central Powers in 1918
faced them with a terrible dilemma. Either they must
come to terms with the Western democracies and accept
whatever terms they offered or they must throw in their
lot with Communist Russia, and " turn the war of
imperialist nations into a war of classes "

The decision was made by the mass of the people.
Weary of war, hating the military dictatorship under
which they had lived for two years, they rose in revolt
against their governments. But the German revolution
of 1918 was not a consciously proletarian movement,
but simply a demand for bread, peace and democracy.
Neither in Vienna nor in the industrial centres of Germany were the Communists more than an insignificant
fraction and the old Socialist leadership was able without
much difficulty to retain control, to hold constituent
assemblies and to set up constitutional democracies on
the Western model. This done, they were compelled to
accept the new position allotted to their nations by the
Versailles powers. Germany proper, her foreign invest-
ments gone, her heavy industries dismembered by the
new frontiers and her armies disbanded, became a debtor
nation with a secondary influence in the affairs of
Europe ; while the Germans of Austria-Hungary were
now either minorities within the new succession states,
or citizens of a truncated Austria with no economic
basis for survival.

Had the Western democracies acted with foresight,
and collaborated in an effort to rebuild the economic

structure of Europe, the German peoples under their new democratic leaders might have been content with their lot. The man in the street wants security and a livelihood; he does not succumb to revolutionary propaganda unless these are denied him for a considerable time, and in Germany, right up to the end, a majority of the people remained loyal to the democracy in spite of all its faults. But the majority seldom determines the fate of nations, and the humiliation of national pride had deeply affected the old ruling class, the bureaucracy and the middle classes. Swept from power by the 1918 revolution, their savings destroyed by the inflation, these classes would have accepted democracy reluctantly under the best conditions. In the post-war world, where democracy and defeat were inseparably connected, and the Covenant of the League formed part of the Treaty of Versailles, they tolerated representative institutions only so long as they appeared to be the sole alternative to Communism. The industrial workers alone welcomed democracy as a positive blessing and used it both in Austria and in Germany for the building of social services considerably in advance of those in France and England; but the classes which should have provided democratic Conservative parties in Parliament remained sullen participants in the new régime. Moreover, the centre of balance of German nationalism had shifted. The disappearance of Austria-Hungary meant that Germans outside Germany now looked to the German state with an undivided patriotism. Before 1918 there were two German nations; now there was only one, and inevitably a centripetal movement took place. The ideas of *Gross-deutschtum*, which had been shattered in 1848, revived once more and gained the fanatical devotion which only national humiliation can bring. In Poland, and Czecho-Slovakia, in Austria and Italy, German minorities now turned to Germany as their spiritual home.

Hitler is the personification of this new idea of *Gross-deutschtum*, National Socialism is its myth, and the Third Reich will, if he completes his task, be its realization. Unlike Italian Fascism, which is a direct descendant of Imperialism, National Socialism was originally a purely nationalist movement which tried, not to organize an already unified nation state for the conquest of empire, but to create a nation state for the first time. It was attempting to do for the German peoples what was accomplished in the middle of last century for the Italians. True, it now aims at Empire, but the dynamic of National Socialism is in its original purpose and not in its new ambitions.

Ein Reich, ein Volk, ein Fuehrer (one realm, one people, one Leader), this is the essential myth. " Reich " does not mean " empire " in the sense of colonies, but refers to the old German ideal of the Holy Roman Empire, the supremacy of the German people as the ruling race in Europe. " Volk " does not mean " nation " but refers to all the German peoples in Central Europe whether inside or outside Germany. " Fuehrer " does not mean " dictator " in the sense that Mussolini is a dictator, but the person who incarnates that German unity which has not yet been realized. The myth, like that of international Communism, springs from a conception of unity in contradiction to all existing frontiers. It does not attempt to consolidate and strengthen an old nation state, but challenges Bismarck's creation as much as the Treaty of Versailles.

Hitler's Austrian origin is a key to the understanding of National Socialism. In opposition to the cool statesmanship of the Prussian, who regarded the nation state as an instrument of policy, and sought to draw its frontiers according to principles of strategy, economics and the balance of power, Hitler put forward the simple notion of German unity. For the fine compromises of Bismarck, his solicitous attention to the claims of the component states, his tacit acceptance of the old European order and attempts to fit Germany into it, Hitler substituted the uncompromising claim to German unity and German supremacy, come what may. Like all revolutionary leaders, he believes in the impossible, and, when matched against statesmen who think the age of miracles is passed, he is a formidable adversary. Only a man brought up outside the Prussian influence, among the talkative dreamers of the Austrian Pan-German movement, could have ranted such nonsense and made it come true.

The very vagueness and vastness of his Pan-Germanism gave his ideas a genuinely revolutionary flavour. They made no immediate appeal to the Prussian army or bureaucracy which " understood " politics, but they did appeal to the lower middle classes, to the students and to the black-coated workers who, while rejecting the Marxist propaganda, were in search of a revolutionary creed. Hitler and his followers could rightly feel themselves to be the opponents not only of Communism and of democracy, but also of the old reactionary order as well. They spoke for the forgotten man in Germany and the forgotten Germans outside. Against a Prussian tradition far more loyal to Prussian supremacy than to German unity, they voiced a simple unreasoning Germanic nationalism.

With regard to the institutions of the new Third Reich, National Socialism was vague. It was not to be Democratic or Bolshevik (on these points Fascism and National Socialism agree), not capitalist or Socialist, but a Germanic community in which a new and genuine aristocracy, recruited from the Party, must impose its will without let or hindrance and abolish class-conflict by the imposition of German discipline and morality. This doctrine, which clearly owes something to Rousseau's mystical concept of the General Will, conceives of the leadership as the natural expression of Germanism. Denying the whole tradition of Western democracy which sought to divide political power and to ensure the protection of minority rights by representation, it asserts the paramount claim of the nation as a whole and the indivisible absolute sovereignty of the new leadership. In so doing, it reverts from the individualism of Liberal democracy to a tribal notion of community. Instead of aiming at the equality of individual rights within the state, it seeks to subordinate every individual to the demands of national self-assertion : instead of building the state with the express purpose of preventing the concentration of power in the hands of a few, it renders illegal any check upon the will of the leadership : instead of the Marxist dictatorship of the proletariat, Hitler created the dictatorship of the German people, which means in effect the mobilization of the German people for the sole purpose of Germanic self-assertion against the outside world. No other purpose, or right, should interfere to prevent the maximization of German power.

This philosophy only makes sense in a world of warring national groups : it is the supreme expression of the principle of national self-determination, and it asserts that this principle should be the sole consideration of statesmanship. But it is combined with a theory of Race which renders it even more formidable. This theory maintains the peculiar superiority of Aryans over the rest of humanity. The human race is divided into rulers and subjects and there is a fundamental inequality between the two classes. Germans may be divided by the frontiers of nation states, but they are united by an affinity of blood, and their racial superiority gives them the right to world domination. Thus the National Socialist statesman must make it his first objective to purify the race of impure elements, to multiply its numbers, and to educate its members to a true sense of their racial superiority.

Racialism was bound to thrive in Vienna, where Hitler lived before the war. It is the philosophy of a national minority threatened by nationalities which it despises but cannot overrule, and its correlative anti-Semitism was equally popular. The German minority, terrified that democracy and Socialism would undermine its privileges, was forced to look round for a scapegoat—and found it in the Jew, who in Vienna was a leading force not only in capitalism, but in the progressive movements. Anti-Semitism therefore became the nationalistic substitute for class war, and racialism the alternative to the materialist conception of history. Marxism had taught that democratic government was the " executive committee of the ruling class " : Racialism replied that it was the system which enabled Jewry to sap the German will. Marxism had denounced the narrow nation state and dreamt of a day when the world revolution would sweep its frontiers away;

Racialism, too, had its dream of a German people united across the divided frontiers and supreme all over the world. Marxism believed that the destruction of capitalism would usher in the millennium, Racialism that the extermination of the Jews would bring the true Germanic paradise.

In Central Europe, where the economic interpretation of history was the myth of the working class movement, Racialism became the revolutionary philosophy of a discontented German middle class which projected upon the Jews all the resentment and lust for power which it felt. Hitler's picture of the Jew contriving the destruction of civilization is a picture, exquisitely true in all its details, not of the Jew but of his own nature. He conjures up an imaginary opponent, ruthless and without scruple, and then argues that against this foe only ruthless men without humanitarian scruples will avail.

What had been a romantic farrago of pseudo-science, which caused a mild flutter in the municipal politics of pre-war Vienna, was suddenly given a European significance by the Treaty of Versailles. Then the anti-Semites had used it to castigate the pro-Slav policy of the Habsburgs; now it became the criticism of the new Europe created by the democracies of the West. Then they could point only to the " Jewish " capitalism and " Jewish " social democracy of Vienna, now they could evolve the legend that Bolshevik Russia was in league with the bankers of London and Paris, and the social democrats of Berlin. The petty local feuds of the Austrian capital were enlarged into a world picture of the German peoples oppressed by the unholy alliance of Western capitalism and Eastern Bolshevism, and the old municipal objective swelled suddenly into the gigantic plan to purify Germany of the Jewish virus, capitalism, socialism and democracy, and to lead the regenerate nation against the enemies which encompassed it.

It is fashionable for self-made men to seek a family tree, and the College of Heralds are prepared to do their best in such cases. Academic philosophers are rapidly performing the same service for Nazi doctrine, and already it can claim a very respectable ancestry with Plato, Herder, Fichte, Rousseau, Hegel and Nietzsche as its most illustrious forbears. Such manipulations of history are, however, misleading and divert attention from the fact that Hitler, unlike Mussolini, has no background of philosophical reading in either the Liberal or the Marxist tradition. It is unlikely that he read either Gobineau or Stewart Chamberlain except in quotations selected by anti-Semitic pamphleteers; it is certain that he never studied either Marx or Hegel in the original. Hitler's writings are the result of discussion and of desultory newspaper reading, and the peculiar fascination of *Mein Kampf* is that it elaborates the half-formed ideas of the streets into a comprehensive secular religion. Breaking altogether with the traditions of German literature and the standards of educated public opinion, it expresses, not a new version of the Liberal or authoritarian or working-class ideology, but the ideology of the petit bourgeois. In this sense it is an epoch-making book, and those who seek to derive its ideas from earlier thinkers are underestimating its originality. *Mein Kampf* is derived from Hitler's personal experiences, and its author has made these experiences into the creed of a nation.

It is here that National Socialism differs from

Fascism. Mussolini is a brilliant thinker whose philosophy, though unorthodox, flows out of the true European tradition. If he is a myth-maker, he is, like Plato's guardians, conscious that "the noble lie" is a lie. Hitler, in this sense, is not an educated man, nor is *Mein Kampf* an educated book. He is not a myth-maker, but the personification of a myth, not, like Mussolini, an advocate of irrationalism but really irrational. Like Mahomet, he has his place not in the history of political theory but in the history of world events. For he is the instrument of the ideas which inspire him and not their fashioner.

Thus his creed is really the destruction of the ideas of the West, of its culture and of its religion. Personifying (but not elucidating) those romantic aspirations which we traced in the thought of nineteenth-century Germany, he is the whirlwind which destroys, before history constructs a new social order.

It is futile to underrate the majesty of the National Socialist myth. It is indeed a *Weltanschauung*, a complete dogmatic religion which explains everything with an all-embracing German logic. All its premises are false, but they are of immense emotional appeal. Racialism is the supreme example of wish-fulfilment in the history of political ideas. It gave an explanation of world history which freed the German people from all responsibility for its plight; and provided a philosophical justification for an attack upon an unpopular democracy and for unbridled nationalist aggression. In short, it created the basis for a popular pan-German movement so conspicuously lacking both in Bismarck's pre-war creation and in the post-war Weimar Republic. That this movement could capture power, however, is partly due to the policy of the Western democracies which between 1918 and 1933 permitted the institutions of democracy and the Covenant of the League to become obstacles in the way of legitimate German aspirations. The Jew has become the scapegoat for the sins of the Versailles powers.

V. THE TECHNIQUE OF POWER

Unlike Fascism, which is largely the personal creation of a single man, National Socialism is a genuinely popular movement. Mussolini intrigued his way to power and formulated a philosophy afterwards to justify his actions; Hitler was the mouthpiece of a movement which, though it compromised with the old powers, always had a dynamic of its own. Mussolini is a modern Prince after Machiavelli's heart, Hitler a reformer with the incoherent zeal and peasant shrewdness of Martin Luther. He has changed the shape of the world not to satisfy personal ambition, but because he expressed the German resentment against the failure of Western democracy to reorganize the world according to its own principles, and the failure of Communism to realize the proletarian millennium. Since neither of these philosophies could shape the world to suit the German peoples, a third movement has arisen, exclusively German and directed to the destruction both of the tradition on which they are based, and the institutions which they created.

But the popular movement of National Socialism would never have achieved power without the tacit connivance both of foreign powers and of classes in

Germany which regarded its ideals as moonshine. The bureaucracy and the post-war Reichswehr, for instance, and above all President Hindenburg and his entourage, could have annihilated the Party, had they wished to do so, as late as the autumn of 1932. The French and British governments could have smashed the régime in 1934 or 1936, if not in 1938, with a minimal risk of war. Its success, like that of the Japanese militarists, depends upon the non-intervention against its imperial schemes of those whose interests seem at first sight to be most vitally endangered. This is the new factor which makes post-war politics profoundly different from those of the previous hundred years.

The explanation of this lack of resistance to National Socialism is to be found in democracy itself. We have seen how, at the end of the war, the ideals of democracy could only have been advanced by statesmen prepared to move beyond the narrow confines of the nation to a higher form of political organization, and larger units of economic co-operation. Against this advance, the forces of tradition and nationalism made strenuous resistance, and not only perpetuated the nation state but actually increased the number of the nations. But within the state itself there was a crisis of democracy. The war had vastly increased the bargaining power of the working-class movements and strengthened their political parties, and the old conflict of Conservative and Liberal was now giving place to one between the parties of the bourgeoisie and the parties of social democracy. Just as at the beginning of the 19th century, the polite battle of Whigs and Tories was ended by the emergence of a new Liberal movement demanding a new economic programme, so now it seemed *pressure groups*

as though the stage was set for a battle between Liberal and Social democracy.

Although the demands of the post-war Social Democrats were far less revolutionary than those of their Liberal predecessors, they were given an adventitious revolutionary flavour by the success of the Russian Revolution. The Trade Unions which were well content to ensure a little security to their members became suspect as "red" organizations, and the whole democratic Left was credited with a dynamic which its speeches may have suggested but for which there was little evidence in its actions. As a result, the middle classes and in particular the growing class of black-coated workers became timidly susceptible to appeals for national unity against the advocates of class war.

It was easy enough, especially in a period of acute economic depression, for well-organized pressure-groups representing great business and banking interests to exploit these appeals for the fortifying of their privileged position, and the prevention of those measures of public control of investment, trade and industry which were essential to the general interest of the modern community. Both in the great industrial countries of Europe and in the U.S.A., the necessary plans of reconstruction were labelled as "red" and discreetly shelved.

These manoeuvres brought discredit not only on the Left, but on Democracy too. The feeling began to spread that representative institutions were a system rigged by politicians which brought no advantages to the mass of the people, and when the Great Slump came in 1929, the critics of Democracy won a great deal of support. In Germany, National Socialism was particularly vigorous in its attack on big business

and the Prussian landlords, and exposed their undue
influence upon Democracy. This attack upon Democracy found a considerable measure of support among
precisely those groups whom Hitler was attacking in
public. Though they could rig free institutions, certain
industrialists believed they would do even better if
they abolished them altogether, and then broke the
Trade Unions whose existence made wage-reductions
and cuts in the social services somewhat difficult. They
began therefore to finance the National Socialist movement and finally, when it began to ebb with the return
of business in 1932, deliberately engineered a coalition
government between their own forces and the National
Socialists. In this intrigue the army and the old
monarchists were tacit accomplices. Against this
alliance between the reactionary and the revolutionary,
it was difficult for the constitutional democrats to
offer any resistance. With deep divisions in their
own ranks and inspired by a respect for law and order,
they were an easy prey for their opponents.

But the victory of 1933 was only the first and easiest
battle in Hitler's campaign. The next stage was the
destruction of his reactionary allies in Germany, and
the attack upon the Versailles powers. The German
industrialists soon discovered that, like Frankenstein,
they had created a monster more powerful than they.
They dared not dispense with Hitler, since he alone
protected them from the popular wrath : on the other
hand, they could not resist him once he had created the
Totalitarian State. While he destroyed the Trade
Unions and the political movements of the Left and
began a rearmament programme which restored their
profits, they were well content, but when in 1935 he

began to " co-ordinate " their activities as well, they discovered that resistance, without the right of free speech, was difficult. By 1938 Hitler had succeeded in introducing a war economy in which the whole economic and social system was brought under the control of the state, and the army, the bankers and the industrialists had become the servants of National Socialism. With state control of currency, investment and foreign trade, the National Socialist planners had as much power as the central executive in Russia. By conspiring with Hitler to destroy an imaginary Communist revolution, the anti-democratic reactionaries destroyed their own power and permitted a state control of their activity far more drastic than anything which the Social Democrats had envisaged in their wildest dreams.

Both the Fascists and the Nazis were counter-revolutionists; they claimed and obtained supreme power in order to prevent revolution. But it would be unwise to draw the conclusion that there has been no fundamental change in Italy or Germany as a result of the counter-revolution. On the contrary, in both countries a real shift of power has occurred as the result of the destruction of Liberal Democracy. We have seen in a previous chapter that the Liberal revolution, which started as a movement against state interference, ended by permitting and actually encouraging an even larger measure of state interference, and the concentration of executive and legislative power in the cabinet. Thus the national Liberal state was inevitably a compromise between the individualistic principles of Liberalism and the collectivist necessities of modern industry. This compromise usually left to the organized pressure-

groups of capital and labour the regulation of wages
and conditions, and permitted an independent judiciary
to interpret the Law, while the state bureaucracy, working under Parliamentary control, managed the social
services and the armed forces. Democracy rested upon
a delicate equilibrium of social forces, and Parliament
became increasingly the representative not of single
citizens but of well-organized economic and social
groups. Indeed, the only group which was not represented there was the general public.

The Fascist state has destroyed this equilibrium.
By suppressing all political parties except one, it has
practically amalgamated the political party and the
state bureaucracy ; by attacking the independence of
the judiciary, it has destroyed the security both of the
individual and of the group or economic interest against
the arbitrary decisions of the state. In brief, it has
substituted for the checks and balances of *Civil Government* a new and monstrous *Leviathan*. Once more there
is a sovereign supreme over the nation, against whose
decisions there is no appeal. The Liberal movement
in Europe, which for two hundred years had sought
to tame the sovereignty of the executive and place
it under the control both of Law and of public opinion,
has been reversed. Now Law and public opinion are
once more instruments of state policy.

This change has given the leadership enormous
powers for good and bad. Since it has nothing to fear
except revolution, it is free to carry out any policy
which it likes. Since the time of Hobbes, the advances
of science have all facilitated a concentration of power
of which he could not dream. Equipped with modern
methods of communication, warfare and propaganda,

the statesman who controls the Fascist state is liberated
from every human limitation upon the policy which he
seeks to pursue. He is in the position of a general
upon the field of battle, and can deploy his economic
forces as the general deploys his divisions. If we wish
to describe Fascism in a sentence, we can say that it
is the destruction of civil life and the militarization of
the activities of a whole nation. Whereas the Liberals
conceived of the state as an evil, necessary to the good
life of the individual and tolerable if it was kept in
check by popular representation and impartial law,
Fascism has once again created a sovereign power which
is a law unto itself and to whose interests every individual right may ultimately be sacrificed.

VI. THE TOTALITARIAN STATE

In the previous chapter we saw that Marx, in spite
of his contempt for Liberal practice, was a fervent
believer in Liberal ideals and conceived of the dictatorship of the proletariat as a brief transition stage on the
way to the international class-less society, when the
state would wither away. The failure of the world
revolution, therefore, and the attempt to build socialism
in one country necessitated a far more permanent form
of dictatorship than he expected or desired. By an
ironical twist of history, a party, pledged to destroy the
necessity for centralized coercion, was compelled to
construct a state far more efficiently centralized than
the Tzarist despotism, and Communist Russia became
the first example of the *Totalitarian State*.

Although Fascism and National Socialism are move-

ments primarily designed to defeat the Third International, they have borrowed their political institutions
almost exclusively from Soviet Russia. Beelzebub has
been employed to cast out Beelzebub, and the two
ideologies confront one another arrayed in closely similar
panoplies of war. This need not surprise us. Both
Communists and Fascists are convinced that any and
every means must be employed to realize their ideals,
and it was only natural that, once the Russians had
proved the effectiveness of the Totalitarian State for
their ends, the Fascists and the Nazis should adopt it
for theirs. Though two opposing armies may be fighting
for different ideals, this difference will not be reflected
in the armaments which they employ.

The common characteristic then of the Totalitarian
states is that they are instruments designed by a small
and compact body of determined revolutionaries for
the furtherance of their plans. Representative institutions and liberal democracy developed as instruments
for the *prevention* of despotic power : all the western
liberals were concerned first and foremost to break
autocracy, and they built their political institutions in
order to prevent any party or interest imposing its plans
without restraint upon the people. They had no cut
and dried scheme for salvation, but held that salvation
comes through free discussion and by compromise
between conflicting groups. Though they admitted
the necessity for force in moments of acute crisis, they
believed in the possibility of peaceful change ; though
they realized that some people are impervious to rational
argument, they thought that most people could be
persuaded to be reasonable.

Liberal democracy rests therefore upon an optimistic

estimate of human nature, which is flatly contradicted
by the protagonists of the Totalitarian State. Since
both Fascists and Communists are convinced that their
opponents are not open to rational conversion, they
are forced to conceive of politics as permanent warfare
and of the State as an instrument of pure coercion;
and by holding these beliefs themselves, they make
democracy unworkable. Not only do their principles
justify them in the methods they adopt, but they
inevitably compel others who do not agree with them
to adopt those methods too. An uncompromising
revolutionary makes the state, which he is attacking,
totalitarian. In such a situation democrats who wish
to survive must curtail democracy. It is no good
believing in the reasonableness of human nature at
the moment when a pistol is pointed at your head.

The Totalitarian state therefore is the product not
only of Totalitarian philosophies but of resistance to
them. Democracy ceases to function so soon as influential sections of the community believe that it cannot
function. The Nazis justified their revolution by the
failure of Democracy, but one of the chief causes of
that failure was the uncompromising behaviour of the
Nazis themselves. The same is true of the Bolshevik
attitude to the Constituent Assembly in Russia.

Once this deadlock has been reached, a new form of
state must be evolved. The administrative machinery is
preserved and the cabinet, which even in democracies has
been steadily encroaching on the rights of parliament,
becomes the supreme legislative and executive body.
But no Totalitarian state starts by being completely
totalitarian. In every case the party which seizes power
is honestly determined to liquidate only its special

enemies and to preserve both for its own supporters and for groups which are friendly to it the right of criticism and of participation in government. Mussolini took many years to evolve his complete autocracy, and in Russia it was only after 1933 that the opposition groups within the Communist Party were destroyed. *Totalitarianism is not an objective in itself, but a consequence of the determination to tolerate only " constructive criticism "*.

Beginning therefore with the monopolization of political power and the liquidation of its enemies, the state develops into a One Party State. With the destruction of the opposition and the elimination of any alternative Government which can be peacefully substituted by electoral means, the representation of the people is centralized in the single party, and this becomes the vehicle both for the dissemination *downwards* of the views of the régime and the percolation *upwards* of the discontents and grievances of the people.

But the destruction of political opposition is never in itself a sufficient safeguard. For immediately it is accomplished, opposition runs underground and permeates every non-political organization. Trade Unions, Churches, Sport Associations and above all friendly gatherings in private houses become centres of political discontent and, since constitutional opposition has been forbidden, they are bound to be subversive. Thus a movement which starts with the intention of eliminating only avowed enemies is forced to suppress every form of voluntary association or to bring it under state control. This is the process known as *Gleichschaltung* [1] in Nazi Germany, and it is inevitably accompanied by the growth of a secret police.

[1] Roughly = bringing into line.

Once this step has been taken, it is clear that the press, cinema and radio and all forms of literature and academic research must be similarly organized. Discussion, alike in the spoken and in the written word, and the whole system of education are suppressed and in their place propaganda, centrally directed, is instituted   In these conditions it is reasonably safe to re-introduce the plebiscite or even democratic institutions.

At this stage the Totalitarian State has three pillars of support, the old bureaucracy and the armed forces, the new secret police and the Party.   These three are generally at loggerheads and the next stage is the struggle between the revolutionary Party and the new state.   For the Party, a genuinely popular movement, is bound to become steadily more extreme in its demands when it finds that it has lost the pleasures of violence which it enjoyed under democracy and has become merely an instrument of propaganda for its old leaders who are now its masters.

The *Gleichschaltung* of the Party is the most difficult task which faces the masters of the Totalitarian State. Men whose qualities were useful in the revolutionary days must be disposed of, and usually it is " the old guard " who disappear.   From a militant army, the Party is gradually transformed into a vast hierarchy of functionaries which in many cases duplicates the administrative machine.   In all but the extreme cases of idealism, however, safe employment is a sure sedative of political discontent.

Meanwhile, three other aspects of the nation's life must be brought into line.   The democratic state could afford an independent judiciary because its objective was the elimination of despotic power. But in the One Party state law and the judges who interpret it are bound to appear " oppositional ". Like education and religion, they too must be *gleichgeschaltet*, and law, instead of being the defence against an arbitrary over-lord, becomes yet another instrument for the accomplishment of the Total Will. So, too, with the employer and the employee. Since, each in his own way, can sabotage the state, if left to himself, they must be organized in state associations. Whatever the pretensions of the Party (and Fascism claims to protect private enterprise against Communism), its leaders are compelled gradually to bring the whole economic life of the country under state control.

Every institution of the Totalitarian state arises from the fact that it is instituted not to facilitate peaceful change, but to destroy its opponents. The nation is gradually deprived of freedom that its rulers may be entirely free and, once the process has begun, it can only be stopped by revolution. With each advance of centralization, and extension of control, it becomes increasingly difficult to avoid the next, until at last the nation is divided into a ruling hierarchy of officials, and a subject people.

In their revolutionary phase both the Communist and the Fascist states displayed profoundly democratic traits. Through the Russian Soviets the common people participated actively in government ; and in Germany and Italy the Fascist parties challenged the old social and industrial oligarchy and secured political power for many members of the middle and lower middle classes. In all three countries a social revolution occurred, though the Fascist method of co-operation with the Conservative forces tended to disguise it, and social equality is still more real in these than in France and England, where the upper middle-classes hold a paramount political influence. But[the destruction of class distinction in the Totalitarian states was only a transient phenomenon, and in all of them the pyramid of social classes is being replaced by a pyramid of political classes in which the mass of the people have no status at all.]

This does not mean that the masses are necessarily discontented. The destruction of civil liberties and of the political parties has affected only a tiny minority of the politically conscious individuals, and some compensation is afforded by the social services which the Totalitarian State can and must afford, and by the security of employment which state control of economics renders possible. For the millions to whom political freedom meant unemployment and a scanty dole, the new régime, with its regimentation and espionage and even with its constant pressure on their standard of living, is not intolerable. Economic security, holidays with pay, family allowances and well-organized health services are inevitably of greater importance to the majority of Europeans than any political principle. Provided they are not asked to fight a war or to accept too sudden a reduction of wages or increase of hours they will serve Totalitarianism with few regrets for Liberal democracy.

This acceptance is inevitable, since, with modern methods of centralized control, opposition, except inside the state machine, is virtually impossible. Only in time of war is a popular revolution possible, and then only in the hour of defeat. This fact explains why the

Totalitarian régimes, though militaristic, are profoundly unwilling to risk a major war. Militarism—the introduction of military discipline into every sphere of life—is an essential feature of their institutions, and righteous warfare the highest activity which they can conceive. Because they began as organizations for civil war, and the only justification for their continued severity is fear of attack, they must still behave as though they were menaced by internal and external foes, and, if there are none, they must create them in imagination. They remain, therefore, in a chronic state of apprehension not because there is anything to fear, but, because, if there were nothing to fear, their whole paraphernalia would look ridiculous. And yet, while glorifying war and challenging each other to battle, each of them knows that a major war would probably bring its own destruction.

For, in spite of its outward appearance of unanimity, the Totalitarian State is not free from internal conflicts. The suppression of opposition, and the construction of a new political oligarchy creates not unity, but a new struggle of rival personalities and groups; and economic depression and internal tension tends to recreate opposition and to set the Party once more against the State. In spite of their display of overwhelming force, none of the Totalitarian states gives an impression of solidity or of permanence. The greater the violence with which the people are stretched upon a Procrustean rack of national unity, the weaker their real unity: the more feverishly they seek to inspire by propaganda a national fervour of self-sacrifice, the more listless and apathetic the response of their subjects.

Once one has rejected the general assumption of the beneficence of *laissez-faire*, it is idle to deny that the Totalitarian state can achieve for its subjects certain advantages which the Liberal state could not. By capturing the control of economic activity, it can plan and co-ordinate the productive wealth of the nation and curb the ambitions of vested interests in finance and industry. But this public co-ordination and control, which is necessary to any modern economy, could well have been achieved without the destruction of civil liberty and the independent judiciary. The tragedy of Liberalism was that by thwarting the just demands of Social Democracy, it produced a movement which destroyed every value, of Liberal civilization. Not only in Germany and Italy, but in every country in the world, there is urgent need for a public control of urban development, the location of industry, the flow of investment and foreign trade. Where this need is not satisfied by democracy, democracy will disappear; where the great economic groups seek to prevent an orderly and civilized co-ordination of their activities, they will be dragooned by an uncivilized militarism. Once again, we must realize that Fascism, like Communism, arises from the failure of Liberal Democracy to adapt itself to new conditions. The task which should have been carried out by democrats according to the principles of democracy, is now being undertaken by militarists; the co-ordination of production and distribution which should have produced benefits for the whole community, is now accomplished for the sake of an imperial dream which can benefit no one, but only satisfies the lust for power of the mythmakers spell-bound by their own myth.

VII. THE BALANCE OF IDEAS

The re-emergence of Germany as a militant force in Europe upset the uneasy hegemony of France and Britain, and re-introduced a balance of power. From 1935 on, the smaller nations had to choose which of the two opposed blocs should " protect their independence " and a long-drawn battle began between the Fascist Axis and the Versailles group which Russia had joined in 1934.

In this struggle Hitler adopted the same technique which he had used in his seizure of power inside Germany. By proclaiming himself the protector of Europe against Bolshevism, he gained the sympathetic attention of certain groups in England and France who were susceptible to the myth of the Communist terror. By playing on the divisions between his opponents he was able to destroy their confidence in one another and thus to weaken an enemy which, united, had an overwhelming superiority of armed force. If war had broken out at any time between 1933 and 1938, Germany would have suffered overwhelming defeat ; and yet by the threat of war, Hitler, with his satellite Mussolini, and his distant allies in Japan, was able to destroy the Treaty of Versailles, while each of them made large territorial acquisitions.

For the growth of National Socialism had produced a domestic conflict in each of the states which were arrayed against it.   For the first time for generations, France and England were torn by an internal conflict on foreign policy. The parties of the Left, in strange unison with the old-fashioned imperialists, demanded

collective democratic resistance to Fascist aggression
and found themselves on occasion defending a status
quo which they had previously denounced. The parties
of the Right, traditionally the defenders of national
rights and imperial interests, became now the advocates
of pacifism and appeasement. Anxious to collaborate
at all costs with the anti-Bolshevik forces in Europe,
they were willing to accept untold sacrifices of strategic
and economic interests, if this was the price to be paid
for security against Communism.

This deep internal conflict made it easy for Hitler
to win a spectacular series of bloodless victories. The
collective aggression of Germany and Italy was far more
effective than the collective security of the Versailles
powers, whose conservative politicians were both unwilling to collaborate with Russia and terrified of the
results which might follow from the defeat of Fascism
in Italy or Germany. Moreover, the Totalitarian régimes, instituted by Mussolini and Hitler, could pursue
a far more active foreign policy than their collective
pacifist rivals. Holding up their creditors to ransom,
and exploiting a state-controlled foreign trade as an
instrument of policy, they were able, even apart from
open threats of war, to dominate the smaller nations
and to paralyze the greater. In 1933, Italy was a second-
rate power, and Germany impotent to prevent her
encirclement. In 1938, Italy was the strongest power
in the Mediterranean and Germany had accomplished
the encirclement of France. Without a major war,
the central powers had nearly won the hegemony of
Europe from the Western democracies and reversed
the results of the world war.

This reversal was not, however, merely a change in

the balance of power of the great nation states. It was a reversal of the *balance of ideas*. In 1918 the progressive ideas of Western democracy were in the ascendant ; at least they were sufficiently powerful to compel the statesmen to accept them in theory even if they did not put them into practice. By 1938, however, these ideas and the forces which supported them were fighting desperately for survival against the new Totalitarian imperialism of Germany, Italy and Japan, which openly and triumphantly asserted their intention of ending the era of Liberal democracy and inaugurating a new epoch of exclusive nationalistic militarism. The myths which the old anti-Liberal forces had hoped to exploit in order to check the progress of Social Democracy, had become the permanent forces in world affairs and had succeeded already in destroying the world order of Versailles. Instead of a motley collection of semi-independent nation states, a new type of political unit was appearing, the Fascist empire absorbing into itself foreign minorities as subject masses, and organizing the whole life of the empire under the most drastic type of militarist planning. In these new empires, the culture and religion of the old bourgeois civilization was suppressed in favour of a centralized propaganda for the new racial and nationalist myths. The world, which for close on four hundred years had struggled to emancipate itself from the rule of inequality and from the irrationalism of superstition, was now threatened with a new absolutism which would utilize all the weapons of science not for the dissemination of knowledge and the emancipation of the oppressed but for the maintenance of a new tyranny and the re-enslavement of the human mind to tribal superstition.

The issue of this struggle is still undecided. In America the democratic forces are still in the ascendant ; in Russia it is just possible that the drastic discipline of Stalinism may bring her millions to the economic level where Social Democracy becomes a real possibility. In Great Britain and her Dominions there is still a vast potential source of democratic idealism, at present dispirited and dismayed, which could be tapped by leaders of courage and determination. But one thing is clear : the epoch of National Liberalism is over. Economics and politics alike demand both a co-ordinated public control of industry and finance, and a larger unit than the old nation state. Whether these larger units will be formed by Fascist aggression, or by democratic co-operation, whether this centralized planning will be directed to imperial expansion or to the happiness of the individual, whether lastly, their philosophy will be based on the rational motive of social equality or the irrational myth of racial inequality—all these things will be decided by the actions of democrats in England and America during the coming years.

BIBLIOGRAPHY

In this book list I wish to indicate not so much the books which have been useful to me as those which may be useful to any reader who seeks to study more thoroughly the problems I have discussed. It is therefore limited to books which people without any special knowledge of political theory or social history can read with ease. Unavoidably some books of an advanced character have been included.

A. GENERAL

FISHER, H. A. L. *History of Europe.* Edward Arnold.

HUBERMANN, L. *Man's Worldly Goods.* Gollancz.

JOAD, C. E. M. *Guide to Philosophy of Morals and Politics.* Gollancz.

LASKI, H. J. *Grammar of Politics.* Allen & Unwin.

MAYER, J. P. (Editor) *Political Thought: the European Tradition.* Dent.

SABINE, G. H. *History of Political Theory.* Harrap.

B. ORIGINAL SOURCES

(These are discussed in the text and can mostly be read by beginners)

BAGEHOT, W. *English Constitution.* World's Classics.

BOSANQUET, B. *Philosophical Theory of State.* Macmillan.

BRUCK, M. VAN DEN. *Germany's Third Empire.* Allen & Unwin.

BURKE, E. *Appeal from the New to the Old Whigs.* World's Classics: Burke, Vol. V.

GREEN, T. H. *Lectures on Principles of Political Obligation.* Longman.

HITLER, A. *Mein Kampf.* (German edition only)

HOBBES, T. *The Leviathan*. Everyman.

HUME, D. *Political Essays* (Social Contract) World's Classics.

LENIN, V. I. *Imperialism*. Lawrence & Wishart.

„   *State and Revolution*. Lawrence & Wishart.

LOCKE, J. *Essay On Toleration*.

„   *Two Treatises of Civil Government*. Everyman.

MACHIAVELLI, N. *The Prince*. Everyman.

MARX, K. *Civil War in France*. Lawrence & Wishart.

„   *Communist Manifesto*. Lawrence & Wishart.

„   and ENGELS, F. *German Ideology*. Lawrence & Wishart.

MILL, J. *Essay on Government*. C.U.P.

MILL, J. S. *Autobiography*. World's Classics.

„   *Utilitarianism, Liberty, and Representative Government*. Everyman.

MUSSOLINI, B. *The Political and Social Doctrines of Fascism*. Hogarth Press.

PAINE, T. *Rights of Man*. Everyman.

Protocols and World Revolution—including translation of *Protocols of Meetings of Zionist Men of Wisdom*. Small, Maynard & Co. Boston.

ROUSSEAU, J. J. *Social Contract*. Everyman.

SOREL, G. *Reflections on Violence*. Allen & Unwin.

SPENGLER, O. *Decline of the West*. Allen & Unwin.

WILSON, W. *The New Freedom*. Chapman & Hall.

C. SUPPLEMENTARY READING

CHAPTER II

DAWSON, CHRISTOPHER. *The Making of Europe*. Sheed & Ward.

DYER, L. *Machiavelli and the Modern State*. Ginn.

FIGGIS, J. N. *The Divine Right of Kings*. C.U.P.

HEARNSHAW, F. J. C. *Social and Political Ideas of Some Great Thinkers of the Renaissance and Reformation*. Harrap.

LINDSAY, T. M. *Luther and the German Reformation*. T. & T. Clark.

POWER, EILEEN. *Medieval People*. Methuen.

SHAW, BERNARD. *Saint Joan*. Constable.

TAWNEY, R. H. *Religion and the Rise of Capitalism*. Murray.

CHAPTER III

GOOCH, G. P. *Political Thought in England from Bacon to Halifax.* H.U.L.

GOUGH, J. W. *The Social Contract.* O.U.P.

HEARNSHAW, F. J. C. *Social and Political Ideas of Some Great Thinkers of the 16th and 17th Centuries.* Harrap.

LASKI, H. J. *Political Thought in England from Locke to Bentham.* H.U.L.

LASKI, H. J. *The Rise of European Liberalism.* Allen & Unwin.

MORTON, A. L. *People's History of England.* (Early chapters) Gollancz.

STEPHEN, LESLIE. *Thomas Hobbes.* Macmillan.

WOODHOUSE, — (Editor). *The Clarke Papers.*

CHAPTER IV

ADAMS, J. T. *Revolutionary New England.*

BEARD, C. *The Economic Basis of Politics.* Allen & Unwin.

BEARD, C. and M. *The Rise of American Civilization.* Cape.

MACCUNN, J. *Political Philosophy of Burke.* Edward Arnold.

STEPHEN, L. *History of English Thought in the 18th Century.* Murray.

CHAPTER V

BRAILSFORD, H. N. *Voltaire.* H.U.L.

DE TOCQUEVILLE. *L'Ancien Régime.* Translated by M. W. Patterson. Blackwell.

ELTON, LORD. *Revolutionary Idea in France, 1789-1871.* Arnold.

FISHER, H. A. L. *Bonapartism.* O.U.P.

MARTIN, K. *French Liberal Thought in the 18th Century.* Benn.

WRIGHT, E. H. *The Meaning of Rousseau.* O.U.P.

CHAPTER VI

HALEVY, E. *The Growth of Philosophic Radicalism.* Faber & Faber.

„ *History of the English People.* Benn.

SMELLIE, K. B. *A Hundred Years of English Government*. Duckworth.

STEPHEN, L. *English Utilitarians*. Duckworth.

CHAPTER VII

BARKER, E. *Political Thought in England from 1848 to 1914*. H.U.L.

CARRITT. E. F. *Morals and Politics*. O.U.P.

CROCE, B. *History of Europe in the 19th Century*. Allen & Unwin.

GARVIN, J. L. *Life of Joseph Chamberlain*. Macmillan.

HEARNSHAW, F. J. C. *Social and Political Ideas of Some Representative Thinkers of the Victorian Age*. Harrap.

ROSENBERG, A. *The Birth of the German Republic*. O.U.P.

RUGGIERO, G. DE. *History of European Liberalism*. O.U.P.

CHAPTER VIII

BEER, M. *History of British Socialism*. Bell.

CARR, E. H. *Michael Bakunin*. Macmillan.

  „   *Karl Marx*. Dent.

HOBHOUSE, L. T. *Metaphysical Theory of the State*. Allen & Unwin.

HOLLIS, C. *Lenin*. Longman.

HOOK, S. *From Hegel to Marx*. Gollancz.

  „   *Towards an Understanding of Karl Marx*. Gollancz.

LASKI, H. J. *Communism*. H.U.L.

MAYER, G. *Friedrich Engels*. Chapman & Hall.

ROSENBERG, A. *History of Bolshevism*. O.U.P.

TROTSKY, L. *History of the Russian Revolution*. Gollancz.

CHAPTER IX

BARNES, J. S. *Fascism*. H.U.L.

BORKENAU, F. *Communist International*. Faber & Faber.

BRAILSFORD, H. N. *Property or Peace*. Gollancz.

FINER, H. *Mussolini's Italy*. Gollancz.

COUDENHOVE-KALERGI, COUNT R. N. *The Totalitarian State Against Man.* Muller.

GOAD, H. E. *The Making of the Corporate State.* Christophers.

HEIDEN, K. *History of National Socialism.* Methuen.

NIEBUHR, R. *Moral Man and Immoral Society.* Scribner.

ROSSI, A. *The Rise of Italian Fascism.* Translated by P. & D. Wait. Methuen.

SHAW, BERNARD. *The Apple Cart.* Constable.

VOIGT, F. A. *Unto Cæsar.* Constable.

INDEX

Printed in Great Britain by Charles & Read, Ltd.
London.

THE ECONOMY
OF
BRITAIN

A HISTORY

By

H. M. CROOME
Author of *The Approach
to Economics*

and

RICHARD HAMMOND

With an Introduction by
Sir William Beveridge

" Deserves to be welcomed as the best
short summary of our mediæval and
modern economic history available."—
Listener

" Manages to pack the whole of English
economic history into one small and
attractive volume."—Professor Postan
in the *Spectator*

" Useful and illuminating. . . . . The
value of the book lies in its simple style,
its orderly arrangement and its handy
size."—*Times Literary Supplement*

8/6 *net*

CHRISTOPHERS

THIS
MODERN AGE

*An Introduction to the Understanding
of our own Times*

By

F. C. HAPPOLD
D.S.O., LL.D.

" What makes his attempt so convincing
is the brilliant clarity both of his outlook and
his writing. . . . A most ingenious series
of charts and plans illustrating the progress
and development of 'essential' factors
like foreign trade, Parliament and the Press
add a great deal to the value of a very
valuable book."—*News-Chronicle*

" A piece of very valuable pioneer work
in the modernisation of teaching."—MR.
H. G. WELLS

" This is an excellent book, clear
and admirably expressed, for the plain
man. The plans, maps and charts are
conceived and executed well."—*Oxford
Magazine*

5/- net

CHRISTOPHERS

THIS
MODERN AGE

An Introduction to the Understanding
of our own Times

By

F. G. HAYFOULD,
D.B.C., LL.D.

"What makes his attempt so convincing
is the brilliant clarity both of his outlook and
his within.' . . . A most ingenious series
of charts and plans illustrating the progress
and development of essential factors
like foreign trade, Parliament and the Press
add a great deal to the value of a very
valuable book."—News-Chronicle

"A piece of very valuable pioneer work
in the modernising of teaching."—Mr.
H. G. Wells

"This is an excellent book, clearly
and admirably expressed, for the plain
man. The plans, maps and charts are
conceived and executed well."—Oxford
Magazine

6/- net

CHRISTOPHERS

{ Laisser faire
                    utilitarianism,
                L of N (no coercive auth
{ Poly + Capitalism (laissi faire)
J.S Mill - liberty, with
                    safeguards agst
                    class prejudice.

Imperm + Nat —
(national   Joe Chaberla
  Liberalism   Mandates
- ld
  laisser   Fascism + othe Total^m
  faire
  nationally
  + internationaly)

Planned econ — ed. For change
                    (Mannheim)